THE NEW
TRAVELER'S ATLAS

A QUARTO BOOK

First edition for the United States and Canada published 2007 by Barron's Educational Series, Inc.

All inquiries should be addressed to:
Barron's Educational Series, Inc.
250 Wireless Boulevard
Hauppauge, NY 11788
www.barronseduc.com

Library of Congress Control Number: 2006931304

ISBN-13: 978-0-7641-6018-9
ISBN-10: 0-7641-6018-4

QUAR.TVAT

Conceived, designed, and produced by
Quarto Publishing plc
The Old Brewery
6 Blundell Street
London N7 9BH

Project Editors Gilly Cameron Cooper, Mary Groom
Art Editor Natasha Montgomery
Designer Alpana Khare
Assistant Art Director Penny Cobb
Copy Editors Nigel Rodgers, Maggi McCormick
Cartographer Julian Baker
Indexer Diana LeCore
Picture Researchers Gill Metcalfe, Claudia Tate

Art Director Moira Clinch
Publisher Paul Carslake

Manufactured by Modern Age Repro House Ltd, Hong Kong
Printed by SNP Leefung Holding Limited, printed in China

9 8 7 6 5 4 3 2 1

---

opposite page: Rice terraces in Bali
pages 4–5: Namburg National Park, Australia

THE NEW
TRAVELER'S ATLAS

A global guide to the places you must see in your lifetime

JOHN MAN • CHRIS SCHÜLER

GEOFFREY ROY • NIGEL RODGERS • MARY-ANN GALLAGHER

CONTENTS

INTRODUCTION

"Travel, in the younger sort, is part of education; in the elder, a part of experience."
–Francis Bacon

The author, John Man, on the trip to the Waorani Indians that changed his perception of his own life and culture.

THE LONGEST JOURNEY EVER MADE was to a place already known, researched, and intimately described. Yet that journey, which might have done nothing but confirm established views, provided all humankind with a revelation. The journey was, of course, to the moon. And the most striking discovery of the first lunar journey in 1969 was an insight into what had been left behind—that image of a marbled dot standing in an infinite void. It was a strange irony of that voyage to travel for 3 days to the moon and rediscover the earth.

It should not have been all that surprising, for that has always been the true purpose of travel: to see, experience, feel, and understand distant places, but then find another reward: to gain a deeper knowledge of home, one's culture, one's self.

The first time I traveled, I mean really traveled, I found myself beside a small airstrip in the Amazon jungle in eastern Ecuador. I had come to write about a tribe that had been contacted not much more than 20 years previously, the Waorani (now usually spelled Huaorani). The adults of the small group I was to live with had been born into the Stone Age, without metal tools of their own. They hunted with blowguns and spears, were renowned for their ferocity, and had no clothing. I arrived with tape recorder, camera, and notebooks. The shock of the first meeting was one of the most intense of my life. To have naked men and women, their earlobes vastly extended to accommodate plugs of balsa wood, crowding around, pulling my shirt up to examine my skin, touching me everywhere, fingering my precious possessions, it all made me very, very nervous. I had no idea what was happening or what to expect. I had never felt so helpless.

My worries faded, my interest grew. I was accompanied by one of the few guides who spoke the language. The group was peaceable. I learned names, and a few words of the language. What surprised me later was how quickly I became used to my new surroundings. It would have taken years to absorb the culture, but within days I felt at ease

enough to go naked myself (except for shoes—feet take 6 months or so to harden). The simple body decoration and the dangling earlobes seemed quite natural. It made other tribes, my own included, seem wildly eccentric.

Within 2 weeks—a time span that will be applied to many of the journeys in this book—my sense of what was normal acquired new dimensions. I came to see several things in my own culture differently. For instance, I had uncritically assumed that Freud was right, that sex is the fundamental drive. But here it took a backseat to survival. Marriage was dictated by the overwhelming need for a joint economy: a man to hunt, a woman to grow manioc. I marched briefly to the rhythm of a different drum. I came back changed.

A World to Share

Why not simply read? Why travel at all? Couldn't we all be happy stay-at-homes, and simply read, or zap or surf our way through the world's wonders, and absorb them that way? No. Books, videos, and the Internet are never substitutes for life-changing experiences. Like me, you will find, if you haven't already, that there are sights and experiences and feelings that change lives, and you cannot know what they will be in advance. The joy of travel is the surprise, the tingle factor. For a while, perhaps no more than a few minutes, you feel again the rush of joy and astonishment that comes from the onset of youthful love. Oh, my God, you say, I had no idea this mountain or that temple would be so small, or big, or beautiful. The moment passes because human beings cannot sustain such bliss, but the memory remains branded by emotion. Can anyone be quite the same after their first sight of the pyramids, or Everest, or the Grand Canyon?

Tasmania, the only island state of Australia, is a land of high rainfall but great unspoiled wildernesses of mountains, lakes, and waterfalls.

The Global Village: The places visited in this book are plotted on a map of the world's climatic zones.

Arctic Circle

Vancouver ★   ★ Banff

Yosemite ★   Adirondacks ★

San Francisco and ★
the West Coast   ★ The Grand Canyon

Tropic of Cancer

★ Hawaii   ★ La Ruta Maya

Costa Rica ★

Equator _____ ★ _____ ★ The Amazon
Galapagos Islands

The Inca Trail ★

Tropic of Capricorn

★ Tahiti and Easter Island

Polar

Cool temperate

Desert

Warm temperate

Tropical

Mountain

★ Patagonia

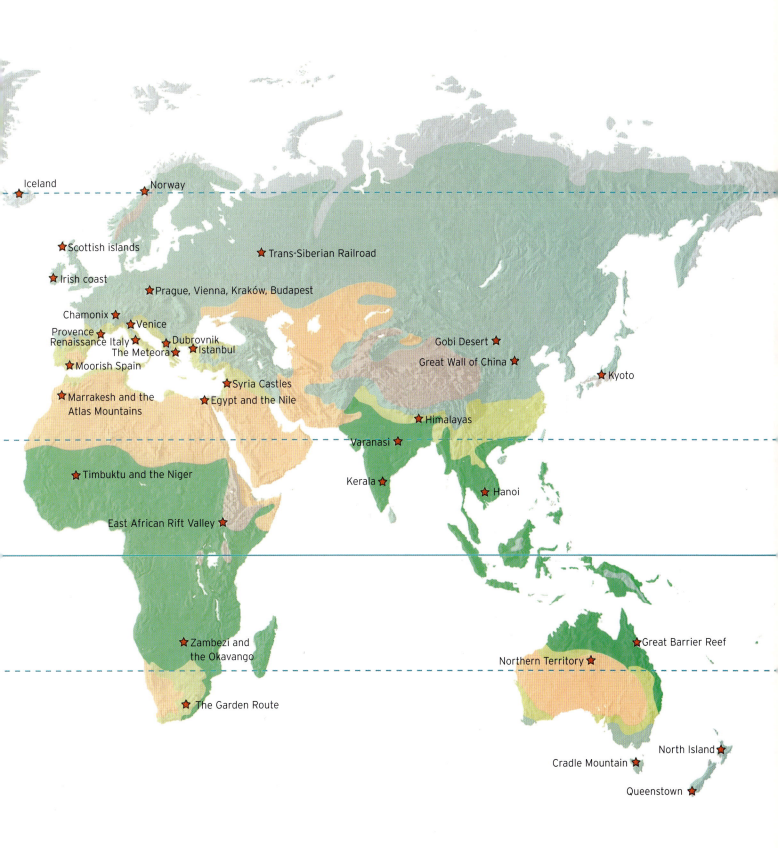

Iceland

Norway

Scottish islands

Irish coast

Trans-Siberian Railroad

Prague, Vienna, Kraków, Budapest

Chamonix

Venice

Provence
Renaissance Italy

Dubrovnik

The Meteora

Istanbul

Moorish Spain

Gobi Desert

Great Wall of China

Kyoto

Syria Castles

Marrakesh and the
Atlas Mountains

Egypt and the Nile

Himalayas

Varanasi

Timbuktu and the Niger

Kerala

Hanoi

East African Rift Valley

Zambezi and
the Okavango

Great Barrier Reef

Northern Territory

The Garden Route

North Island

Cradle Mountain

Queenstown

Leave your cup of tea behind at home, to journey to the source of tea, the plantations of *Camellia sinensis*, a native plant of the mild, moist mountain region between India and China.

Don't think the experience will change the world directly. Its effect is utterly private, and if it is not private, it can easily be as tedious as a vacation shot bliss recycled as cliché. Thousands see such visions every year, and the world remains unimproved by their reactions. If and when something tremendous happens, it is only to you. There is no sure way, unless you are a poet or artist, that you can transfer the feeling into the mind of another. Best not to try, but to hug it to yourself, and know that you have gained something ineffable.

But even through us nonpoets, the experience has an effect indirectly. Look at it the other way around. These things are part of a common heritage. It is not simply that you are enriched by the experience of travel to exotic places, but that if you do not seek them out, you remain impoverished, cut off from what should be truly yours as an inhabitant of the world in a new millennium.

Once humans were limited to the speed and distance they could cover on their feet, on a horse, in a canoe, or on a ship. It took weeks, or years, to seek out and experience new worlds. The grand tour of Europe, undertaken by the wealthy in the 1700s, took many months. One of the greatest of medieval travelers, Ibn Battuta, ranged across northern and eastern Africa, to the Middle East, to the Volga, to India, to China, but it took him 30 years of solid travel. Now we can all see what he saw, or at least the modern equivalents. Travel at its best allows us to share our world, and our heritage. As inhabitants of the global village, we had better be aware of what we should inherit and what we should pass on.

The Right Time

Never was there a better time to go. Today, a traveler can be in Miami in the morning and with the Waorani the same night (though they are not as they were when I first saw them). All of Ibn Battuta's destinations could be visited inside a few months. It is not just the difference between them and us, between here and there, that would have astonished Ibn Battuta or our traveling 19th-century ancestors, but the speed of transposition.

Such experiences are yours for the asking. Of all the places in this book, almost all can be visited within 24 hours, from anywhere in the world. You can, if you wish, chug for days up the Amazon to the rubber-boom town of Manuas; but you can also fly in straight from Rio. A Londoner or New Yorker can be in the world's remotest habitable spot, Easter Island, within a day and a night. A rich and dedicated traveler could taste every place and journey mentioned in this book in the space of a single year.

But don't even think of trying it. Travel, or rather arrival, may indeed broaden the mind, but only if it is done with discrimination. One purpose of this book is to show you how to slow down to

—> A CHECKLIST OF TIPS

FOCUS FIRST ON WHAT SUITS YOU Wilderness or a city; a new culture or your own; near or far. See what you can accomplish in the time available. Compare costs: there's almost always a cheaper way, and it may be better.
HEALTH Check out the risks.
EQUIPMENT Usually best bought in advance, but sometimes it's better to buy locally on arrival.
INSURANCE Get it well in advance. Check the small print. Can you be sure of reparation and/or treatment locally? Will it get you home?
EMERGENCIES Have a backup plan in case of trouble. Know your contacts. Check alternative travel possibilities.
LANGUAGE In an unfamiliar culture, a good local English-speaking guide is the key to enjoyment. A bad one is a nightmare. Be warned: there are no guarantees.
COMMUNICATIONS Consider taking a mobile cell phone with international dialing. In an emergency it can save time, money, the lives of professional rescuers, even your own life.
NUMBERS One is scary. A group is often bland. Between two and four offers a good balance.

experience in depth, to absorb, for the flip side of ready access is overload and superficiality, the curse of instant travel. "If this is Tuesday it must be Rome" is not just a joke on mass tourism—it's a sad truth.

So another purpose of this book is to broaden the mind by narrowing the vision. Every destination and journey offers something of significance, something that should take time to savor, something that rewards commitment. Of course, few have world enough and time, let alone money, for detailed study. Most, though, can steal a week or two from a busy life. This book strikes a balance between expertise and instant access. To know Kyoto, one would have at least to live with the language and culture for years; wildlife experts and geologists make careers out of studying the Grand Canyon or Yosemite; but 2 weeks in these places is enough to gain a sense of them, thanks to modern transportation. A vacation spent in relative safety traveling across the Karakorams into China can provide insights as deep (though different) as those acquired by walkers or riders obsessed by concerns about whether they and their horses can make it over the next ridge.

Narrowing the vision fulfills another purpose—it provides an objective. To fulfill an ambition is itself a satisfaction, whatever the nature of the experience when you arrive. One final thought: you can choose to fine-tune that satisfaction by not always taking the easiest option. Modern travel allows room for you to take a path slightly less traveled: the ramshackle rather than the air-conditioned, the slower rather than the faster. A little suffering helps. To venture by bus into Tibet's chilly and barren highland is a risky business, but it makes the arrival in Lhasa all the more rewarding.

John Man

Travelers can take a riverboat journey along the Li Jiang river in southwest China, to where the extraordinary geological formations of the Guilin Hills erupt from a sea of flooded paddy fields.

NORTH AMERICA

"Travel is more than the seeing of sights; it is a change that goes on, deep and permanent, in the ideas of living."
MIRIAM BEARD, AMERICAN WRITER, B. 1901

BANFF NATIONAL PARK

"I never, in all my explorations of these five chains of mountains throughout western Canada, saw such a matchless scene.... I felt puny in body, but glorified in spirit and soul."–Explorer Tom Wilson, 1882

A gold-mantled ground squirrel is among the denizens of Banff's untouched forests.

THE CANADIAN ROCKIES run 1,000 miles (1,600 km), right up the western edge of the country and on into Alaska, but their heart–and most accessible region–is the area around Banff. Every summer, every winter, millions of hikers, climbers, and skiers come here. Despite the crowds, anyone can feel as puny and as glorified as Tom Wilson, for the wilderness is as matchless as ever.

These are young mountains, formed as part of the crumple zone when the two American continental plates rammed into the Pacific plate 70 million years ago. Youthfulness in mountains, as in body sculpting, leads to great definition. Ice, snow, wind, frost, and rain have chiseled out peaks and sheer cliffs, leaving edges unblunted by time. From high ice fields, glaciers grind down, turning rock to powder that clouds the icy lakes. Thick forests of aspen, pine, fir, and spruce flow over the lower slopes and lap the lakesides. Higher up, alpine meadows splashed with bluebells and heather give way to bare and wind-blasted heights. The varied wilderness, once the domain of moose, black bear, and grizzlies, was opened up little more than a century ago. In 1858, Dr. James Hector, exploring the Bow River valley, was kicked unconscious by his packhorse. His Indian guides, thinking him dead, prepared to bury him, but he opened his eyes and survived to see Kicking Horse Pass named for him. Soon afterward, pioneers discovered that the cold above ground is matched by the heat below ground. Subterranean furnaces warm the meltwaters and percolate them back to the surface. Sulfur springs turned Banff into a spa renowned for its surrounding glories, and the area became Canada's first national park in 1885–a mere 10 square miles (26 sq km).

Now the heart of this heartland is Banff National Park, 2,580 square miles (6,680 sq km) of peaks, meadows, lakes, and glaciers running for 150 miles (240 km) along the borders of British Columbia and Alberta. It is only one of three other parks–Jasper, Yoho, Kootenay–that form an even vaster wilderness, all loosely laced with trails. Banff National Park alone has 1,000 miles (1,600 km) of them.

Once, the Canadian Pacific Railroad brought in most visitors. Today, the railroad is mainly used for freight, although special sightseeing trips are operated from Vancouver, Jasper, and Calgary. Visitors mostly drive or bus in from Calgary, 90 minutes away, arriving in one of the two main centers, Banff and Lake Louise. Be warned: both places are packed in high season, both winter and summer.

A Victorian Monster

Banff's hot springs, once the town's equivalent of a gold mine, are as crowded as ever, especially the Upper Hot Springs near the base of the cable cars (known as gondolas) that shoot up the 7,440-foot (2,263-m) Sulfur Mountain. The town is still dominated by one of its original resorts, a 578-room monster of Victorian gothic, the Banff Springs Hotel, the world's largest hotel when it was built in the 1890s. About 11 miles (18 km) south, another gondola combines with a chairlift to reach the Continental Divide.

Banff hosts an annual arts festival, but most

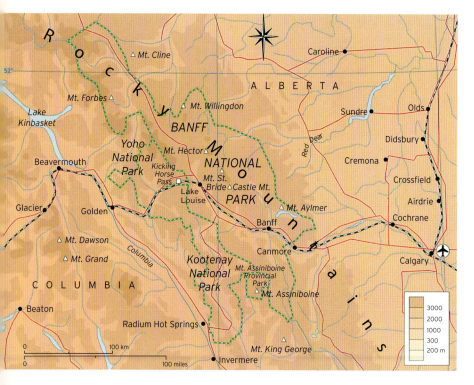

Glaciers and waterfalls wash out silt, giving the waters of Lake Moraine its particular pearly radiance.

-> FACT FILE

AIRPORTS Calgary, Edmonton.

WINTER SPORTS HIGH SEASON March.

COLUMBIA ICE FIELDS CENTER Open mid-April to mid-October, www.columbiaicefield.com.

AVERAGE SNOWFALL 100 inches (251 cm).

BANFF LAKE LOUISE TOURISM Tel: +1 (403) 762-8421; web: www.banfflakelouise.com.

PERMITS Permits are required to enter all Canadian National Parks, including Banff National Park. Daily fees range from one day ($8) to annual ($55) with concessions available for children and seniors. A family/group permit is available for one car with up to seven passengers ($16 for one day or $107 for an annual pass), www.pc.gc.ca/pn-np/ab/banff/ visit/tarifs-fees_e.asp?park=1.

BEARS Black bears and grizzlies are dangerous, though rarely encountered. Follow the guidelines in local literature. In brief: don't approach, don't feed, don't run. Back away slowly.

people come not for the town but for its surroundings. Day hikers can head up the Spray River and Sulfur Mountain from the Banff Springs Hotel; more serious backpackers start outside the town, and higher up. Two highways follow the railroad north along the Bow River, whose emerald waters come crashing down from Kicking Horse through a wilderness that still retains its pristine grandeur. From the faster Highway 1A and the scenic Bow Valley Parkway, five trails—from 3 miles (5 km) to 17 miles (28 km) long—lead up past waterfalls and lakes to stupendous outlooks.

Some of these interlink with the trails surrounding Lake Louise, 37 miles (59 km) from Banff. The resort is both a village and the lake itself, which is 3 miles (5 km) away. It is the lake that is

Crystal-clear waters thunder over the rocks in this spellbinding waterfall, just one of many that feed pristine Lake Moraine.

Lake Louise (right), beneath the bastion of Mount Victoria, is one of Canada's most visited sights, while the heights above Bow River (below) attract only the intrepid.

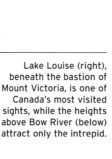

the draw. Known as the "gem of the Rockies," its waters are made pearly by "rock flour," the powder ground out of the mountains by glaciers. The result—despite the intrusive presence of a 1920s hotel—is an image of postcard perfection, which at sunset and sunrise reflects the surrounding snowcapped peaks and forested slopes in colors "distilled from peacocks' tails," in the words of one awed writer.

Naturally, in summer lakeside trails are crowded. The trail around Lake Agnes, less than a mile from Lake Louise, is said to be the most heavily used path in the Rockies. But for the more ambitious, the wilderness is within easy reach. Just 8 miles (13 km) away is Lake Moraine, a sight so beautiful, with its vivid turquoise waters and backdrop of 10 peaks, that it was used on old Canadian $20 bills. Of several trails leading away from the lake, one leads up to 8,600 feet (2,605 m), the highest point

reached by a major trail in the Canadian Rockies. This is also Canada's prime winter playground, with seven major ski resorts, two near Banff and one near Lake Louise (the others are Nakiska, Fortress Mountain, and Jasper). Between them these places offer downhill and cross-country skiing, dog sledding, ice climbing, skating, snowmobiling, snowshoeing, heli-hiking, heli-skiing, canyon crawling, and fishing. Mount Norway, just north of Banff, is popular with advanced downhill skiers and also offers the area's only night skiing.

Giant Ice Field

Those seeking wilderness of a different sort can head north toward Jasper along Highway 93–the Icefields Parkway. Though a million people a year make the journey, it is still surprisingly underdeveloped. In 143 miles (230 km) there are only three service stations, and snow often closes the road between October and May.

Some 75 miles (120 km) north of Lake Louise is the Columbia ice field, 120 square miles (325 sq km) of ice and snow that is the largest glacial area south of the Arctic Circle and north of the equator. It is the source of six major glaciers, three of which can be seen from the parkway. An Icefield Center offers views and information about ice walks, which for those with the right equipment–good boots, and clothing to ward off the bitter winds, for the temperature plummets beside the ice fields–provide a dramatic insight into the forces that are still carving these wild peaks.

THE GRAND CANYON

"Whoever stands upon the brink of the Grand Canyon beholds a spectacle unrivalled on this earth."–Early canyon geologist François E. Matthes

Bighorn sheep can be seen in less accessible parts of the canyon.

AFTER ALL THAT IS READ AND HEARD about the Grand Canyon, the first glimpse of this World Heritage Site, designated one of the seven natural wonders of the world, still takes your breath away.

The mile-deep gorge averages 10 to 12 miles (16-19 km) wide between the North and South rims. Flowing in a southwesterly direction from its source in the Rocky Mountains, the Colorado River carves 277 river miles (446 km) through the bottom of the canyon from Lees Ferry to Lake Mead.

Colorful hues of geologic layers dating back more than 2 billion years blend shades of gray, green, brown, and red. Some of the rocks can be dated by embedded fossils. Sheer cliffs, hiding caves and arches, rise 400 to 500 feet (120-150 m). Iron oxide leaches and stains the face of these rocks adding additional color to this palette. As sunlight, sometimes mixed with cloud covering, traverses the canyon, brilliant hues cast a changing visual and magical image, a dreamy sight for a photographer, artist, or the wondrous gaze of more than 4.5 million annual visitors.

Congress established Grand Canyon National Park in 1919. Its current boundaries, which encompass 1,904 square miles (4,950 sq km), were determined by the Grand Canyon National Park

The secluded forests of the North Rim's Kaibab Plateau contrast with the bare, crowded South Rim.

Enlargement Act in 1975. Today, visitors can enjoy scenic overflights originating at the Grand Canyon Airport located in the gateway community of Tusayan. Others might choose to travel 80 miles (130 km) from the city of Flagstaff, while some may opt to ride the Grand Canyon Railway, approximately a 2-hour one-way ride from Williams, Arizona.

The easiest way to get around the South Rim developed area is to park your vehicle and use the free shuttle bus system. The five hotels on the South Rim are anchored by the 78-room recently renovated El Tovar Hotel built in 1905 and Bright Angel Lodge, built 30 years later. There is also the 201-room Grand Canyon Lodge located at the less-visited North Rim, a winding 215 miles (344 km) further north. In the bottom of the canyon on the north side of the Colorado River along Bright Angel Creek, Phantom Ranch offers stone cabins with toilet facilities but no showers, plus four bunk-style dormitories, segregated by sex, each with toilet and shower facilities. Reservations to stay at these

–> FACT FILE

LENGTH 277 miles (443 km).

DEPTH 1 mile (1.6 km).

WIDTH Average width 10 miles (16 km), narrowest point 600 feet (180 m), widest point 18 miles (28.81 km).

BEST TIME TO GO Mid-May through mid-June, to avoid the worst crowds and heat.

BEST TIME TO VIEW Morning and evening, when it's cool and the sun casts a slanting light.

CLIMATE Summer high over 100°F (38°C); winter low down to 0°F (-18°C).

WHAT TO TAKE Good boots, water bottles.

INFORMATION Park information, Tel: +1 (928) 638-7888; web: www.nps.gov/grca.

White-water rafters make stately progress past the sheer cliffs of Marble Canyon, but elsewhere the Colorado River displays its cutting edge.

properties should be made 6 months to a year in advance, although it may be possible to get last-minute cancellations. Access to Phantom Ranch is by strenuous hiking, riding a mule, or river rafting.

Mules plod the 9.6-mile, 4,385-foot (15.4-km, 1,336-m) descent down Bright Angel Trail bringing supplies and tourists to the ranch. On the North Rim, Canyon Trail Rides offers half-day rides descending 1.8 miles and 1,415 feet (2.9 km and 431 m) down the 14-mile (22.5-km) North Kaibab Trail to Supai Tunnel. There are weight and height restrictions for mule rides, and yes, they do weigh you.

Intrepid hikers can escape the crowds and see an intensity of the canyon not available to those peering over the rim or viewing the trail from a mule. The National Park Service posts signs on the trails in several languages with warnings such as:

do not attempt to hike down to the river and back in one day; stay hydrated; avoid hiking in the heat of the day; eat frequently; make shady rest stops; and keep your shirt, hat, or bandana wet.

Easier hikes include the Rim Trail, which follows the South Rim for miles. Sections of the trail are paved and wheelchair accessible. On the North Rim, the Bright Angel Point, Transept, and Widforss trails provide excellent views.

It would be foolish not to be fit and conditioned to tackle the more difficult Bright Angel, South Kaibab, and North Kaibab trails.

In 4 to 6 hours a hiker can descend Bright Angel Trail (9.6 miles/15.4 km from the trailhead to Phantom Ranch), but the return requires twice the time. Descent can wear on knees and toes; the upward grind can be grueling on heart and lungs. Bright Angel, unlike South Kaibab Trail, has both

rest stops and availability of drinking water at Indian Garden, 4.6 miles (7.4 km) from the rim. The South Kaibab Trail is steeper but only 7.1 miles (11.4 km) to Phantom Ranch.

The North Rim is 1,000 feet (305 m) higher than the South Rim; 1.5 miles (2.4 km) north of Grand Canyon Lodge, the North Kaibab Trail descends 13.8 miles (22 km) to a fork near Phantom Ranch. One route leads over the Silver Bridge to the Bright Angel Trail, while the other leads over the older Black Bridge to the South Kaibab Trail.

Havasu Canyon: A World Apart

Havasu Canyon trailhead, remotely located northeast of Peach Springs, or 90 miles (144.8 km) north of Seligman, Arizona, begins on Hualapai Hilltop. This 8-mile (12.9-km) trail on the Havasupai Reservation leads to the village of Supai. Located next to the crystalline blue-green waters of Havasu Creek, the village is known as the home of the "people of the blue-green water." The first 1¼ miles (2 km) of the Havasu Trail winds through a series of switchbacks, losing 1,100 feet (335 m) in elevation. It's an additional 900 feet (274 m) in elevation and less than 7 miles (11.2 km) to the village. The trail is well traveled by 25,000 visitors a year who come to visit the wondrous Navajo, Havasu, and Mooney waterfalls. Colorado River rafting parties bushwhack 10 miles (16 km) just to see Mooney Falls. There is a public campground (tribal permit required) near the falls and a 24-room lodge. Nonhiking trail options include riding a horse and flying in a helicopter. The only reminder of civilization is the noise of Supai tractors tilling fields of corn, beans, squash, and sunflowers on the canyon floor.

There is no better way to see the canyon than rafting through it. From Lees Ferry to Lake Mead, the Colorado River churns and gouges its way through ripples and major rapids. Trip options vary from 3 to 16 days. Grand Canyon uses its own 10-point scale to measure rapids. Hance, Horn Creek, Crystal, and Lava Falls are 10-pointers during high-water flows. Trips use smaller oar-powered rafts or dories, paddleboats (smaller rafts where the passengers do the paddling), or larger 35-foot (10.6-m) motorized self-bailing rafts. Reservations for rafting trips should also be made well in advance.

The Grand Canyon can be enjoyed by everyone; no one ever doubts that it is truly one of the wonders of the world.

Those who book well in advance can ride mules down the vertiginous trail from the South Rim to the canyon floor.

Cascades in the Havasupai Indian Reserve, where "the people of the blue-green water" live in a remote and verdant outpost of the Grand Canyon.

The Grand Canyon is a cross section of the uppermost level of the earth's crust. If you were to cut a slice out of an African, Asian, or Australian plateau, the visual effect would be much the same.

TOWERING CLIFFS OF YOSEMITE

John Muir, Yosemite's founding father, wrote that the valley was like a mountain mansion into which "Nature had gathered her choicest treasures."

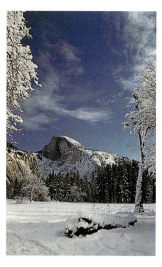

IN 1851, A TROOP OF CALIFORNIA VOLUNTEERS deep in the Sierra Nevada Mountains chased some Native Americans into a hidden refuge on the Merced River, and found themselves in a wonderland of granite monoliths, giant trees, and foaming waterfalls. One of the troop, a young physician named Lafayette Bunnell, learned that the local tribes called the place after their word for "grizzly bear"–Yo-sem-it-y. Its fame spread, and in 1864 it became state property. In 1890, the 750,000-acre (303,000-ha) valley with its surrounding area became one of the first three U.S. national parks.

Some 10 million years ago, the Sierra Nevada

arose. Then two other forces–the flowing waters of the Merced and the scouring action of ice-age glaciers–succeeded each other, several times. The glaciers, which once filled this valley to a depth of around 3,000 feet (almost 1,000 m), scooped out bowls, or cirques, below the peaks, and sliced vertiginous cliffs like the drop of Half Dome and the sturdy prow of El Capitán–at 3,500 feet (1,066 m) the world's biggest slab of exposed granite. When the ice vanished the last time, meltwater lakes silted up to form fertile valleys.

Milder forces of erosion are still at work, as shown by glories like the 620-foot (189-m) Bridalveil

With a mantle of snow, Half Dome stands guard over the valley floor.

The vertical cliff of Half Dome was formed when a glacier moving through the valley undermined the mountain, causing it to split.

-> John Muir, the First King of Conservation

-> John Muir, the First King of Conservation

Yosemite was made a national park largely at the instigation of John Muir (1838-1914), the Scottish-born father of American conservation. When he arrived in San Francisco in 1868, he asked directions to "anywhere that's wild" and learned of the Yosemite Valley. It was he who realized the valley was the product of glacial erosion. His visits there and to other pristine western landscapes inspired him to take a lead in protecting the Sierra range. This in effect established both the conservation movement and a pressure group to inspire federal action, which, in 1890, gave birth to the first national parks. In 1892, he was the cofounder and secretary of the Sierra Club, whose members still work to keep the wilderness unspoiled and accessible. The club's members soon established regular summer camps in Yosemite's Tuolumne Meadows, and John Muir is memorialized in the trail named for him, part of the Pacific Crest that leads from Yosemite Village through the Meadows and southward to Mount Whitney, 120 miles (192 km) away.

Cathedral Spires are among the Yosemite peaks that were exposed after glaciers and rivers eroded surrounding softer rock.

Falls and the double waterfall, the Upper and Lower Yosemite, which together form the highest falls in North America at 2,425 feet (739 m).

The soil's fertility is reflected in the 1,000 species of wildflowers and the variety of trees—black oak, incense cedar, ponderosa pine, and giant sequoias. Though not as tall as the related coastal redwoods, the sequoia is bulkier, making it the largest living thing on earth. In three separate groves, the sequoias soar over 200 feet (60 m). In the largest, the Mariposa Grove, a veteran known as the Grizzly Giant is an estimated 2,700 years old.

Most of the 4 million visitors a year stick to Yosemite Village, with its visitor center, shuttle buses, and campgrounds, and the scenic drive along Tioga Road, once a wagon route to mines on the far side of the Sierra Nevada. Strollers have ready access to Yosemite Falls, Mirror Lake, and Half Dome. Walkers prefer the hiking trails northeast to the alpine slopes of Tuolumne Meadows, or to the south through Mariposa Grove to see the Grizzly Giant and a "tunnel tree" with a road through it (there were two until one fell in 1969). But these trails, too, can be extremely crowded.

Far from the Milling Crowds

Intrepid visitors prepared for longer stays can head away from the roads and popular trails. There are climbing classes for beginners, and the experienced can choose from thousands of feet of granite cliff. Half Dome claims the continent's sheerest cliff—only 7 degrees from vertical—and Glacier Point, at 3,200 feet (969 m), less than a mile from Half Dome, offers stupendous views. Hiking permits are limited: 60% are issued in advance on application to the park authorities; the rest are issued daily on a first-come, first-served basis from ranger stations. Hikers then have access to rough mountain campgrounds and more than 700 miles (1,120 km) of trails. They will discover a staggering range of ecologies reflecting very different environments. From dry foothills with pines and oaks, trails climb along streams and through meadows to forests of maple, dogwood, and Douglas fir. Higher up, white bark pines thin out as they approach the timber line, above which the crest of the Sierra Nevada rears, with two peaks (Lyell and Dana) reaching over 13,000 feet (almost 4,000 m).

Hikers share the backcountry with coyote, fox, skunk, and racoon. The grizzlies for which the valley and park are named have long since vanished, but in the backcountry hikers may see mule deer–so-called because of their long ears–grazing in meadows. Occasionally, visitors stumble on a black bear scavenging for anything to eat, from berries to discarded candy. Black bears–which are in fact mainly brown–are rather aggressive and may attack if alarmed. Hikers should make plenty of noise, and campers should store food safely out of bears' reach. Never feed them!

One trail that strikes a balance between the excessively rigorous and overly popular is the 17-mile (27-km) ascent of Half Dome. A steep path along the Little Yosemite Valley leads up nearly 2,000 feet (600 m) past the Vernal and Nevada Falls, on behind Half Dome, then upward over the rock's vast humped back with the aid of steps and fixed cables to the near-vertical 4,800-foot (1,450-m) drop. It is possible to do this in a day, but you do need to be fit and start early.

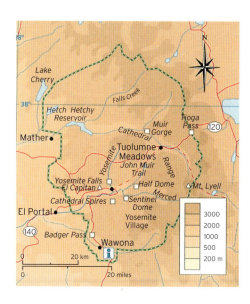

–> FACT FILE

DIMENSIONS OF VALLEY 7 miles (11.2 km) long, and up to 1 mile (1.6 km) wide.

SIZE OF NATIONAL PARK 1,200 square miles (3,108 sq km).

INFORMATION Obtainable from the Visitors' Center, Yosemite Village–Tel: +1 (209) 372-0200; web: www.nps.gov/yose.

BEST CLIMBING SEASONS April-May; September. In winter it is snowed under.

WILDERNESS PERMITS Wilderness permits (for long treks) are available in advance between May 15 and September 15: book online, by calling +1 (209) 372-0740, or by writing to Yosemite Association, PO Box 545, Yosemite, CA 95389.

SPECIAL NOTE Crowds in this national treasure can be avoided by entering a lottery (yosemitepark.com). Selection allows the visitor to choose a hike with a guide and a mule option to overnight in established camps that serve meals. The traveler only needs to carry a pack with water and essentials.

The Bridalveil Falls were known as the "spirit of the puffing wind" to the local tribes.

SAN FRANCISCO AND THE WEST COAST

In 100 miles (160 km), from San Francisco Bay to Big Sur, city life at its most sophisticated turns to nature in the raw.

Night lights show off San Francisco's unique combination of bayside and hill, low-rise and high-rise.

IT WAS THE DISCOVERY OF GOLD in the Sierra Nevada that stimulated the growth of San Francisco in the mid-1800s. That, combined with its superb setting overlooking a natural harbor, has produced a city that to its inhabitants and million of visitors often seems golden. Its strait—the Golden Gate—between California's largest bay and the Pacific Ocean is bridged by one of the world's engineering glories. Its climate—cold waters and warm lands combining to create quick changes in the weather—architecture, culture, and setting all match its golden origins. With a population of 750,000 and an area of just 46 square miles (116 sq km), it combines small-town charm with a big-town zest, all shot through with a unique liberalism. Here beatniks, hippies, and gays have all found a congenial home.

Part of the city's charm comes from its accessibility. Although on the edge of one of the country's largest metropolitan areas (the Bay Area), it is constrained by the rugged peninsula on which it lies. It is one of the few American cities that does not demand a car. In good walking shoes or sneakers, the city is yours, if you carry a jacket to counter the sudden chill of fogs and are prepared to tackle hills—there are more than 40 of them—that rise like flights of stairs. If exhaustion threatens, the city's three ancient and revered cable car lines are standbys, carrying commuters and tourists up and down from the bayside.

The starting point, historically and geographically, should be the docks. A triangle of land to the south, its 6-mile (9.6-km) perimeter, marked by Van Ness Avenue, Market Street, and the bayside Embarcadero, is the city's heart or downtown. Fisherman's Wharf, with its touristic shops and restaurants, backs onto North Beach, which still retains the bohemian feel that made it famous as the base of the Beat generation in the 1950s. A short climb brings you to Telegraph Hill topped by Coit Tower, a monument to the city's firefighters decorated by fine murals.

Or from Fisherman's Wharf visitors can take a cable car up to Union Square, where tourists gawk at the sumptuous art deco lobby in the St. Francis Hotel. Nob Hill, as its name suggests, like neighboring Russian Hill, has the mansions and grand hotels that catered to the rich who made their fortunes in the skyscrapers of the financial district below. To the south lies Chinatown, a seething neon-lit world served by its own schools, banks, temples, and newspapers, as well as more than 100 restaurants. Southwest lie the disconcerting slums of the Tenderloin district, which contrasts with the grandeur of the neighboring Civic Center. But there is more to San Francisco than can be revealed in one day's walking. Westward from Fisherman's Wharf is Golden Gate Bridge, the world's first great suspension bridge, with a span of three quarters of a mile (1.2 km). Though completed back in 1937, it still holds its own as an arresting piece of architecture, one that becomes magical when fog blankets its base. Its lure is occasionally fatal as well: every month, half a dozen people jump from the midway point to their deaths in the water 260 feet (80 m) below.

A mile south is Golden Gate Park, designed by Frederick Olmsted, creator of New York's Central Park. This is a glorious 1,000-acre (404-ha)

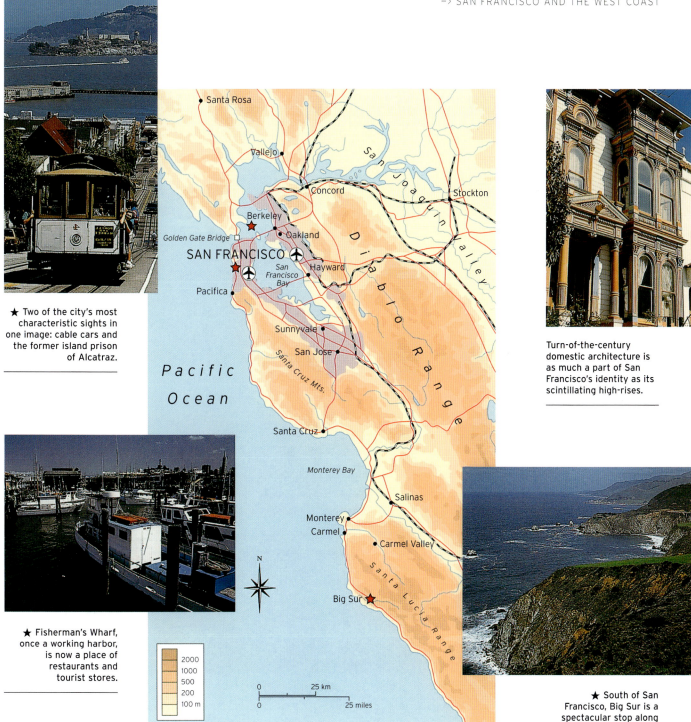

★ Two of the city's most characteristic sights in one image: cable cars and the former island prison of Alcatraz.

Turn-of-the-century domestic architecture is as much a part of San Francisco's identity as its scintillating high-rises.

★ Fisherman's Wharf, once a working harbor, is now a place of restaurants and tourist stores.

★ South of San Francisco, Big Sur is a spectacular stop along the cliff-hugging coastal Highway 1.

playground, with meadows, lakes, and gardens, numerous museums (including the stunning new de Young museum), a buffalo paddock, and the tallest artificial waterfall in the West, overlooking the massive–but forbiddingly cold–Pacific surf.

Surf, Whales, and Wilderness

The city has contrasts enough for a lifetime, let alone 2 weeks, but many visitors seek out greater privacy and peace by driving south along the dramatic coastal road Highway 1. Fifty-five miles south of San Francisco, the wild and lonely sand beaches at Año Nuevo Point are home to the

world's largest mainland breeding colony for the northern elephant seal. Admission to the state reserve is by permit only (available in advance from the park authorities), but the spectacle of these extraordinary creatures courting, mating, and giving birth among the sand dunes is unforgettably moving. Some 75 miles (120 km) south lies Santa Cruz, a city founded by a Spanish missionary in 1791. There is little sign of Spanish Catholicism now, apart from a replica 1792 mission. The Pacific waves rolling into Monterey Bay, and a giant roller coaster, make it a sensational beach playground.

Monterey itself arose as a sardine and a canning

Pelicans fly with slow, heavy deliberation, like prehistoric birds, over the beaches of Monterey and Carmel.

town, but Cannery Row—immortalized in the title of John Steinbeck's novel—and the Fisherman's Wharf are now glitzy shopping arcades, bars, and discos. The city's best known sight is the Monterey Bay Aquarium, with its kelp forest, a pool where visitors can stroke rays, and a vast window, claimed to be the world's largest, which provides an underwater view of the Pacific environment, complete with turtles, sunfish, sharks, and man-o'-war jellyfish. The 17-mile (27-km) drive around the Monterey peninsula, which swings through forests of Monterey cypresses, offers a chance to see seals basking, then skirts the shopping mecca and artists' colony of Carmel where music is banned in public places.

The true glory of the coast, and the ultimate contrast with the urban areas to the north, lies south of Monterey along the stretch known as Big

-> FACT FILE

BEST TIME October, for Halloween's gay parades in The Castro, and with fewer people and less fog along the coast.

CITY DRIVING On the many steep hills, park with the wheels turned into the curb, if facing downhill, and turned toward the street if facing uphill. This is the law.

CITY ACCOMMODATION Seldom a problem. Tourism is the city's greatest business, and you'll never be stuck for a room.

BIG SUR TRAVEL Public transportation is poor. Best to use a car, and then walk.

The 1,400-yard (1,272-m)-long Golden Gate Bridge spans the entrance of San Francisco Bay to the Pacific Ocean.

Sur. Here a line of surf-battered cliffs marks the border between the Los Padres National Forest and the Santa Lucia range. It is one of the world's great unspoiled coastlines, along which Route 1 snakes past rocky coves and through canyons. One of the few places you can reach the shore is Pfeiffer Beach where a sea-cut arch stands out at the foot of massive cliffs and visitors can spy pelicans fishing beyond the icy breakers.

Here, camping is virtually a way of life. There are half a dozen major campgrounds, while a mile inland from Pfeiffer Beach on the Big Sur River is a campground that acts as a gateway into the Pfeiffer Big Sur State Park. Dozen of trails lead away into the Big Sur and Los Padres hinterland, where deer and bobcats roam. A tough 2-hour climb up the tortuous Buzzard's Roost Trail leads to a panoramic view over the whole region. In spring the wildflowers are glorious, but October through November offers glimpses of sea otters and gray whales, with fewer foggy days.

In complete contrast to the misty cliffs and pounding surf south of San Francisco, the Lassen Volcanic National Park, about 260 miles (416 km) to the north, presents a striking, diverse landscape of active volcanoes, gurgling hot springs, and swirling lava formations set amid extensive forests dotted with translucent lakes. The park is traversed by a spectacular highway, but, to fully experience the park's natural beauty, strike out on one of the numerous excellent hiking trails.

AMERICA'S LARGEST WILDERNESS

"Stanley had found Livingstone in darkest Africa before most New Yorkers knew much about the wilderness at their back door."–Nature writer Lincoln Barnett

White-tailed deer are common in the forests, feeding on grass, ferns, and trees, and in summer often splashing through lake shallows seeking out aquatic plants.

THIS WILDERNESS IS SOMETHING OF A PARADOX. It is larger than several states, larger than some countries, being almost the size of Belgium. Yet it lies close to the most densely populated part of the U.S.–the Adirondack State Park is just 200 miles (320 km) from New York City.

The area's 5,000 square miles (12,950 sq km) of lakes, forests, rivers, and low rounded hills were virtually unknown until the 1830s. Lake Champlain on its northeast borders had been fought over between French, British, and Indians for almost two centuries, for it was a fine water route between Canada and the Hudson River. But the wilderness itself was not even named until 1838, when geologist Ebenezer Emmons proposed it as an anglicized form of a name given to a tribe of Algonquin Indians. Supposedly, the name arose from their habit of living on tree buds and bark during the harsh winters, for which they were known as "ratirontak"–eaters of trees–by their Iroquois enemies. The region became one of the nation's first state parks when in 1894 New York State declared that "this forest preserve shall be forever kept as wild forest land."

Until the 1980s, it was the largest park in the U.S. (now Wrangell-St. Elias in Alaska is larger). It incorporates land in a range of categories, from the 1,500 square mile (3,885 sq km) wilderness areas kept entirely undeveloped, and where access is only on foot or horseback, to areas with many well-maintained state campgrounds, ski centers, public beaches, and boating facilities.

Ancient Formation

The Adirondacks are part of one of the most ancient mountain systems on earth. There are no fossils–the rocks were formed 700 million years before life emerged on earth. Back then, the area's foundations were a seabed that became gorged with lava and sediments. Later, a primeval continental collision buckled these rocks upward into 20,000-foot (6,095-m) peaks, in five ranges running northeast to southwest–lines that can still be traced today.

By roughly 500 million years ago, as the drifting continents parted again, erosion had worn the mountains to stubs. About 425 million years ago,

FACT FILE <–

TIME TO AVOID Blackfly season (early June to mid-July).

INFORMATION ON HIKING AND CAMPING The Adirondack Mountain Club on Lake George (tel: +1 (518) 668-4447), Lake Placid (tel: +1 (518) 523-3441), or High Peaks Information Center, 3 miles south of Lake Placid.

TRANSPORTATION Buses run from Albany to lakes Placid, Tupper, and George.

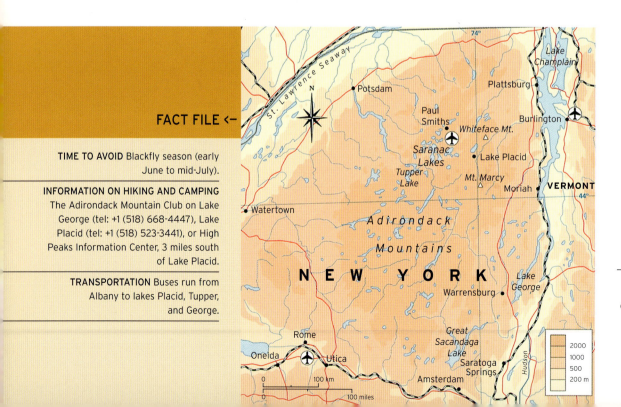

The heartland of this huge region (right) is dominated by the ancient eroded stumps of once-high mountains and hundreds of small lakes.

Lake Placid's wooded shores and central island are sheltered by the broad shoulders of Whiteface Mountain.

A hotel on Lake Placid's secluded banks (below) provides a haven from which to walk and fish.

North America collided again with Europe, throwing up the Appalachians, building a new edge to the American continent, and shielding the Adirondacks. For hundreds of millions of years the area seems to have been tranquil. Then came the last climatic chapter in the region's formation. Over a period of a million years, four great ice sheets blanketed North America, grinding off the surface, gouging out valleys. As the ice retreated for the last time 10,000 years ago, valleys and depressions filled with water, creating river systems and the Adirondacks's 2,000 lakes.

So the soil is thin and the mountains are low, but the forests are varied, from softwoods like spruce and balsam fir in wetlands to hardwoods on the valley sides, to the alpine plants and naked rocks above the 4,900-foot (1,493-m) timberline. Trail walkers favor the northeast, the High Peaks area, where 46 summits of around 4,000 feet (1,219 m)

The ribbon of Long Lake stretches for 13 miles (21 km) through the center of the National Park but is in parts only 100 yards (91 m) wide.

cluster around the highest point in New York State, Mount Marcy at 5,334 feet (1,625 m). From here the view is spectacular—as its first conqueror, John Cheney, described in 1837: "Old Champlain, though 50 miles off, glistens below you like a strip of white birch bark when slicked up by the moon on a frosty night; and the Green Mountains of Vermont beyond it fade and fade away, till they disappear as gradually as a cold scent when the dew rises."

Land of the Deer Hunter

Though there are black bears in the mountains, they are seldom seen around campgrounds because garbage is no longer left out in the open, but lone campers should heed the guidelines about food storage. The most common creatures are white-tailed deer, which live off grass, ferns, and goldenrod in the summer and hemlock, ash, and maple in the bitter winters. Since their predators—chiefly wolves—vanished long ago, the deer population would boom, destroying their winter food sources, if they were not contained by humans: this is prime deer-hunting country.

The human population is sparse—some 125,000—but every year about 9 million come in to ski, fish, camp, hunt, and climb (there is a club for those who have climbed Mount Marcy and its 45 neighbors: the Fortysixers). Most of them come in summer, after mid-July (before then, for about 6 weeks, mornings and evenings can be made a torture by biting blackflies).

Lake George is a popular and ever-expanding resort. But with 2,000 miles (3,200 km) of trail, hikers can spend days without seeing anyone, and campers can pitch tents freely as long as they are 150 feet (45 m) away from a trail, road, water source, or campground, and no higher than 4,000 feet (1,219 m). Canoers can use a 170-mile (275-km) network of lakes and streams, for which Lake Saranac is a good starting point. There are a dozen skiing centers—Lake Placid, with a speed-skating oval in the middle of town, hosted the 1980 Winter Olympics. Cross-country skiers have 60 miles (96 km) of groomed trails, and for downhill skiers Whiteface Mountain has 65 runs and 10 lifts.

-> The Hudson's Secret Source

Of the Adirondacks's countless rivers, the best known is the Hudson—by name, at least, for this section of the river is known to very few. At its mouth 306 miles (490 km) away along the New York-New Jersey border, it sustains the world's largest seaport. But here the Hudson is a stream that flows from Henderson Lake—or so it was believed when the first maps were made. In fact, the river's headwaters originate 6 miles (9.6 km) up from Henderson, in a little pool first seen only in 1872 by the state surveyor Verplanck Colvin. It was, he reported, a "minute, unpretending tear of the clouds, a lovely pool shivering in the breezes of the mountains." The phrase appealed to his bosses, and they named it accordingly: Lake Tear. Like most of the region's ponds, the lake is silting up as plant debris and silt washes from the slopes of Mount Marcy. But in other ways the area remains much as Colvin found it.

VANCOUVER

"To describe the beauties of this region will, on some future occasion, be a very grateful task to the pen of a skilled panegyrist."–Explorer George Vancouver, 1757-1798

Eight beautiful totem poles stand in a corner of Stanley Park. Their stories are explained in an interpretive center.

VANCOUVER IS CONSISTENTLY RANKED as one of the best cities in the world to live in, as well as one of the most alluring holiday destinations. It's easy to see why: few cities can match its sublime natural setting surrounded by harbors and a backdrop of the Coast range, cosmopolitan buzz, and relaxed way of life, and even fewer are as green, as safe, or as friendly. Where else in the world can you ski down world-class slopes in the morning, then stop for a dim sum lunch on your way to a championship golf course? The lively heart of the city is packed with great shopping, dining, and entertainment. There are numerous ethnic neighborhoods ranging from Chinatown to Little India, all providing a colorful alternative window on the city.

Despite all the big-city pleasures on offer, Vancouver's greatest allure is its magnificent natural setting. To the north are spectacular mountains (Whistler, the celebrated mountain skiing resort, is just a 2-hour drive away); the Pacific Ocean has worn the coast into a series of beautiful creeks and inlets. This spellbinding coastline, flecked with offshore islands, is home to a spectacular variety of marine life, including orcas (killer whales), dolphins, porpoises, sea lions, and otters. Across the strait, the charming port city of Victoria sits pretty at the southern tip of Vancouver Island. Its 19th-century colonial-style buildings and British customs are perfectly preserved after more than a century. Between Vancouver and Vancouver Island are the scenic and remarkably unspoiled Gulf Islands, which have become a summer paradise for thousands of visitors yearning for the slow, unhurried lifestyle of the islands.

Exploring Vancouver

Downtown is the heart of Vancouver, containing most of the city's shops, restaurants, and hotels, along with a business and financial district, a forest of glassy skyscrapers. You can get a 360-degree bird's-eye overview of the city from the lookout at

The glittering steel and glass of downtown Vancouver is a magnificent sight from across the bay.

Harbor Center Tower, a needle-thin glass tower housing the downtown campus of Simon Fraser University, with continually changing views of Burrard Inlet Harbor, the Coast Mountains, English Bay, and False Creek. Gastown is the historic heart of the city, and some of the city's earliest buildings are conserved along cobblestoned streets bustling with shops and its original steam clock. The pedestrianized area was originally named for a garrulous innkeeper nicknamed "Gassy Jack." Plunge from here into the noise and color of nearby Chinatown, just one of Vancouver's many ethnic neighborhoods. (Though if you are hopping between Chinatown and Gastown, take a taxi through the east side neighborhood.)

Travel by water taxi to Granville Island, one of the most popular attractions in Vancouver (along with the Vancouver Aquarium Marine Science Center), where the public market is piled high with fabulous fresh produce and gourmet items. Former warehouses have been converted into shops, restaurants, and studios for local artists and craftspeople. This was one of the first industrial areas to be reclaimed, but it was quickly followed by others that have become hip places to shop, eat, and drink. The Robson and Burrard street area hosts great international stores, including Louis Vuitton and Tiffany's (coming). Granville Street also has great shopping, including many antique stores.

West of downtown is the magnificent green expanse of Stanley Park, one of the largest public parks in the world. It's neatly edged by the

Make the heart-stopping journey across the Capilano Suspension Bridge—230 feet (70 m) above the Capilano River in North Vancouver.

looking south over the city or from the Gross Mountain tram in North Vancouver are considered the best possible views.

Vancouver boasts numerous beaches, and the mild climate ensures that they are always filled to capacity during the balmy days of summer. The best of the central beaches is Third Beach, along the south side of the Stanley Park Seawall. Further afield, the beaches at Jericho, Locarno, and Spanish Banks share one long golden stretch of sand curving around two pretty bays, while iconic Wreck Beach (where clothing is optional) at the end of Point Grey has been popular since the 1920s.

Victoria and the Gulf Islands

Victoria, at the southern tip of Vancouver Island and about 80 miles (130 km) from Vancouver as the crow flies, is a quaint little island city replete with historical buildings and oodles of charm. It's a popular daylong excursion from Vancouver, and can be reached by ferry (1 hour and 35 minutes) or floatplane (40 minutes). Victoria's fortunes peaked during the mid-19th century, but the city was soon eclipsed by Vancouver and it sank into a genteel decline. Little has changed since, and Victoria remains proud of its architectural heritage and of its colonial importance under the British Empire. Even now, the city retains many typically British customs, and afternoon tea (complete with scones and clotted cream) at the historic Empress Hotel remains a highlight of any trip. Several of the carefully preserved old houses are open to the public, and the city's Buchart gardens are famous throughout western Canada. Numerous whale-watching, fishing, and sea-kayaking excursions also depart from the lovely harbor (the best time to see whales is from late July to September).

The Gulf Islands are strung prettily along the Strait of Georgia between Vancouver Island and the mainland. They are linked by ferry and floatplane to Vancouver Island. The Islands are famous for their relaxed way of life, unspoiled scenery, and large artistic communities. Of all the islands, Salt Spring is the most popular, though Galiano (population 800) is perhaps the wildest and most beautiful (as well as the driest and sunniest). Among its many parks and reserves is the Montague Harbor Provincial Park, where gorgeous beaches made of finely crushed white seashells can be found in the midst of the wilderness. In 2003, the Gulf Islands National Park Reserve of Canada was established to protect the area's unique ecosystem, which supports a rich diversity of plant, animal, and marine life. Orcas, porpoises, sea lions, harbor seals, and otters call the surrounding waters home; eagles, falcons, and turkey vultures soar overhead. Most extraordinary of all are the orca whales: this region is one of the best places in the world to see these magnificent mammals.

celebrated Seawall Promenade—continually filled with joggers, cyclists, and in-line skaters—which offers breathtaking views across the city to the mountains and the harbor. The park offers plenty to keep both adults and kids amused. In addition to the world-class aquarium, there is a water slide park, a miniature railway and golf course, and beaches for swimming, along with an Olympic-size pool. Adults can also find tennis courts, lawn bowling, cricket games, and more. This is just one of the clutch of beautiful parks that fringe Vancouver and offer numerous activities from kayaking and fishing to hiking and mountain biking.

Lighthouse Park is a perfect picnic spot for visitors with a rental car who want to explore West Vancouver, with some of the region's oldest trees; Cypress Park, high in the mountains, offers spellbinding views from hiking trails and ski slopes. Not far from the University of British Columbia, Pacific Spirit Park, the furthest western point of the city, has extensive walking trails that meander through wooded ravines, estuary marshes, and pebbled shores. There are several splendid botanical gardens, including the nearby magnificent University of British Columbia's Botanical Garden, the VanDusen Botanical Garden, and the Bloedel Conservatory where tropical birds inhabit the lush rain forest. The Dr. Sun Yat-sen Classical Chinese Garden provides a tranquil oasis in the heart of Chinatown, and the Nitobe Memorial Garden is utterly enchanting. The exquisitely manicured gardens at lofty Queen Elizabeth Park offer lovely views within the city limits, although the view from either Stanley Park's seawall at the 9 o'clock gun

CLIMATE Vancouver has a temperate climate with considerable rain during the winter months, particularly November–February. When it is raining in the city, snow falls on Vancouver's north shore Coast Mountains, where there are three ski slopes.

WHEN TO GO June to early October, when the city's foliage and flowers are in bloom. The peak season for skiing and other winter sports is January and February, and the slopes of Whistler are ranked among the best in North America. Whale watching is best between late July and September.

CURRENCY The Canadian dollar, which is divided into 100 cents.

TIPPING Tipping is customary in restaurants and taxis. Tip around 15% or 20% if the service was excellent. A dollar per drink is normal in bars, or around 15% if you are buying a round. Canadians rarely tip more than 10%; 15% is considered generous.

POPULATION Downtown Vancouver 550,000. Metropolitan area 2.2 million.

NOTE Metropolitan Vancouver and Whistler will host the 2010 Winter Olympics.

Barkley Sound, on the west coast of Vancouver Island, is scattered with tiny islands and delightful coves.

CENTRAL AND SOUTH AMERICA

"Too often...I would hear men boast only of the miles covered that day, rarely of what they had seen."
LOUIS L'AMOUR, AMERICAN WRITER, 1908-1988

LA RUTA MAYA

Trace the marvels of a once great civilization by following the Mayan Route via stepped pyramids deep in the rain forest and dramatic ruins on the edge of the blue Caribbean Sea.

The ceremonies of the Toltecs, a warlike nation from central Mexico, are recalled in the carving of a skull storage rack.

LONG BEFORE THE AZTECS ARRIVED, a brilliant civilization flourished for many centuries in what is now southern Mexico, Guatemala, and Belize. The Mayas constructed massive cities and temples of stone without metal tools, pack animals, or the wheel. Most were mysteriously abandoned before the Spanish arrived in the 1500s, but in their heyday the Mayas had a hieroglyphic writing still not completely deciphered and, thanks to their remarkable astronomy, a highly accurate calendar.

To see all of the Mayan cities—there are hundreds —would take years, but it is possible to visit the main sites by following the 1,500-mile (2,400-km) Ruta Maya (Mayan Route), by bus or jeep, in 2 to 3 weeks. The journey—a modern, not an ancient route—goes through still remote areas, where old Spanish churches molder in quiet squares, the descendants of the Mayas follow their traditional way of life, and many—especially women—still wear traditional costume such as *huipile* (a decorated cotton blouse). Many travelers, once bitten by the Mayan bug, return venturing further off the beaten track to visit temples lost deep in the rain forest.

The best base is the fine old Spanish colonial town of Mérida in the north of the Yucatán peninsula. With an air of faded grandeur, it is noted for excellent hammocks. Near Pisté, a small town 60 miles (100 km) on the road east, stands the most famous, most visited Mayan city, Chichén Itzá. Too many visitors can destroy its atmosphere, but fortunately there are hotels in old houses and haciendas nearby, so it is possible to arrive in the evening and see the ruins early the following day, before the bus parties arrive.

Chichén Itzá is unlike any other Mayan site. Its architecture and sculpture reveal the influence of the warlike Toltecs of central Mexico, who occupied the city in the 900s A.D. Everything is aligned with mathematical and astronomical precision; if you add up all the steps of the huge pyramid of Kukulkán that dominates the site, they total 365. At the spring and autumn equinoxes, the parapet at the top casts long zigzag shadows down the side of the pyramid to meet the stone serpents' heads at the bottom, creating the effect of giant snakes descending. Inside the pyramid, a long slippery staircase climbs to the temple at the top, where the red-painted jaguar throne has jade eyes and flint fangs. Beneath the pyramid, Chac Mool—the Toltec rain god—reclines in the courtyard, holding a cup to receive the heart of the sacrificial victim.

The Sorcerer's Pyramid

Some 45 miles (72 km) south of Mérida stand the awesome ruins of Uxmal, a city that flourished between 600 and 900 A.D. The place is dominated by the astonishing pyramid known as El Advino—the sorcerer. Unlike other Mayan buildings, it appears almost modern: its smooth, round-cornered slopes soar at an alarming gradient to its 100-foot (30-m) summit, where a squat temple looks out over the Puuc Hills nearby. Climbing the almost vertical stairs to the top is a dizzying experience, closer to rock climbing than climbing a staircase. The

so-called Nunnery Quadrangle, on a small rise just to the north, shows the power and sophistication of the Mayan architects in a different way. The lower half of its long facade is plain honey-colored limestone, punctuated by square openings; the upper half is completely covered with an intricately carved geometric frieze.

Moving south through the state of Tabasco and into Chiapas, it becomes increasingly hot and steamy, and the landscape is more densely wooded. Chiapas has the largest indigenous population of any Mexican state. Since 1994, Zapatista rebels have been fighting Mexican government forces in the region, demanding rights for the *campesinos* (peasants). Except for occasional security checks, this is unlikely to affect visitors along the Ruta Maya, but check for news of the situation before setting out.

Just where the highlands of Chiapas begin stands Palenque. The natural setting is superb—the ruins rise from a clearing in the emerald jungle amid the constant chirrup of insects and the screech of howler monkeys. This is a hot, humid place, so stay in the new village 4 miles (7 km) up the road and visit the archeological zone in the early morning; not only is it cooler, but the sight of the temples emerging from the morning mist is marvelously atmospheric.

Three broad tiers of steps lead up to the long porticoed facade of the palace complex, to one side of which stands the four-story astronomical tower,

Chichén Itzá's forceful pyramid was probably built by Mayan architects for the Toltecs.

Uxmal's Pyramid of the Sorcerer soars with tremendous verve above the elegant Nunnery Quadrangle.

looking like a Chinese pagoda transported to the Central American rain forest. The decoration throughout the site is exquisite, especially on the Temple of Inscriptions pyramid, to the right of the palace complex. A dank and eerie tunnel leads into the heart of the 80-foot (25-m) stepped pyramid, to a crypt that houses the stone sarcophagus of the Mayan king Pacal. He ruled Palenque during the 7th century A.D., when the main buildings were constructed.

Mayan High-rises

There is a bus connection from Palenque, via the border town of La Palma, to Flores in the remote, densely forested Petán region of Guatemala, near the Mayan ruins of Tikal. A more enticing way to arrive, however, is by boat along the Usumacinta and Pasion rivers. A path leads beneath the canopy of trees; suddenly, improbably, a tall steep-sided pyramid of blackened limestone soars up. Then another, and another: the pyramids of Tikal are the skyscrapers of the Mayan world, 20-story temples with almost impossibly sheer stairways to their summits. Only a fraction of the site has been excavated, and it's thrilling to look out over the treetops from a pyramid and contemplate the undiscovered temples still beneath the dense foliage all around.

Palenque is one of the most graceful of all Mayan sites, a 7th-century ensemble of palaces and temples crowned by a tower for astronomical observations.

From here, make the short excursion across the Honduran border to another classic Mayan site, Copán, or continue to the former British colony of Belize. With its Afro-Caribbean population, this small, laid-back English-speaking nation feels more like the West Indies than Central America. Just off the coast is the largest coral reef in the Western Hemisphere, ideal for snorkeling and scuba diving in blue Caribbean waters as schools of exotic fish swim past

you. Yet despite these advantages, Belize attracts surprisingly few visitors. Visiting the impressive Mayan ruins of Altun Ha, just north of Belize City, you feel like an explorer as you come upon the great pyramid of Caracol deep in the rain forest of western Belize—at 140 feet (42 m), still the tallest building in the country.

From Belize City, you can return to Mexico through Quintana Roo, the easternmost state of the

Yucatán peninsula, stopping at Tulum. It is not the biggest of Mayan cities, but it is the only one on the coast, and the location is dramatic. The place was still occupied when the Spanish first came this way, and as you walk along the beach watching the great waves crashing against the limestone cliff beneath the towers, there is little to spoil the illusion that you have chanced upon an outpost of a still-powerful state, whose officials might emerge from the ramparts to check your credentials.

From here, it is about 80 miles (130 km) north to Cancún, with its international airport. The highway runs along the coast beside white sand beaches, but if you prefer not to end your Mayan odyssey in a brash new development, return to Belize City and fly from there.

–> FACT FILE

CURRENCIES Peso, Mexico; quetzal, Guatemala; lempira, Honduras; Belize dollar, Belize. All can devalue suddenly; take U.S. dollar traveler checks.

LANGUAGES Spanish is the official language, except in Belize, but many of the indigenous peoples still speak Maya-related tongues. English is widely understood.

CLIMATE Summer temperatures can easily reach 90°F (32°C) and above, and the climate is intensely humid. It rains May–October.

TIME TO GO October–March.

NEAREST INTERNATIONAL AIRPORTS Cancún, Mérida, Belize City.

WHAT TO TAKE Snorkeling gear, water purifier, insect repellent, sunblock, sunglasses, good hiking boots, waterproof clothing, binoculars.

WHAT TO BUY Hammocks, Panama hats, silverware.

HEALTH Vaccinations against typhoid, polio, and hepatitis A are recommended. Malaria is a problem. Avoid tap water, uncooked vegetables, and salads.

WILDLIFE WATCHING IN COSTA RICA

See the world in its primordial state in Costa Rica, a land of smoldering volcanoes and pristine forests that teem with exotic wildlife.

The cloud forest of Monteverde is home to an extraordinary variety of insect and bird life.

DEEP IN THE CAVERNOUS GREEN STILLNESS of a mist-shrouded forest, a shaft of sunlight falls on the bright splash of an orchid or butterfly. A scarlet macaw bursts from the foliage in a sudden explosion of color and sound. Fantastic bromeliad plants cling to trees, drawing nourishment from the air itself. This is Costa Rica.

This small peaceful country has escaped many of the troubles afflicting its Central American neighbors, thanks mainly to its lack of an army. The capital, San José, is a spruce little city of 400,000 people, remarkable for its orderliness and lack of obvious squalor.

"If San Salvador or Guatemala City were hosed down," wrote travel writer Paul Theroux, "all the shacks cleared and the people rehoused in tidy bungalows... those cities would, I think, begin to look a little like San José." It is an agreeable place to relax and to use as a base for exploring the beautiful Meseta Central region. There are hotels to suit all budgets, lively cafés steeped in the rich aroma of roasting Costa Rican coffee beans, an

attractive blend of colonial and modern Spanish architecture. There are countless restaurants, most of them serving simple Central American fare such as *gallo pinto* (rice and beans with grilled meat or chicken).

Along the Spine of the Continent

From San José it is a 5-hour journey to Corcovado National Park in the southeast of the country, through scenery of epic grandeur, taking you through Alajuela, Costa Rica's dignified second city nestling under the awesome smoking cone of Volcán Poás. The Pan American Highway then climbs up into the Cordillera Talamanca, following the 1,000-foot (300-m) ridge of mountains over steep-sided canyons and forested slopes. The views are unbelievable; perched on the spine of the continent, you can see both the Pacific Ocean and the Caribbean when the weather's clear.

Eventually the road winds down through cane fields to the decaying port of Golfito, looking out onto the Golfo Dulce. Beyond the clear, glassy waters of the gulf, the Osa Peninsula juts into the Pacific. This clump of rolling hills and deep canyons, cloud forests and mangrove swamps, is still a remote, inaccessible region fought over by gold miners and conservationists. Fortunately, a third of it—some 200 square miles (518 sq km)—has been set aside as the Corcovado National Park. Its huge coastal tracts and pristine forests are home to most of the country's endangered species, including jaguars, tapirs, and monkeys; caymans and crocodiles swim in its waters; turtles drag themselves onto the long white beaches to lay their eggs, while the world's largest bird of prey, the harpy eagle, can sometimes be seen wheeling in the skies above.

There is plenty of accommodation in Puerto Jímenez, the main town on the peninsula, which can be reached by boat from Golfito, but it is still several hours' journey by bus and on foot to the park, and better, therefore, to stay in the park itself, at one of the ranger stations at Los Patos or Sirena; camping is also available. The rangers will give advice about self-guided tours through the park. In the stations, biologists and ecologists mingle with hikers and nature lovers, discussing the animals and habitats of the area. But once you are hiking through the reserve, staying at the strategically placed lodges, your only companion will be the sights and sounds of nature in the echoing forests and along the endless, deserted beaches.

The Cloud Forest of Monteverde

Some 50 miles (80 km) north of San José, on the crest of the Cordillera Tilaran, is another reserve remarkable not only for its astounding cloud forest but also for a unique social and environmental experiment. The Monteverde Cloud Forest Reserve was first created by 40 Quakers who left Fairhope, Alabama, in 1950 in search of political and religious freedom—many of them had recently served jail sentences for refusing to be drafted, and Costa Rica had just disbanded its army. They bought land from local Costa Ricans and developed a dairy farm on the steep slopes. Environmentalists before their time, they set aside an area of virgin cloud forest to protect the watershed.

The reserve now protects some 40 square miles (104 sq km) of forest, though it is not an isolated pocket of conservation. Despite sporadic conflicts of interest, the project—and the visitors it has attracted—have inspired other local landowners to set aside forest and create nature trails. Even on the farmland outside of the reserve, you can walk from banana and coffee fields and moist, flower-filled cow pastures into dark, mysterious woods.

The reserve is approached via the ramshackle town of Santa Elena, 112 miles (182 km) northwest of San José (4½ hours by bus) and just 22 miles (35 km) north of the Pan American Highway. A narrow, unpaved road leads from Santa Elena, through the village of Monteverde, and up the mountain slope to the reserve entrance. It is only a few miles, but the road is often made difficult by dust in summer and mudslides during winter.

The forest itself is home to an astounding variety of wildlife, including the brilliant red quetzal bird, toucans, bellbirds, the bare-necked umbrella bird, the endangered tapir, monkeys, armadillos, coatimundis, and the brilliant colored, 2-inch golden toad. Orchids and bromeliads festoon the towering, ancient rain forest trees, while more than 200 species of fern provide moist, rich-smelling undergrowth.

The reserve administrators remain determined not to sacrifice this unique environment to mass tourism, though they have developed a wide range of amenities for visitors, all very discreetly arranged so as not to compromise the area's natural beauty. In Monteverde village, there are several simple but comfortable hotels, cozy pubs and restaurants (vegetarians are catered to), camping facilities, handicraft shops, and bookstores. On the reserve, the visitor center provides maps of the trails, and details of the birds and mammals you may see in the forest; and three simple shelters allow you to hike for days without leaving this enchanted world.

The rolling hills of central Costa Rica are banded by lowlands along the Caribbean and Pacific coasts, while to the south are mountains of volcanic origin.

The white-faced capuchin monkey (right) lives in the understory to midstory levels in the forests of Costa Rica and eats ripe fruit and insects. It is one among many varieties of animal and bird life in the forests.

-> FACT FILE

POPULATION 4,015,000.

CURRENCY Costa Rican Colón, devalues frequently.

LANGUAGES Spanish is the official language, but English is widely spoken.

CLIMATE Cloud forest regions are very humid: rainfall may average as much as 190 inches (483 cm) a year. Temperatures seldom fall below 72°F (22°C) in San José, and then only in December and January. The coast is even hotter.

TIME TO GO December through March is the least rainy period, also the coolest and the best for birdwatching.

MAIN AIRPORT San José.

WHAT TO TAKE Insect repellent, flashlight, good hiking boots, waterproof clothing, binoculars.

WHAT TO BUY Coffee, Costa Rican artesanía including leather goods and painted woodwork.

HEALTH Malaria and dengue fever (similar to malaria) are prevalent in some areas.

FOOD AND DRINK Among popular dishes are *sopa negra* (made with black beans and a poached egg), *casado* (rice, beans, stewed beef, and cabbage), and *tortas* (tortillas with meat and vegetables). Coffee is excellent.

ACCOMMODATION In recent years, numerous wonderful eco-lodges have opened up, particularly along the west coast.

Follow the trails through Corcovado National Park's virgin forest—the home of the country's highest tree, a 230-foot (70-m) ceibo.

It is even possible to rent a horse and ride to the nearby Río Negro reserve, from where you can see the lowering cone of Volcán Arenal, billowing gray plumes of lava smoke, which at night turn an infernal orange, shot through with sparks. The volcano is no more than 10 miles (16 km) away; to get there you must skirt Lake Arenal, a trip of some 30 miles (48 km). You can rent a four-wheel drive vehicle in nearby Fortuna to take you up the western slope. Looking down from the rim into the crater of bubbling lava gives an awe-inspiring sense of the raw power of nature, but you don't do it without an experienced guide–Arenal is an active volcano, and you definitely do not want to be up there when it blows.

Tortuguero National Park

The Tortuguero National Park, about 90 miles (144 km) north of Limón on Costa Rica's Caribbean coast, encompasses one of the last surviving sections of tropical rain forest in the country, a thrillingly remote region threaded with rivers and canals. Boat trips explore this moist, verdant paradise, offering innumerable opportunities for wildlife watching, including howler and spider monkeys, crocodiles, manatees, otters, and macaws. Most spectacular of all are the giant sea turtles, which nest along the glorious white-sand beaches. Many lodges in this area offer special packages, which include visits to the nesting grounds of these wonderful creatures, on the verge of extinction only 30 years ago. Of the four species found here, the green turtle is probably the most commonly found, while the giant leatherback–a monster that can grow up to 6 or 7 feet (2 m)–is the most striking.

North of Tortuguero, and linked by canal, the vast Barra del Colorado National Wildlife Refuge extends to the Nicaraguan border. This vast refuge protects extensive rain forests and wetlands, accessible only by boat along a network of waterways fringed with raffia palms. Huge jabiru storks circle lazily over the canopy, macaws shriek, and crocodiles and caiman bask on the mudbanks.

The fruit market in San José, Costa Rica's capital city.

Puerto Viejo is one of the many beaches and ports on the Caribbean coast worth visiting.

RIVERBOAT ON THE AMAZON

A thousand miles upriver from the Amazon's mouth, in the heart of the rain forests, lies the exuberant city of Manaus, once the world's rubber capital. Even further beyond is the faded glory of Iquitos in Peru.

Many of the creatures of the rain forest are masters of camouflage, such as the leaf frog.

TO MANY CHILDREN who open a battered atlas to the map of South America and point a finger at the dot labeled Manaus, it looks unspeakably remote in the middle of the continent's green heart on the long ribbon of the Amazon. Later, seeing television wildlife documentaries, or perhaps the image of the demented conquistador floating downstream on a raft in Werner Herzog's film *Aguirre: The Wrath of God*, confirms the impression, and the Amazon becomes an unmissable destination.

There are basically two ways to see it. One is to book a tour, flying into Manaus or Iquitos, from where comfortable boats chug through the backwaters to one of the eco-lodges built in the rain forest. These are usually constructed in the traditional local style of tropical hardwood and thatched with palm leaves, and may float on the river or be perched on stilts amid the treetops. From their observation platforms there are panoramic views across the rain forest; accommodation is in comfortable chalets (huts) with private bathrooms, and most lodges have a restaurant offering local and international cuisine. Take a canoe along the rivers to spot alligators, piranha fish, and animals along the riverbank or one of the organized walking tours in the jungle. The disadvantage is that you travel in a hermetically sealed bubble, seeing the natural environment but detached from local human life.

By Rusting Riverboat

The other way is to go down to the ocean port of Belém, a vibrant city with a splendid market where old Portuguese colonial buildings are framed by a

The old riverboats that ply the Amazon provide a picturesque, if slow (and often uncomfortable), means of traveling from the river mouth at Belém to the river's upper reaches in Peru.

Manhattan skyline of sleek towers, and ask around for one of the passenger boats that ply the river. There's no doubt that this is the hard way to travel. The rusty old riverboats are packed with passengers, livestock, and freight. Accommodation consists of a sweltering shared cabin or a hammock on deck, and often the only source of water is a standpipe that comes straight up from the river. The food served on board seldom varies—fish with rice and yucca, a sweet potatolike vegetable, with the occasional piece of chicken. But its quality varies alarmingly; the fish that was deliciously fresh when it was first taken on board may be served, rotten and slimy, 3 days later. Remember these are lawless parts. When the monotony of the journey is relieved by the occasional stop at a riverside village—often little more than a landing stage with a scruffy bar—a lot of alcohol is drunk and tempers flare. Although most passengers will be scrupulously honest, there's nowhere secure to store valuables, so it is wise to leave them at home.

Another disadvantage is that the riverboats stay close to the main channel of the river—which is

–> FACT FILE

CURRENCY Brazilian real; Peruvian inti. Both currencies have a history of frequent devaluations, so travel with U.S. dollar traveler checks.

CLIMATE Equatorial; expect temperatures of around 90°F (32°C) or higher and heavy rains January–May, especially in eastern Amazonia; central Amazonia, around Manaus, is dryer.

TIME TO GO July–October.

NEAREST INTERNATIONAL AIRPORTS Manaus, Iquitos.

WHAT TO TAKE Sunglasses, water-purifying pills, hammock, insect repellent, flashlight, good hiking boots, waterproof clothing, binoculars.

WHAT TO BUY Duty-free electronic goods (in Manaus), and local craftworks, including bongo drums and terracotta figurines.

HEALTH Vaccination against typhoid, yellow fever, and polio strongly advised. Malaria resistant to drugs is a major problem; mefloquine is recommended. Do not drink water unless bottled or sterilized; avoid salads, uncooked vegetables, unpeeled fruits, and undercooked meat, especially from street sellers.

LANGUAGES In Brazil Portuguese is the official language, but English and Spanish are widely spoken. In Peru, Spanish is the official language but English is understood in some tourist areas.

The Amazon rain forest has the largest number of plant species in the world, dominated by trees that rear 200 feet (60 m) above the forest floor.

Broad Parisian-style boulevards—a relic of the evanescent prosperity of the late 19th-century rubber boom—give Manaus an improbably European feel in the heart of Amazonia.

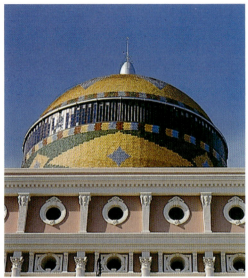

The opera house in Manaus was built in 1896 at the height of the rubber boom.

often 6 miles (9.5 km) wide—and far from the banks, so you won't see so much wildlife. But for the intrepid, travel by local boat has advantages. First, it is astonishingly cheap; as probably the only gringos (westerners) on the boat, you'll learn basic Portuguese and/or Spanish fast, and what you lose in wildlife watching, you'll make up for in human drama.

Time passes slowly as the endless curtain of green jungle slides past the boat. When the boat stops at a riverside settlement, it is a major event. There's a flurry of activity as members of the crew trade staples such as toothpaste and cigarettes for local produce, and passengers get on and off: a farmer bringing home a new tractor part, a woman and her daughters taking chickens to sell in the market, a young man returning crestfallen from the big city where his grand plans have failed. Then it's back to the slow rhythm of the journey, lying on the

baking tin roof of the boat watching birds wheel over the unbelievably wide expanse of muddy brown water. At night, fireflies follow the boat, and the eyes of a cayman glint from the water.

Meeting of the Waters

Approaching Manaus, the river divides into two streams of distinctly different colors—to the left, a yellowish swirl, to the right, a wide band of dark water. This is what gives the Rio Negro its name. The water darkens as the two great rivers join. On the banks of the Rio Negro, 9 miles (14 km) north of the confluence, is Manaus. For travelers, the city is a culture shock: big, glamorous, and sleazy, the one metropolis of all of Amazonia, with a seedy dockland, bustling commercial center, and throbbing nightlife. The turn-of-the-century rubber boom left the town with a grand neoclassical opera house, where international megastars such as Sarah Bernhardt and the Ballet Russe once performed. Then the boom collapsed—rubber plants smuggled out to Malaya broke Brazil's lucrative monopoly— leaving the place almost impoverished. But massive tax concessions have restored the local economy, turning Manaus into the consumer capital of Amazonia; people fly in from as far afield as Colombia and Venezuela to buy refrigerators and dishwashers in its warehouse emporia.

Faded Elegance

The Amazon port of Iquitos, 1,200 miles (1,920 km) further upstream and cultural center of eastern Peru, provides a better idea of how Manaus once looked. Above Manaus, Brazilians call the river the Solimoes, though it is still known to the rest of the world as the Amazon. At Tabatinga, on the three-way frontier between Brazil, Peru, and Colombia, you'll probably have to change boats. This is a grim, gritty modern border town, but its old quarter has a faded elegance and some decent hotels.

Iquitos, the main city of the Peruvian Amazon, is a surreal outpost of European elegance of the 1800s surrounded by virgin rain forest; no roads connect it with the outside world; it can only be reached by plane or riverboat. The town has several improbable relics of the rubber boom, including some grand old hotels, the Tarapaca Pier, and the curious Iron House, designed by the French engineer Gustave Eiffel for the 1889 Paris World Fair and reassembled in Iquitos.

In the riverside quarter of the Puerto de Belém area, traditional thatched houses stand on stilts at the water's edge. Above Iquitos, the river divides, with the Maranon continuing west and the Ucayali

turning abruptly south. Those travelers brave—or demented—enough can push on up the Ucayali to Pucallpa, a raffish port on the edge of the rain forest and the Peruvian highlands. Here is the end of the Amazon basin, within a day's bus ride of the Andean realm of the Incas.

-> Riverboat Journey Times

Brazil	upstream	downstream
Belém to Manaus:	5-6 days	4-5 days
Manaus to Tabatinga:	5-8 days	3-4 days
Peru		
Tabatinga to Iquitos:	4 days	2 days
Iquitos to Pucallpa:	5 days	3 days

The backwaters and tributaries of the Amazon (left) are home to the giant waterlily, *Victoria amazonica* (above), whose leaves are strong enough to support the weight of a child.

THE INCA TRAIL

Follow paved roads built centuries ago by the people of the Inca Empire, through jungles and spectacular mountain passes, to reach the "lost city" of a once-great civilization.

The view from the highest pass on the Inca Trail.

IN 1533, THE INCA EMPIRE FELL to Spanish conquistadors led by Francisco Pizarro, and the complex Inca civilization was totally destroyed. Since the rediscovery of many Inca monuments in the early 1900s, the magnificent and melancholy remains of this lost empire have lured visitors from around the world. Traveling from the old Inca capital of Cuzco through the "Sacred Valley" of the Rio Urubamba to the ruined Inca city of Machu Picchu on its mountain peak, you discover the Inca world still survives in the high mountain: in the Quechua language spoken by some million people (half the population), in the traditional costumes of the Andean *campesinos* (peasants), and in the Catholic saints' days, often a thinly veiled homage to the old gods.

Acclimatization in Cuzco

Cuzco is a graceful colonial town in a valley 11,024 feet (3,360 m) high, ringed by snow-capped mountains. The oldest continuously inhabited city in the Americas, it was half destroyed when the Incas rose against the Spanish in 1536. The amazingly neat Inca masonry has since been incorporated into later buildings, and many—including the baroque cathedral—rest on the foundations of Inca palaces. The main square, the broad Plaza de Armas, was once the ceremonial center of the Inca capital; stop for a meal or a coffee beneath its arcades, and you'll probably find a chunk of Inca masonry beside you.

Arriving by plane from Lima, altitude sickness symptoms may strike: breathlessness, dizzy spells, and nausea, and it is worth spending a few days of acclimatization in Cuzco before climbing to greater heights. There is no shortage of hotels—many of them are old and charming—and Cuzco has delightful cobbled streets with wooden-balconied colonial buildings and mysterious courtyards. In the street market by the station, fruit and vegetables are sold alongside traditional crafts—fabrics made from alpaca (llama) wool dyed with natural colors such as cochineal. Sample a plastic cup of *chicha*, a weak and cloudy beer made from (prechewed) fermented maize, or buy a bag of coca leaves to chew.

On a ridge above the town stand the remains of the Inca fortress Sachsayhuaman. The Inca city was planned in the shape of a puma, and the fortress formed the animal's head. Though damaged during the 1536 uprising, its tiers of zigzag granite ramparts, with characteristic trapezoid doorways, still look powerfully impressive. There were originally three towers at the summit; the circular foundations of one give a good idea of its immense size. From here there are marvelous views of the surrounding mountains and over the tiled roofs and church towers of Cuzco.

On the Inca Trail

To control their empire, which stretched into modern Ecuador and Chile, the Incas built an elaborate network of trails, running more than 2,500 miles (4,000 km) through highlands, Amazon valleys, and coastal deserts. The trail of some 30 miles (48 km) in the Urubamba Valley to Machu

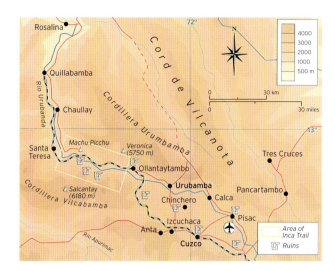

Picchu takes 4 days to walk because there are some big gradients. There are campgrounds and shelters along the way, but take your own food.

Crossing the fast-flowing river on a small suspension bridge, the trail starts amid dense subtropical vegetation before climbing into the bleak highlands; far below, the silver ribbon of the Urubamba runs along the bottom of its gorge, while snow-capped Andean peaks tower above. On the way are Indian villages and abandoned Inca towns, which were cited to control the route. At first, the trail is just a dirt track, but on the third day, after crossing a cold, windy mountain pass, the Abra de Runkuracay, the trail changes to a narrow roadway, paved with close-fitting Inca stones.

Further on, the roofless and overgrown Inca town of Sayamarca ("Dominant Town") clings to a rock above the trail, accessible only by a narrow stairway cut into the stone between an overhanging rock wall and a sheer precipice. Nearby is an ancient stone aqueduct. More evidence of Inca engineering skills appear beyond the next valley, where a 26-foot (8-m) tunnel—wide enough to allow laden beasts to pass through—has been cut into the rock.

The "Lost City"

You emerge from the next pass to an awe-inspiring view of the Urubamba Valley and the glistening glaciers of the 19,000-foot (5,787-m) Nevada Veronica. Just below, the Inca ruins of Phuyupatamarca ("Cloud Level Town") cling to the slope, surrounded by the terraced fields that fed its

In Cuzco's main market, in front of a Spanish colonial archway, Indians from the surrounding countryside sell herbs and traditional crafts alongside more domestic goods.

population. A steep granite stairway cuts down into the forested slopes of the Urubamba Gorge toward another Inca town, Huinay Huayna ("Forever Young"), with a campground and a visitor center nearby. From here, a broad level path leads through scrub and light woodland to narrow stone steps. These lead into a small structure, Intipunku, Gateway to the Sun. Through the rectangular stone doorway, the "lost city" of Machu Picchu appears on its mountain ridge, walls and thatched huts are often wreathed in clouds, and you feel as if you were its first discoverer. From Intipunku, a path leads directly to Machu Picchu itself.

An alternative to the 4-day hike is to travel by train from Cuzco to Aguas Calientes, where buses wind up to the ruins. You might choose to stay in Aguas Calientes, a dilapidated but welcoming little town nestled in a cloud-filled valley beneath densely wooded slopes. Spend a peaceful night in one of the small hotels, listening to the rushing river and strange animal cries from the cloud forest, then set off early next morning to walk the mile along a steep valley, through which the Rio Urubamba gurgles its way to Machu Picchu.

Hewn from a Sacred Mountain

Clinging to the flanks of a steep ridge, tier upon tier of defensive walls, gardens, palaces, and temples rise. Fountains gurgle down through stepped basins. Walls of many-sided stones, so finely worked that you couldn't slip a scalpel between them, loom above. Massive, sloping stone doorways lead onto plazas filled with swaying grass and poppies. At the highest point is an altar, from which a mysterious square pillar known as the "Hitching Post of the Sun" projects. Altar, post, and the steps that lead up to them are all hewn from mountain rock, which the Incas held sacred.

The whole site is overlooked by a towering granite pinnacle, Huayna Picchu. The original Inca stairway

leads through cloud forest festooned with orchids and air plants to the summit, where bright butterflies flutter about your head. From the top, you can see the entire site amid its setting: the cloud-capped peaks, the forested valleys, and the river far below. The ruins are especially impressive at dawn or sunset, but many buildings are currently being restored.

Hiram Bingham, the American archaeologist who discovered the city in 1911, thought that he had found Vilcabamba, where the last Incas held out against the Spanish until 1572. But Machu Picchu dates from the mid-1400s, and the less impressive ruins of the Incas' last capital were later discovered 100 miles (160 km) west at Espiritu Pampa. Machu Picchu may have been a religious center abandoned before the Spanish arrived, possibly as a result of the civil war and smallpox epidemic around 1527. But such theories remain speculation. The purpose and fate of Machu Picchu are shrouded in mystery.

The ruined Inca city of Machu Picchu clings to steep, cloud-forested slopes high above the Urubamba River.

Descendants of the Inca people in Ollantaytambo form a large percentage of the town's population, and Quechua, the main Inca language, is still widely spoken.

-> FACT FILE

CURRENCY New sol (post 1990) and U.S. dollars welcomed in small denominations.

VISAS Citizens of the United States, Canada, Great Britain, South Africa, New Zealand, and Australia do not require visas to enter Peru as tourists for up to 90 days.

PERMITS To hike the Inca Trail you must organize a trek through an officially approved agency at least 1 month in advance (up to 2 months in advance during high season, May–September); independent trekking without an official guide is prohibited.

HEALTH Yellow fever, typhoid, and polio vaccinations strongly recommended. Drink only bottled or boiled water; avoid salads, uncooked vegetables, and peeled fruits. Rest and/or head for lower altitudes if you have severe symptoms of altitude sickness. Diamox is recommended for combating altitude sickness.

LANGUAGE Spanish and Quechua are the two official languages. English is understood in the main centers.

CLIMATE Subtropical but varies dramatically with altitude. It can be very cold high up; heavy rains December–April.

TIME TO GO April–November.

NEAREST AIRPORT Cuzco.

WHAT TO TAKE Pills for malaria, insect repellent, sunscreen, sunglasses, sun hat, hiking boots, windproof, warm clothing, binoculars, flashlight.

FOOD AND DRINK Pisco sour, a potent brandy, is the national drink. *Aji* and *ajo* (pepper and garlic) form the basis of most dishes, along with rice and about 2,000 types of native potato. *Aji de gallina* (chicken in a spicy cream sauce) is popular. Avocados and tropical fruit are abundant.

WHAT TO BUY Handicrafts, alpaca rugs and blankets, ceramics, carved gourds.

IMPORTANT NOTE New regulations mean that the Inca Trail (not Machu Picchu or the shorter 2-day trail) will close for 1 month a year, usually February. The government is considering extending the period to 3 months a year. Check that the trail will be open before you book.

PATAGONIA, ARGENTINA

"...the uttermost part of the earth." –Bruce Chatwin, *In Patagonia*

PATAGONIA IS UNIMAGINABLY VAST, battered by the Atlantic Ocean to the east and bounded by the Andes to the west. At its southernmost point, the archipelago of the Tierra del Fuego traditionally marks the end of the world. The first European explorers in this immense land described the native Patagonians as giants, twice the height of other people, and the bones of the world's largest dinosaur were discovered in the remote town of Plaza Huincul. Most of Patagonia is covered in wild, windswept steppe, where llamalike guanacos skip under a boundless sky, but it also encompasses desert, ice fields, mountains, and some of the most unspoiled coastline in the world.

The communities are linked by plane, but for real road-trip romance, take the legendary highways like Ruta 40 and Ruta 3, which–although little more than dirt tracks in parts–score Patagonia from north to south. Many estancias (traditional Argentine sheep farms with enormous lands) have guest rooms for visitors (though these are incredibly historic, elite, and expensive–some costing U.S. $1,000 per person per day). Most offer numerous activities from horseback riding to fly fishing.

The Chubut Valley and the Valdés Peninsula

Well into the 19th century, few were prepared to settle on Patagonia's inhospitable terrain, but for some it held the promise of freedom. On July 28, 1865 (still celebrated as "Landing Day"), 153 Welsh settlers came ashore near present-day Puerto Madryn. Alarmed by the erosion of their language and traditions in their homeland, this little band set

The romantic Islotes Les Eclaireurs lighthouse is better known as "the lighthouse at the end of the world."

The nimble guanaco is perfectly adapted to Patagonia's wild and craggy landscape.

Patagonia offers spectacular opportunities for observing wildlife. The Southern Right Whale—on the verge of extinction until recently—gathers to breed every year on the Valdés Peninsula. The Atlantic coastline is home to numerous penguin and seal colonies: the most spectacular is the southern elephant seal, which can weigh over 3 tons and is the largest seal in the world. Patagonia's bird life is equally rich and varied, from the Magellanic penguins on the Atlantic coast to the mighty Andean condors found to the west. Patagonia is also home to the southernmost hummingbird and the parakeet living closest to the Pole.

out to establish a Welsh colony, where they could preserve their culture intact (in other parts of the region, German and Swiss settlers had the same idea). Even now, in small communities such as Dolavon, Gaimon, and Trelew, you can still hear the Welsh language spoken, stop off for a Welsh tea, or take in the annual *eisteddfodau*, the traditional celebrations of Welsh music, literature, and song.

Much of the starkly beautiful Valdés Peninsula, close to Puerto Madryn, is a protected nature reserve, its rugged coast and empty beaches home to a rich variety of marine life. Out at the tip of Punta Ninfa, the only continental colony of elephant seals congregate in a sheltered bay, while whales gather to breed in the calm waters of the Golfo Nuevo from May through December. Besides whale-watching opportunities, the area is known as a sub-aquatic paradise, offering excellent cold-water diving and snorkeling.

Wild Patagonia

Ruta 3 heads south through the arid, wind-whipped *meseta* (plateau). About 50 miles (80 km) south of Caleta Olivia, a dirt track splinters westward into

The rugged steppe of El Chaltén encompasses steely lakes and offers beautiful views of the distant Andes.

the eerie Petrified Forest (Bosque Petrificado), which was declared a national monument in 1954. When volcanic eruptions were throwing up the Andes 130 million years ago, this gigantic forest was buried under thick layers of ash, where it slowly turned to stone. Over millennia, wind and rain scoured the region, exposing the prodigious trunks and creating a strange, otherworldly landscape—a fitting home for the Patagonian giants of legend.

There is more spectacular wildlife in the magnificent Monte León National Park, about 30 miles (45 km) southeast of the provincial capital of Santa Cruz. This is one of Argentina's newest parks,

only established in 2004, and remains one of Patagonia's best kept secrets. In this wild and romantic stretch of the Atlantic Coast, the shoreline is dotted with islands and towering stacks and pocked with caves and caverns. It's a walker's paradise, but keep an eye on the treacherous tides that can rapidly engulf the islands and swallow the bays. Guanacos pick their way over lonely cliffs, flamingos gather in pink clouds, and sea lions and Magellanic penguins bask in secluded bays. You can stay in the old estancia de Monte León, where a small museum describes the park's former incarnation as an extensive sheep farm.

This sea of icy peaks can be found in the spectacular Parque Nacional Los Glaciares.

The immense Perito Moreno glacier is Patagonia's most celebrated natural attraction, gliding infinitesimally across Lago Argentino.

FACT FILE ←

AREA 492,000 square miles (787,000 sq km)

POPULATION 1,500,000

CURRENCY Peso, divided into 100 centavos. ATMs are easy to find in larger towns, but get cash before heading into rural areas. Traveler checks are rarely accepted outside Buenos Aires.

BEST TIME TO GO Longer days and warmer temperatures make summer (December-March) the best bet.

LANGUAGES Spanish. English is rarely spoken except in urban areas.

WHAT TO TAKE Windproof, waterproof jacket, sturdy walking boots.

FOOD AND DRINK Try Welsh cakes and *bara brith* (fruit bread) in the Chubut Valley, or freshly barbecued fish or lamb elsewhere. Argentina is also famous for its meat and *asadas*, or barbecues.

AIRPORTS Patagonia has several airports, with regular shuttles between major towns and Buenos Aires. These include Puerto Madryn, El Calafate, Ushuaia, and Río Gallegos.

GETTING AROUND Not all roads—even the main highways—are paved. Don't drive in rural areas at night, when livestock often gather on the roads to stay warm.

Parque Nacional Los Glaciares

The National Park of the Glaciers contains Patagonia's most celebrated natural attraction, the glittering Perito Moreno glacier. Stretching for 20 miles (32 km), this vast mountain of ice is one of only three advancing glaciers in Patagonia. The effects of global warming have caused most glaciers to retreat, but the Perito Moreno performs a curious natural dance: it advances slowly over the enormous Lago Argentino and, on reaching the opposite shore, forms a huge dam. The water pressure finally forces the dam to rupture spectacularly, in one of the greatest natural sound-and-light shows on earth. The last rupture, in March 2004, brought 17,000 visitors from all over the world; it is impossible to predict when the next one will take place.

The main access town is El Calafate, on the shores of Lago Argentino, where boat cruises take visitors right up to the glacier face. Watching the mighty glaciers calving—throwing off huge chunks of ice with a thunderous groan—is an awe-inspiring experience. This southern section of the national park attracts hordes of day-trippers, while the northern section, accessed from the small town of El Chaltén, is considerably quieter. El Chaltén is a 5-hour drive north of El Calafate, the battered road heading through stark steppe with the snow-capped Andes spiking the sky to the west. The town sits at the base of Mount Fitzroy (110,000 feet/3,375 m), and the nearby forests, peaks, and lakes offer excellent opportunities for hiking, climbing, fishing, and adventure sports.

The End of the World

The archipelago at the southern tip of South America is called the Tierra del Fuego ("Land of Fire"). It was formed millions of years ago by the last stutter of the Andes mountain range. Dangerous prisoners were once incarcerated far from civilization in the prison at Ushuaia, the southernmost city in the world, which spills down mountain slopes to the sea on the Isla Grande. Now this friendly community is the gateway to the Tierra del Fuego National Park (and the departure gateway for many cruises to Antartica), where inky lakes and ancient forest, rivers, and sweeping bays cluster at the ends of the earth. The highlight is a scenic narrow-gauge steam train, which chugs through dense forest to Lapataia Bay—quite literally the end of the line. Pleasure boats negotiate the Beagle Channel, passing islands populated by birds, seals, and penguins, and head out to the lonely Lighthouse at the End of the World (which inspired Jules Verne's novel of the same name) on the Isla de los Estados.

AFRICA

"Going up that river was like traveling back to the earliest beginnings of the world, when vegetation rioted on the earth and the big trees were king."
JOSEPH CONRAD, POLISH-BORN ENGLISH WRITER, 1857-1924

MARRAKESH AND THE ATLAS MOUNTAINS

A city seething with life, and snow-fed mountain slopes keep the desert at bay.

Ouarzazate once was nothing but the lonely frontier fort of Taouirt on the desert's edge, but now has dozens of hotels, an airport, and a zoo.

CLIMB TO THE FLAT ROOF of any of the small hotels in the heart of old Marrakesh, and you will see a panorama of mosques, minarets, and towers, with palm trees rising above hidden courtyards. Beyond, seeming very close in the clear air, the peaks of the High Atlas Mountains, snowcapped most of the year, flash white against deep blue skies. Over everything lies a reddish pall, the dust that gives Marrakesh its name, "the Red City," reminding you that, though green with gardens, this city is an oasis amid a desert. But don't spend too long admiring the panorama. Just beneath, throbbing with cacophonous life, is the Djema el Fna, which means Place of the Dead—though nowhere could be livelier than Marrakesh's greatest square. The acrobats, musicians, dancers, snake charmers, fortune-tellers, and storytellers filling the dusty expanse might have stepped from the pages

of *The Arabian Nights*. The square, an oblong surrounded by low buildings, is a stage for their daily performances, but it is at night that the unscripted free show is at its most brilliant—and not just for tourists, for the stories related are all in Arabic or Berber, not French or English. Rows of open-air food stalls are set up where you can eat typical Moroccan food—try *harira*, a thick soup—and sip mint tea, the standard Moroccan drink served with quantities of sugar. Beware, however, of the peddlers who will hassle you nonstop, trying to sell you their services as guides or almost anything else. Don't imagine that pretending ignorance of French, English, or any other language will save you from their attentions: they seem to speak every tongue under the sun.

Guide to Bartering

Unless traveling with an organized tour, it is helpful for first-timers to hire a guide, either from the Tourist Office or, almost as good, from among the more agreeable individuals in Djema el Fna; they cost little. Once with your chosen guide, you are safe from all others as he zealously leads you around. You will undoubtedly end up in a shop in the souks, the maze of tiny covered alleys crammed with stands selling leatherware, silver, silk, wool and cotton clothes, carpets, spices, ornate daggers, and much plastic trash. The shop chosen will probably be run by someone the guide just happens to know, who will—such is your astounding luck—generously offer you an "extra special price." Haggling is not only expected, it is almost obligatory: express utter unbelief at the price first demanded and doubts over whether the item is really what you want. It should be a leisurely process, marked by the consumption of endless mint teas. Once a price is agreed, most shopkeepers prove surprisingly knowledgeable about credit cards and air freight home if the item is too large to carry.

Enduring Glories

But Marrakesh is not just an emporium; it is a former imperial city, with some of the greatest architecture in the Islamic world, reflecting its glorious if turbulent past. Founded in 1062 by the Almoravid dynasty, who ruled an empire from Toledo, Spain, to Senegal, the city has since been

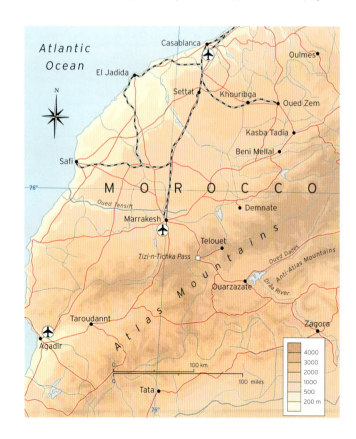

Windows in exterior walls are rare in reclusive Marrakesh, but the few visible often have elaborate iron grills and colorful tilework, reflecting the influence of Mozarabic craftspeople from Granada in Spain.

deserted, ruined, and rebuilt many times. Its golden age was the 1100s, when Moorish craftsmen came from Spain to build mosques and palaces. Unfortunately, non-Muslims are strictly barred from entering mosques, but you can admire the outside of the Koutoubia Mosque tower, a classic of Moorish Andalucian architecture, and actually go inside the Medersa Ben Yousef, a *madrasa* (theological college) of the 1500s, with intricate stucco ceilings. More romantic are the Saadian Tombs, also dating from the 1500s, where among slender cypresses and rosebuds lie the graves of the Saadi sultans. Inside the gloomy but stunningly opulent Hall of Twelve Columns is a dome covered in what looks like gilded lace, another example of Moroccan stucco.

Outside of the city walls stretches the still elegant Ville Nouvelle (new town), built under the French protectorate (1912-1956), with French restaurants and cafés lining busy boulevards planted with flowering orange trees. Here too are luxury hotels set in verdant gardens around swimming pools, where the former British prime minister Winston Churchill used to stay and paint. Unless you really love the hubbub of the old city, this is the best area to stay, only half an hour on foot from Djema el Fna, less by bus or *fiacre* (horse-drawn carriage).

Mountain and Desert

Beyond Marrakesh lie the mountains and desert of what the French called *le Grand Sud* (the Deep South), now accessible by bus or rental car, provided you stick to the main asphalted routes–

Marrakesh, which by day can seem drab and dusty, hums with life far into a night lit by thousands of lamps.

Hidden within the folds of the Atlas, waterfalls such as the one at Ouzand seldom cease their flow, even in midsummer, thanks to the slow-melting mountain snows.

The half-ruined *casbah* (fort) of Telouet rises above fertile cropland irrigated by waters from the Atlas Mountains. The views from its flat roof are spectacular.

the lesser roads can be just tracks over naked rock. Some 30 miles (50 km) beyond the city, the road climbs through green oak woods toward the peaks of the High Atlas. These are the greatest mountains of North Africa, rising over 13,000 feet (3,900 m), and in spring they are covered with wildflowers. The village of Telouet, 12 miles (20 km) east of the highway, is worth a detour: stone houses with unglazed windows and flat earth roofs surround a grim-looking *casbah* (fort). Telouet was once the headquarters of the Glaoui tribe, who governed most of southern Morocco for the French with medieval ferocity until the 1940s, hanging their enemies' heads on the walls of Marrakesh. The highway snakes up to the Tizi n'Tichka Pass, at 7,467 feet (2,275 m) the highest in Morocco and

snowbound in winter, and then descends into a barren, rocky landscape.

Ouarzazarte, about 90 miles (144 km) from Marrakesh, was once a vital frontier fort on the edge of the world's greatest desert. From first sight its red cubes of houses and palm trees look like a movie set for an oasis, and movies have been indeed shot here. There are now several hotels and even a golf course, thanks to the Dra River. The river, fed by Atlas snows, cuts a gorge through a range of the Anti Atlas Mountains, then heads south into the desert where it finally expires. En route, it creates green, intensively cultivated oases with mud-built villages surrounded by palm trees, just like a miniature Nile Valley. The road follows the river, and it is worth stopping at the village of

-> FACT FILE

CURRENCY Moroccan dirhams.

LANGUAGES Arabic and Berber dialects (spoken by 40% of the population), with French and some Spanish and English. Take a phrase book.

CLIMATE Mediterranean/Saharan. Very hot in summer, over 100°F (38°C) in Marrakesh, but often cold in the mountains. It can rain heavily in winter.

WHEN TO GO October-April to avoid the heat, but take warm clothing.

TWO DON'TS Don't drink the tap water and don't go around half naked, especially if you are young and female. Although some tourists do, it upsets Moroccans.

AIRPORTS Marrakesh, Ouarzazarte, Agadir.

GETTING AROUND Reasonable bus services along the main routes, but for freedom rent a car.

WHAT TO BUY Carpets, leatherware, pottery, silver and copper, spices.

FOOD AND DRINK The great national dish is *tajine*, made with fish or spiced meatballs, young lamb or chicken, and prunes, infused with lemon and olives and cooked slowly in a clay dish. Most Moroccans, being Muslim, do not touch alcohol, but go for mint tea or fresh fruit juice, but good potent local wine can be found in restaurants for Westerners. Try Cabernet President among the reds and Oustalet rosé for a refreshing pink. The whites are not recommended.

Agdz to admire the carpets for which it is famous. Zagora, 104 miles (168 km) southeast of Ouarzazarte, and another former frontier fort, is rather drab compared to the surrounding scenery, but useful as a base for exploring the desert and especially for renting camels. If you can ride these strange lurching beasts in comfort—some people get seasick—you can arrange desert expeditions here for up to a week, complete with guides and tents. You sleep under canvas and can see the stars rise with stunning clarity above the desert, which spreads south and east for thousands of empty miles.

Snake charmers, usually Berbers, perform daily in the main square of Marrakesh, the Djema el Fna. The charmers control the reptiles as much by their own body movements as by their music.

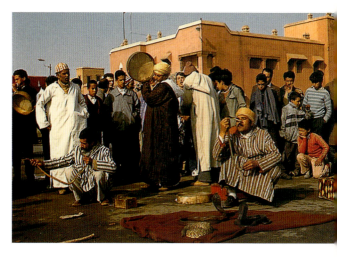

TO TIMBUKTU BY STEAMER

The legendary "city of gold" may no longer quite live up to its former reputation, but the river journey to it cuts through the republic of Mali, the throbbing pulse of West Africa.

THE RIVER NIGER is the main artery of life in the heart of West Africa: a source of food, the home of around 200 species of fish, and along the navigable section from Koulikoro downstream and eastward to the fabled city of Timbuktu, where the vast majority of the population is focused. For the visitor, a passage along one of its navigable sections provides a remarkable insight into aspects of rural Africa.

Timbuktu's former glories may have faded, but taking one of the Compagnie Malienne de Navigation (CMN) boats, along the Niger from Koulikoro to Korioum, Timbuktu's river port, provides a panorama of life sliding by along the river's banks. Small towns and mud-hut villages, punctuated by the spiked towers of the distinctive local mosques, cling to the main source of life amid a barren landscape.

Canvas-covered *pinasses* and canoelike *pirogues* (below) at Mopti, at the confluence of the Niger and the Bani rivers.

FACT FILE ←–

LANGUAGE French is the official language, but there are several local languages.

CURRENCY West African CFA franc.

CLIMATE Rain season June–September. Hottest March–May, 104°F (40°C). The *harmattana*, a dry, hot, dusty wind, blows from the Sahara December–February.

WHEN TO GO The boats run August–November when the river is high enough.

WHAT TO BUY Wood carvings, masks, woolen goods, copperware.

HEALTH WARNING Take precautions against malaria, yellow fever, hepatitis, typhoid, polio, and rabies. Avoid unboiled milk, unbottled or unsterilized water, and uncooked fruit and vegetables.

The Niger, the largest river in West Africa, begins its long journey in the highlands of Guinea and then wanders deep into the ever-expanding Sahara Desert. At Timbuktu it turns south into Nigeria and flows toward the Atlantic Ocean. Most of the river's flow is dependent on rains in the distant Guinea highlands, supplying it both with water and the fertile silt so vital to farming along the only green land in the desert. The steamers themselves resemble floating villages with sweltering cabins, loud music in the bars, and cargo spread everywhere with people piled on top. Accommodation varies from luxe–luxury cabins with air-conditioning–and two levels of first class with beds or bunks, to the very hot and dirty, if very lively, fourth class, which shares the lower deck with cargo. Food is included in first and second, and sometimes third classes, but it is usually uninteresting. Bottled water can be purchased on board or before you travel and is available in all the towns along the way. Otherwise drinking water is simply water drawn from the river–so don't ever drink it!

Ségou is the first sizable town you come to heading downstream toward Timbuktu. Quieter than Bamako and less touristy than Djenné or Mopti further down, it is a thriving, unspoiled African market town. Since it is off the beaten track, harassment by beggars or peddlers is still minimal. The market is open all week and is especially good on Mondays, selling fine examples of Bambara pottery, rugs, and blankets.

The Dogons

The boat's next step is Mopti. Until the French colonial period, Mopti was a small riverside village. Then, situated between the two administrative centers of Bamako and Gao and with commerce expanding along the river, Mopti began to grow. More importantly, Dogon country is only a day

away, in the Bandigara Escarpment. The Dogons are animists, believing that natural objects have souls. Their religion impregnates everything they do, influencing even the design of their villages and homes. Villages are built to resemble the human body, with houses representing arteries and veins. Their art is considered among the finest in Africa, particularly the intricate masks. Their architecture is also distinctive, with multistory houses clinging precariously to rock faces.

Partly because of the Dogon traditions, Mopti has become Mali's premier tourist destination, as well as the most vibrant port on the Niger River, lying on the junction of the Niger and Bani rivers in a vast inland delta. The Grand Marché (Great Market) is in the old town about 10 blocks from the port. Market day is Thursday with Bozo fishermen converging on the city to sell white slabs of salt from the camel caravans from northern Mali. Mopti is also famous for blankets: wool or wool-cotton mix blankets, camel hair blankets, and the ornate (and expensive) Fulani wedding blankets. The town's mosque is of typical Sudanese mud architecture found throughout Sahelian Africa. Each year the gray mud coating is washed off by the rains and has to be replaced during the dry season. The protruding beams are not merely decorative; they make the refacing task easier.

Elegance in a Desert

Djenné, standing amid the floodplains of the Niger further downstream, has a similar task on a grander scale. Its elegant mosque, built in 1905, was based on designs of its predecessor, which dated from the

Djenné's Grande Mosquée has to be resurfaced each year after the rainy season.

11th century. This sleepy, attractive town, founded in the 9th century, reached the height of its importance at the same time as Timbuktu in the 1300s, when it profited from the trans-Saharan caravan trade, Morocco being 55 days by camel train to the north. Today the whole town comes alive on market day (Monday) when the Grand Marché is held in front of the Grande Mosquée.

Timbuktu lies about 7 miles (11 km) north of the Niger. It was once spread along the river's banks, but the river has since changed course. Time has not been kind to the city, with its low gray mud-bricked houses lining narrow sandy streets. But along the alleyways are the ghosts of a time when this was an important center of Islam. There are many mosques, and some fine limestone houses—which recall the architecture of Egyptian temples—built by wealthy Moorish merchants of the 16th century. Many of the grand monuments of a prouder past have gone with the drifting sands of the Sahara, but the magic of its name and its past still give the town a unique atmosphere.

Unglazed earthenware pots can be bought at Mopti.

The village of Songo, around 50 miles (84 km) southwest of Mopti, presents a fine example of the mud and stone Dogon architecture.

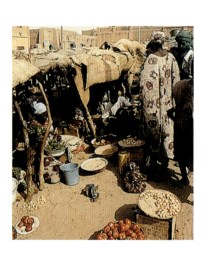

The grand market at Timbuktu sells mainly vegetables, but there is a smaller artisans' market nearby.

-> René Caillié, Discoverer of Timbuktu

In 1824, the Geographical Society of Paris offered a 10,000-franc prize for proof that Timbuktu really existed. The winner had to survive the journey and bring back firm proof. Inspired by the name, René Caillié, a self-educated man with little money, set out for Africa to seek Timbuktu—the forbidden "Golden City." Starting in April 1827, he traveled disguised as an Arab. His notes were kept inside his copy of the Koran, and he recorded his journey by pretending to study the scriptures. On reaching Timbuktu in April 1828, he "experienced an indescribable satisfaction" but was disappointed at finding the city of gold as "ill-looking houses built of mud" and no gold roofs or pavements. He returned to Europe by traveling 1,000 miles (1,600 km) across the Sahara via Morocco in a desert caravan. His "proof" that Timbuktu existed was a sketch of the town and his meticulous notes.

EGYPT AND THE NILE

Egypt, kingdom of the pharaohs, is a land of pitiless desert and cool oases, where extraordinary wealth and sophistication exist side by side with primitive lifestyles—and some of the oldest buildings on earth.

The mortuary temple of Seti I at Abydos is unique in the delicacy of its reliefs, and in its seven sanctuaries dedicated to Osiris and six other deities.

EGYPT WAS DESCRIBED by the ancient Greek historian Herodotus as being "the gift of the Nile." Even today, both urban and rural life depend on the fertile strip of river that divides the Egyptian desert into two. The Nile, the world's longest river, travels 4,160 miles (6,695 km) from its beginnings in Uganda and Ethiopia north to where the Delta meets the Mediterranean Sea, and knits the country together: around 96% of Egypt's population live in the lands of the delta and along the fertile narrow strip. Rainfall is negligible and until the construction

of the Aswan Dam (opened 1970) regulated its flow, Egypt depended totally on the Nile's annual flooding for its continued existence. As a desert country, climatic swings are extreme, with daytime temperatures ranging from 60°F (15°C) in January to 108°F (42°C) at the height of summer. At night in winter the temperature may drop to freezing. Sandstorms are common March through May when the *khamsin*, a dry, hot, dusty wind, blows in from the Western Desert. Winter is generally the best time to visit, particularly if you want to wander

Approach the pyramids of Giza from the desert to the west, preferably by mule or on horseback. They say you can hear them whisper at dawn: certainly you will escape the burning heat of the midday sun and the worst of the tourist buses.

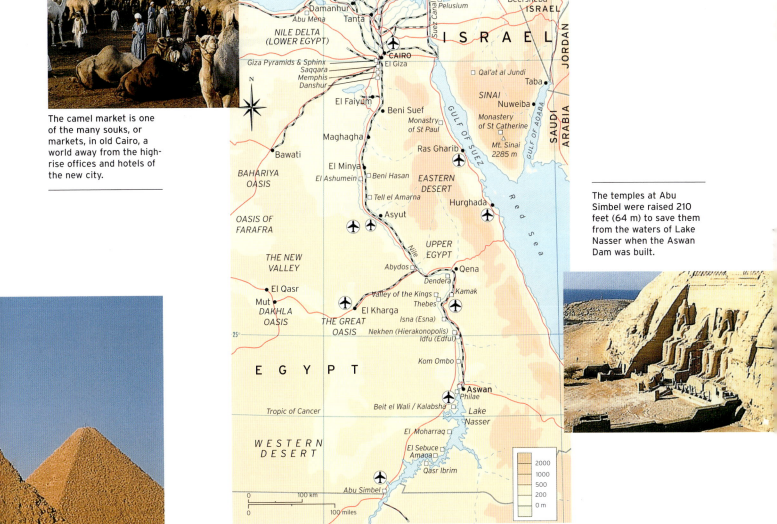

The camel market is one of the many souks, or markets, in old Cairo, a world away from the high-rise offices and hotels of the new city.

The temples at Abu Simbel were raised 210 feet (64 m) to save them from the waters of Lake Nasser when the Aswan Dam was built.

around the ancient sights of Upper Egypt at Aswan and Luxor. In summer these places are unbearably hot. This also applies to visiting some of the desert oases. Cairo is also at its most pleasant in the spring and autumn.

No matter how many clichés have been used to describe them, the pyramids remain unique, the only one of the seven wonders of the ancient world still intact today. There are other pyramids on the west bank of the Nile, but the three at Giza are the largest and the finest of them all. They were built as royal tombs over 4,500 years ago, overlooking the river northwest of the ancient capital of Memphis, whose mud bricks have now all disappeared back into the Nile or are buried deep beneath modern Cairo. Today the site is an easy

30-minute taxi ride from the center of Cairo, but such an approach misses their awe-inspiring scene of scale and mystery, as there is no real desert left between the Cairo suburb of Giza and the ancient site. Instead, hire a horse or a camel for a couple of hours from the nearby village of Nazlat al-Samman and ride across the desert sands from the far side. Negotiate the fare in advance (haggle!) and pay only on completing your trip. From this direction you can appreciate the perfect geometry of the pyramids set against the desert landscape, and imagine how they once looked, for part of their original coating of smooth white ashlar remains on their western sides.

There are three main pyramids, each of which can be entered, but only the Great Pyramid, the

The vast temple at Karnak, of Amun, the "king of the gods," is approached by a row of ram-headed statues. Amun was often shown with a ram's head.

tomb of the Pharaoh Khufu (known as Cheops by the Greeks), who died in 2567 B.C., holds anything of interest. Visitors can clamber through its claustrophobic passageways to reach three chambers within, including the king's chamber with its impressive granite sarcophagus. The museum behind the great pyramid is worth a visit to see the Solar Boat of the Pharaoh, unearthed from a nearby vault. It is the breathtaking scale of these monuments that makes them so dramatic. Cheops is the largest pyramid ever built, incorporating more than 2,250,000 blocks of stone, weighing an average of more than 2½ tons each.

Cairo itself is a colorful, cosmopolitan city, where east meets west, north meets south in culture, religion, and lifestyles. Fine mosques and a skyline of minarets reflect Cairo's long history as one of the greatest of all Muslim cities, but the crowds beneath them are made of Coptic Christians, Jews, northern Europeans, and black Africans. Ever-increasing numbers of migrants arrive daily from the countryside, many of them sleeping in the cemeteries.

The old walled city to the south encloses 400 mosques, vibrant bazaars, whitewashed stone houses, and narrow streets, and the relative quiet of the Coptic Christian quarter. To the north and west is the modern Cairo of broad avenues, designer shops, smart hotels, and international business, as befits Africa's largest city.

The Egyptian Museum houses Tutankhamen's treasures among one of the best collections of Pharaonica and Byzantine art and sculpture.

By Felucca on the Nile

No journey to Egypt would be complete without sailing along the Nile from Aswan to Luxor in a *felucca*, a traditional sailboat. The Nile's current flows from south to north, but the prevailing wind blows the opposite way, up the Nile Valley from the Mediterranean, so boats can flow effortlessly downstream with the current and use sail power to return easily and elegantly. You see life going on along and on the river as it has for millennia: fishermen with their nets, *fellahin* (peasant farmers) plowing with oxen, mud huts, waterwheels, and date palms. Feluccas can be chartered for groups of travelers, but cruising between Luxor and Cairo is discouraged because of the dangers of terrorism by Islamic fundamentalists.

Most travelers fly or take the train down to Luxor, one of Egypt's premier attractions, and then spend a few days cruising on one of the many comfortable, often luxurious, Nile steamers. Luxor, built on and around the 4,000-year-old site of ancient Thebes, capital of Egypt under the New Kingdom (c. 1700-1000 B.C.), is almost a huge open-air museum.

On the west bank of the Nile, some 300 miles (500 km) south of Cairo on the edge of the desert, lie the monuments and necropolis of ancient Thebes, including the staggering temple and tomb complexes of the Valley of the Kings and the Valley

of the Queens—the sites of tombs of Tutankhamen and Queen Hatshepsut, and giant images of 64 pharaohs carved into the rock.

On the east bank is the lively city of Luxor itself, with picturesque if decrepit balconied houses. In the nearby village of Karnak is the immense and the well-preserved temple of Amun, whose obese columns make it the most grandiose in all Egypt, along with

The tomb, at Luxor, of Queen Hatshepsut, who gained unprecedented power for a queen during her reign (1503-1482 B.C.)

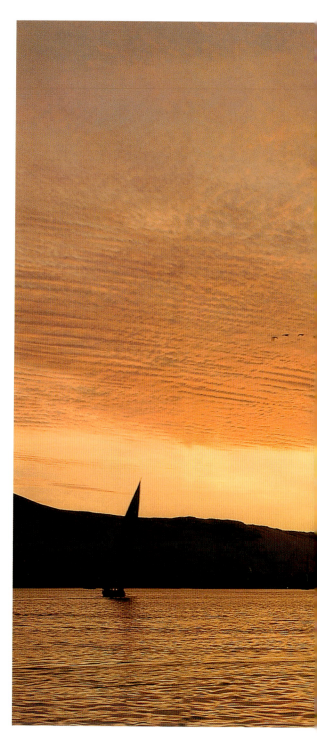

other ancient sites scattered among gardens and palm groves. Karnak is also a pleasant spot for eating out, though Egyptian food outside Cairo is too often a bland mingling of Western influences. However, Egyptian brandy and beer are good.

A 4- or 5-day cruise from Luxor is Aswan, gateway to sub-Saharan Africa, a city with a delightful island of gardens in midriver. There are relatively few antiquities here, and the Aswan Dam is immense but dull, but it is a short flight to Abu Simbel, the great temple of Ramses II. The temple was moved by a Herculean UNESCO effort in 1964 from its original site, which now lies beneath the waters of Lake Nasser, to its present site 210 feet (64 m) above.

Traditional *feluccas* (below) can be chartered as more peaceful alternatives to steamers and motor cruisers.

–> FACT FILE

LANGUAGE Arabic (official); Berber, English is widely spoken.

BEST TIME TO GO November–March.

CLIMATE Hot and dry year round. Summer: Cairo 97°F (36°C); Aswan 108°F (42°C). Dust storms in April. Very little rain except on the coast. Dust storms affect the country from late March to June.

MAJOR AIRPORTS Cairo and Luxor.

BARGAINING Part of everyday life in Egypt and applies to everything. It's expected!

WHAT TO BUY Gold and silver jewelry (seek advice when buying), papyrus paintings, leather goods, carpets, perfumes, spices, and alabaster (best in Luxor).

WHAT TO TAKE Insect repellent and high-factor sunblock.

SPECIAL NOTE The security situation in Egypt is volatile and should be checked out in advance. Contact your Foreign Office. Note that security authorities may insist on escorting travelers in some areas. Many people choose to travel with an organized tour.

THE EAST AFRICAN RIFT VALLEY

The Rift Valley is a vast depression of land that encompasses soda lakes and flamingos, volcanic craters and sulfur springs, and simmering plains that teem with wildlife.

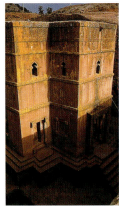

An Ethiopian rock church in Lalibela. The geographical seclusion created by the Rift Valley helped a distinctive culture to be preserved.

TEN MILLION YEARS AGO, a huge wedge of land, stretching over 4,000 miles (6,400 km) from Jordan and the Red Sea to southeast Africa, subsided to create a depression known as the Great Rift Valley. Plateau lands rise gradually toward the valley rim, and then drop up to 3,000 feet (900 m), at a series of fault lines in the rocky crust of the earth. In places in the East African part of the Rift Valley, such as Tanzania, the forces of erosion have obscured the effects of this massive earth movement, but elsewhere there are high cliffs bordering fantastic broad valleys, like lost worlds, between 30 and 40 miles (48-64 km) wide. Distinct ecosystems developed, the sheltered lands of the depression often providing conditions in which a wealth of wildlife could flourish. While tropical

forests thrived to the west, the rain-shadow area created by the Rift Valley cliffs evolved into dry grassland, the savannah plains and the heart of East Africa's safari land.

Much of the valley is made up of a series of troughs and swells along the fault lines. The troughs are around 25 miles (40 km) wide, and along the western branch of the rift have filled with fjordlike lakes, whose depths often plunge below sea level. They include Lake Tanganyika—the second deepest freshwater lake in the world after Lake Baikal—which covers 12,700 square miles (32,900 sq km). Along its shores are fine beaches and abundant wildlife.

In the eastern branch of the East African Rift Valley, which runs through Ethiopia, Kenya, and Tanzania, shallow soda lakes like Lake Natron have formed. Their alkaline waters are low in fish, but the algae and other tiny organisms attract gawky flamingos in the thousands, startling pink against mirror-dazzling water and relentless blue sky. Along

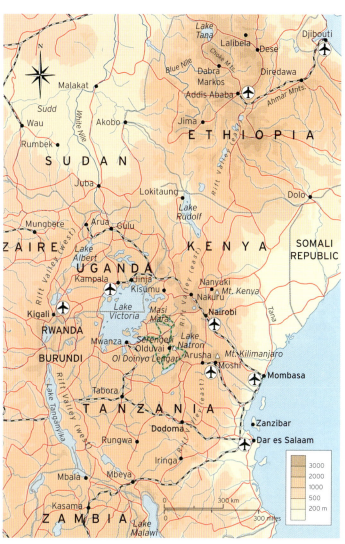

The full impact of the land that slid between two faults to create the Rift Valley is seen from the top of the escarpment rim at Lake Manyara in Tanzania.

Flamingos feed on the algae and other minute organisms in the soda lakes of the eastern branch of the East African Rift Valley. Their pink coloring comes from the pigments in the algae.

this eastern branch, too, are mighty volcanic uplifts where molten rock has burst through the thinned continental crust into volcanoes such as Ol Doinyo Lengai—"Mountains of God" to the local Masai people—Mount Kilimanjaro, and Mount Kenya. As you climb Mount Kilimanjaro—at 19,340 feet (5,895 m) Africa's highest mountain—you pass through the world's vegetation zones, from desert through tropical forests, to permanent snows.

West of Ol Doinyo Lengai is the Serengeti Plain in Tanzania, whose dusty soils are probably a fallout of volcanic ash. The endless grasslands that flourish here are the home of the African elephant, and grazed by giraffe, zebra, wildebeest, impala, and eland, as well as their predators—lions, leopards, and hyenas. Every year, in July and August, more than a million wildebeest move north from

Tanzania's Serengeti National Park across the Mara River and into Kenya in search of the fresh pastures created by the seasonal rains; the ungainly beasts, accompanied by the more graceful zebras, move en masse often at a gallop and in single file. When the rains come again in November, they head back south to Tanzania and the cycle begins all over again. Although migrations occur in other parts of Africa, nowhere else are the numbers so prolific or the sight so easy to see. It is possible to rent a trip in a hot air balloon to view the spectacle.

Human Development
The grasslands that formed as a result of the earth's great rift also proved more suitable than the surrounding tropical forests for an upright, two-legged, sharp-eyed species to evolve. In a small

Although Mount Kilimanjaro (below) is only 3 degrees from the equator, its summit is permanently covered in snow; banana, coffee, and maize are grown on the fertile lower slopes.

Giraffes are animals of the savannah, feeding mainly on acacia leaves. They are a protected species.

place called Olduvai in northern Tanzania, not far from the town of Arusha, Dr. Louis B. Leakey and his wife Mary had been searching intermittently for the best part of 20 years when in 1959 they found part of a hominoid skull, which they called Zinjanthropus (*Australopithecus boisei*). The skull fragments were dated at 1.8 million years old, making it part of the oldest discovered hominoid at that time.

In 1979, Mary made another important discovery at Laetoli, some 40 miles (64 km) away, of footprints in a riverbed made by a man, woman, and child. Subsequent investigation dated these footprints at 3.5 million years. Since they were made by hominoids that walked upright, the discovery pushed the dawn of humankind much further back in time than previously thought. Today

you can see where the Leakeys excavated in a hole, now roofed over with a pipelike opening. Here the layers of soil and rock mark the journey back in time as you descend into the earth, an awe-inspiring experience. At the top of the gorge, there is a sense of overwhelming peace as you sit and reflect on the fact that you could be sitting on the very spot where Eve, the "mother" of all human beings, once sat admiring the same landscape several million years ago.

A Land That Time Forgot

The geological complexity and pure raw beauty of the East African Rift Valley is nowhere more obvious than in Ethiopia. The very nature of the landscape has kept invaders out and the inhabitants in, allowing the country to develop its own very distinct culture and religion far removed from external influences and fashions. Ethiopia's style of Christianity—and much else about Ethiopian life—has changed little since Christianity was first introduced by Egyptian Coptic monks in the 2nd century.

At Lalibela in the central highlands, there are 11 churches carved out of solid rock. But the real treasure of Ethiopia is found further north at Axum, where lies the very basis of Ethiopian religion and culture. In the church of St. Mary's of Zion lies the Tabot. This is, according to local legend, the original "Ark of the Covenant"—the vessel holding the original Ten Commandments that was given to Moses by God on Mount Sinai and later stolen from King Solomon by Menelik I, Solomon's son by Makeda, Queen of Sheba.

-> FACT FILE

BEST TIME TO GO
Tanzania: June-July and December-January;
Kenya: June-October;
Ethiopia: October-January.

CLIMATE East Africa has two rainy seasons: April-May; and late October and early November. Coolest June and July when average daytime temperature is 72°F (22°C).

THINGS TO BUY Native handicrafts, Makonde carvings, batiks, soapstone carvings, and *kiondos* (woven sisal bags and baskets).

AIRPORTS Nairobi and Mombasa in Kenya; Dar es Salaam and Kilimanjaro International Airport in Tanzania.

THINGS TO DO Wildlife safaris, camel safaris, mountain trekking, white-water rafting, scuba diving, dhow sailing, balloon and cycling "safaris."

GETTING AROUND Generally easy with buses, trains, planes, and cars widely available.

HEALTH Malaria, cholera, and yellow fever are all prevalent, so take relevant precautions. Don't drink the water or eat salads or uncooked vegetables. Vaccinations against meningitis, polio, tetanus, diptheria, and rabies are recommended.

Children of the Masai, a nomadic cattle-herding people of Tanzania and Kenya, on the shores of the soda lake, Natron.

THE ZAMBEZI AND THE OKAVANGO

The Zambezi takes you from a raging river gorge and the world's largest waterfalls to a delta in a desert.

The lilac-breasted roller is just one of over 400 bird species that live in the delta lands of the Okavango.

JUST A PLANE RIDE TRANSPORTS YOU between two dramatically contrasting faces of Africa—from where water falls with such force that its spray is visible from 25 miles (40 km) away, to the sluggish waters of a river and the world's largest inland delta. Both have unique and remarkable ecosystems: the microclimate of the Victoria Falls rain forest, and the swamps and reed beds, rich in wildlife, of the Okavango Delta in the heart of the Botswana desert.

The Smoke That Thunders

Mosi oa Tunya—the "smoke that thunders"—is the resonantly poetic name the local Makololo people give the immense series of waterfalls that make up the Victoria Falls. The whole area shakes perpetually as the Zambezi River, 1½ miles (2.5 km) wide, cascades an average 1,200 million gallons (550 million liters) of water 330 feet (100 m) into the Zambezi Gorge every minute, creating the largest waterfalls on earth. The falls are divided

The Zambezi has attractions for geologists, wildlife watchers...and adventure seekers.

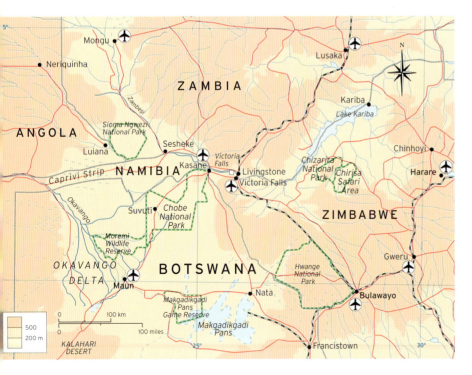

between Zambia and Zimbabwe (which has most of the best sites), but you can walk easily across the border.

The sheet of water that plummets suddenly from gently rolling grassland into the rocky canyon of the Zambezi Gorge is split into three main sections by jutting rock islands on the lip of the falls: the Maind Falls, the Rainbow Falls, and the Eastern Cataract. The clouds of spray create an unusual and ecologically significant rain forest, particularly rich in great ferns found nowhere else in Zimbabwe or Zambia. You can walk through the rain forests in a perpetual—and very wet—mist, beneath arcs of spray.

"No one can imagine the beauty of the scene... scenes so lovely must have been gazed upon by angels in their flight," the British explorer Dr. David Livingstone wrote on seeing the Victoria Falls. His words live on today in the "Flight of Angels," a journey by plane, helicopter, or microlight over the gorge. The aircraft follows the zigzagging course of the river, seemingly only feet above the dense clouds of spray and rainbows created from them. The effect of light at different times of the day

The river cuts through vulnerable cracks in hard basaltic rock of the Zambian plateau, while the Victoria Falls cascade over crosswise fault lines.

-> FACT FILE

GETTING THERE Fly into Harare in Zimbabwe (the Falls are only a few hours away by bus, car, or train), or directly to Victoria Falls Airport.

BEST TIME TO GO Okavango Delta, July–September; Victoria Falls, all year.

CLIMATE Zimbabwe's location on a high plateau converts tropical temperatures to those of a Mediterranean summer. Botswana is predominantly desert with searing daytime temperatures plunging to near-freezing at night. The delta, although hot in the day, is quite pleasant at night.

HEALTH Inoculations for cholera, typhoid, polio, and possibly rabies; take malaria prophylactics.

WHAT TO TAKE Insect repellent, raingear, sunscreen.

FOOD AND DRINK International food at most main hotels and lodges. Zimbabwean beer is popular, as is the traditional maize beer, *whawha*.

WHAT TO BUY African handicrafts.

SPECIAL NOTE Zimbabwe is politically unstable and the current situation should be carefully researched before travel to the region.

THE ZAMBEZI AND THE OKAVANGO

The waterways of the Okavango (left), with their extraordinary range of wildlife, can be explored in the *mekoro*, the dugout canoe of the native Ba Yei, a tribe of aquatic hunters.

as it refracts through the ever-present mists is quite ethereal. Beneath a full moon, there is a delicate silver, ghostly glow, and even, maybe, a lunar rainbow.

The chasm cut by the Zambezi has become a focus for adventure activities, including one of the highest bungee jumps in the world from the Zambezi Bridge—2 seconds of sheer terror strapped to a giant elastic band plummeting head first 330 feet (100 m) toward the river—and running the 23 sets of rapids that make up the lower Zambezi.

River rafting is graded from I to VI—from gentle rapid to impossible to run. The Zambezi rapids clenched between steep cliffs up to 700 feet (213 m) high, are mostly grades IV and V, making this a serious roller-coaster ride in a flimsy rubber boat. Trips downriver vary from a half day and 12 rapids to a full day and the whole river. There are opportunities for recuperative wildlife watching in the nearby Zambezi National Park, where sable, antelope, and other wild animals graze in a parkland setting.

Each year millions of wildebeest migrate across the plains of Africa, seeking water and fresh grazing.

Hippopotamuses help maintain the waterways of the Okavango as they trudge through them in their quest for food.

The Jewel of the Kalahari

For the ultimate contrast to the roar of the Zambezi, take a short plane flight from Victoria Falls to the Okavango Delta in neighboring Botswana. Landing at one of the region's lodges or campgrounds provides an eagled-eye view of the world's largest delta, which runs into a desert rather than the sea. The Okavango River flows from the highlands of Angola and ebbs into the northwestern Kalahari Desert. And there it runs its course; it doesn't flow out again but subdivides into smaller and smaller streams, channels, and lagoons before evaporating or soaking into the sand.

The 6,000 square miles (15,000 sq km) of delta is one huge oasis, a pristine habitat for many species of wildlife on the many islands created by the streams and channels. About 20% is protected in the spectacular Moremi Wildlife Reserve. Among the 36 species of mammal are lion, elephant, giraffe, buffalo, wildebeest, zebra, and numerous species of gazelle. Hippo and crocodile, fish eagles, cormorants, and cranes are all permanent residents. There are no roads, only the occasional four-wheel drive vehicle, and no crowds.

To make the most of this tranquil habitat and its wildlife, explore the delta in a *mekoro* (dugout canoe) poled by a local fisherman and accompanied by a guide. You can spend days winding your way through 250 miles (400 km) of waterways, floating from island to island, camping wild under the stars and eating fresh-caught fish. Alternatives include a tented camp such as Xaxaba and luxury safari lodges.

THE GARDEN ROUTE, SOUTH AFRICA

As warm a welcome as its climate makes the Garden Route the most visited area in this part of the world.

These pretty houses painted in ice cream colors are found in Cape Town's Bo Kaap neighborhood.

CAPE TOWN, WITH ITS CONSTANT influx of travelers and merchants, has long been proud of the welcome it offers to strangers, and over the last decade it has become the most visited city in South Africa. From here, South Africa's ravishing Garden Route stretches for almost 500 miles (800 km) to Port Elizabeth.

The Outeniqua Mountains sweep down to the Indian Ocean, meeting forests, lakes, and sheer sea cliffs. Charming seaside resorts are piled around glorious white-sand beaches; parks and reserves protect dramatic capes, virgin forests, and beautiful lakes; and, on the Overburg Coast, the endangered southern right whale breeds in the turquoise waters. The coast is also a popular destination to see and dive with great white sharks.

Cape Town

Few cities can boast Cape Town's superb natural setting. Sprawled around a magnificent harbor, and dominated by the curiously flattened silhouette of Table Mountain, it is surrounded by white-sand beaches, islands, and dramatic capes. Affectionately known as "the Mother City," the first European settlement in sub-Saharan Africa was established here in the late 17th century, and the colonial legacy is still apparent in opulent Victorian buildings and attractive terrace cafés.

A visit to its most famous landmark, Table Mountain, is essential, either by climbing up numerous hiking paths or swooping up in the cable car. From here, the whole city unfolds magically (except when the notorious mist, known as "the tablecloth," descends). Among the forests on its eastern slopes, the shady Kirstenbosch National Botanical Gardens provide a tranquil retreat from the city bustle, or you can catch the classic view of Table Mountain from the golden sands of Blouberg Beach. Most of the best museums and cultural attractions are neatly lined along the "Museum Mile," and down by the harbor the Victoria and Alfred Waterfront offers bars, desirable shopping, and smart restaurants for al fresco dining. From here, boats depart regularly for trips out to Robben Island, where 3,000 political prisoners, including Nelson Mandela, were incarcerated between 1962 and 1991. Now Robben Island is a museum, where ex-inmates run guided tours and provide moving testimony to the hardships suffered under the apartheid regime.

The townships (nonwhite communities established under apartheid) are still poverty stricken, but much has improved since the transition to democracy, and residents are eager to share their life stories and culture with visitors. A local guide is essential, but a visit to the

The vine was first introduced here in the 17th century. Excursions to the nearby vineyards are popular day trips from Cape Town.

townships may well be one of the most memorable events of any trip to South Africa. Behind Table Mountain, a chain of peaks extends to the legendary tip of Cape Peninsula, where a cable car swings up to the historic lighthouse at Cape Point. The nearby Cape of Good Hope is popularly but erroneously believed to be the southernmost point in Africa, but it offers dramatic views of sheer cliffs circled by wheeling seabirds. (If you bring a packed lunch, make sure that the cheeky baboons don't steal it!)

The Garden Route

The N2 highway heads southeast of Cape Town to Hermanus, piled around a salty old port, which is world famous for land-based whale watching. The endangered southern right whale breeds close to shore between August and November, their distinctive V-shaped blows clearly visible from the coastal paths that snake around the town, but other whale species are present year round.

The De Hoop Nature Reserve, which spreads eastward toward Mossel Bay, offers extraordinary

views of these beautiful beasts from its lichen-covered cliffs and undulating sand dunes. The Agulhas National Park, at the southernmost tip of Africa, encompasses silvery wetlands and protected coastline, which is home to seals, whales, dolphins, and porpoises. Pretty whitewashed fishermen's cottages are preserved in nearby Struisbaai, which overlooks endless sandy beaches. Witsand is a small family-friendly resort town at the mouth of the Breede River. Like Still Bay, further east, it offers good whale watching and excellent facilities for water sports.

For more adventurous activities, head up to Albertinia, where thrill seekers can bungee jump from the highest single-span bridge in the world. And, if that's not enough, visitors can meet the great white shark face to face in Mossel Bay (near the fishing village of Gansbaai), which offers—among numerous other attractions—shark cage dives. This historic town is where the Portuguese explorer Bartholomeu Dias, who was the first European to navigate the Cape of Good Hope since ancient times, set foot in 1488, and it retains a cluster of elegant old buildings.

The splendid white-and-gold edifice of Cape Town's Old Town Hall is one of the city's most recognizable landmarks.

The historic Outeniqua Choo-Tjoe steam train puffs along the coastline near Wilderness National Park.

It's a very popular holiday resort, with a year-round balmy climate and wonderful beaches, but it can get too crowded in high season. George is the only major town along the Garden Route, and it is the starting point for the Outeniqua Choo-Tjoe (or Choo Choo), a vintage train that steams through magnificent scenery to Knysna. The Blue Train, South Africa's answer to the opulent Orient Express, makes an even more spectacular voyage along the Garden Route from Cape Town to Port Elizabeth. Chic Herold's Bay is a quieter resort, 25 miles (15 km) east of George, with beautiful coastal walks and plenty of opportunities for spotting whales and dolphins.

The largest surviving stretch of indigenous forest in South Africa spreads east of George, scattered with shimmering lakes and rivers, and backed by lofty mountains. This is perhaps the Garden Route's most spectacular region, much of it protected in a trio of national parks. Wilderness and Sedgefield are the main access towns for the watery paradise of the Wilderness National Park, where nature trails meander through lush forest and down to surf-pounded coves. Among the many activities on offer is the peculiarly South African sport of kloofing, which entails scrambling (or leaping) into river gorges and canyons.

The lively community of Knysna is perched winsomely on the shores of a beautiful lagoon, with a sea channel guarded by a pair of massive sandstone cliffs. The lake is preserved as part of the Knysna National Lake Area and is home to the Knysna seahorse, a tiny delicate creature that is in danger of extinction. The lake also supports an oyster farm, and these delicious morsels are readily available in the town's many fine restaurants.

Extensive forests, such as those at Goudveld or Diepvalle, offer more great hikes, and treetop chalets provide some of the most unusual accommodations on the Garden Route. Perfect sweeps of golden sand enclose Plettenburg Bay, a picturesque resort splayed around a sheltered natural harbor that is a nursery to the endangered southern right whale. There are several nature reserves in the area, including Robben Island, which you can reach by sea kayak. Storm's River famously offers the world's highest bungee jump, which descends for a gut-wrenching 710 feet (216 m) over the Bloukrans River. Nearby Storm's River Mouth is the gateway to the Tsitsikamma National Park, a breathtaking natural wilderness of forests, rivers, and canyons that stretches right out into the Indian Ocean. The famous Otter Trail is an arduous but exhilarating 5-day trek, named for the elusive clawless otter.

The Garden Route culminates in Port Elizabeth, a bustling resort that owes its popularity to 25 miles (40 km) of dazzling white-sand beaches. Every tourist whim is catered to, from countless water-sports facilities to Bayworld, which incorporates an Oceanarium and Snake Park among many other attractions.

MEDITERRANEAN
AND THE NEAR EAST

"The real voyage of discovery consists not in seeing new landscapes, but in having new eyes."
MARCEL PROUST, FRENCH WRITER, 1871-1922

MOORISH SPAIN

Amid the gardens and orange groves of southern Spain, the relics of the old Moorish civilization of Andalucía still survive almost magically.

Moorish decoration is distinguished by its delicate symmetry as in these filigree arches at the Alhambra in Granada.

IT IS SOMETIMES SAID that old Moroccan families still keep the keys to their long-lost houses in Spain. At a time (800-1000 A.D.) when most of Europe was still barbarous, a brilliant civilization flourished in the Muslim realm of *Al Andalus*–Andalucía. The Moors, a mixed race of Berbers and Arabs, crossed into Spain from Morocco in 711, and within 4 years had conquered most of the peninsula. Gradually, over almost eight centuries, the Spanish regained their lost territory. Though they tried to erase all traces of the Moors, much glorious architecture survives. The Moors also left a more subtle mark on Andalucía: in its proud independence (it now has its own regional government); in the landscape, which they lovingly irrigated; in the gardens and squares that decorate its cities; in the passionate Arabic cadences of the flamenco; and even in dishes such as lamb stewed with almonds, or *ajo blanco*, a soup made with garlic, grapes, and almonds that is directly descended from a medieval Moorish recipe.

The old Moorish quarter of Córdoba is still full of narrow streets with balconied houses set around quiet, leafy courtyards.

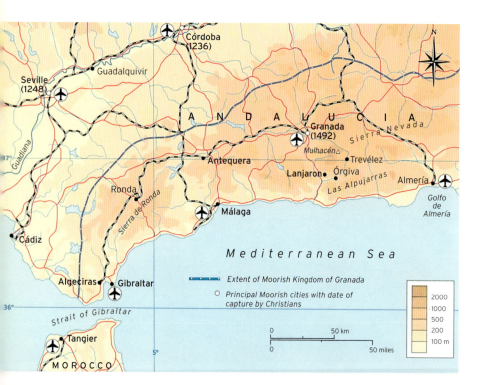

At the heart of Moorish Spain is Córdoba, a modern city that has one of the best preserved medieval quarters in Europe. For three centuries the country was ruled from this great metropolis of commerce and learning. The Moors created a network of irrigation channels in the surrounding countryside, which fed the city's gardens and outlying vineyards and orchards. Vestiges of this horticultural luxuriance can be seen in the riverside gardens of the Alcázar, an ancient palace.

Other Moorish splendors can be glimpsed in the Great Mosque–"La Mezquita"–once the largest in the world after the Kaaba in Mecca. After the Christian Reconquest in 1236, it was converted into a cathedral. The minaret was left standing, but was later encased in a baroque facade. Inside, a hypnotic succession of red and white marble arches is supported by 600 columns. Outside, rows of orange trees still grow in the courtyard, where worshippers once washed at the fountain before entering the mosque.

Under the tolerant Moors, always a minority in Spain, Córdoba became a great center of Jewish culture. North of the Mezquita is a labyrinth of narrow streets still known as Judería (Jewish quarter); many of its old houses are now fashionable restaurants. At the heart of the Judería is a small half-ruined synagogue of 1315, one of the few to survive in Spain. Like much other Spanish architecture that looks Moorish, it is *mudéjar*—work done by Christians or Jews in a Moorish style.

City of Vitality

After the caliphate of Córdoba collapsed in the 11th century, power shifted to Seville, 70 miles (110 km) down the Guadalquivir River. Seville—the largest city in southern Spain—throbs with life, its inhabitants packing its cafés and bars all day and night. Thanks to its gardens, all this urban excitement is accompanied by the scent of jasmine and the sound of birdsong. In spring comes the *Semana Santa* (Holy Week) procession, where hooded penitents are followed by floats bearing images of the Virgin or Christ, followed by the *Feria de Abril*, a week-long party in which men parade on horses and women dance in gypsy dresses. It is possible to stay in hotels in restored old mansions around courtyards, but book early. Everywhere in Seville you will seldom be out of sight of a striking remnant of its Moorish past: the 320-foot (92-m) minaret La Giralda. It was built in the late 1100s, just 50 years before the Reconquest, and now serves as a tower to the cathedral that supplanted the mosque. Adjacent to the cathedral is the Alcázar, the royal palace where Spain's Muslim and Christian traditions met in a brief but extraordinary fusion. Begun in the 9th century, but completed by Muslim craftspeople after the Reconquest, its elegant pavilions, decorated with arabesques and inscriptions in both Arabic and Gothic script, face

The Andalucían countryside is a harmonious blend of patterned agricultural land, whitewashed towns such as Arcos de la Frontera, and distant sierras.

-> FACT FILE

POPULATION 7.4 million (about 18% of Spain).

AREA 54,250 square miles (87,300 sq km)—17.3% of Spanish territory.

CURRENCY Spanish peseta.

CLIMATE Mediterranean; July-August 104°F (40°C), snow in winter.

TIME TO GO Winter and spring to avoid the crowds and see the snow on the Sierra's peaks.

NEAREST AIRPORTS International airports at Seville, Málaga, Granada, Almería, Jerez de la Frontera. Córdoba has good bus and rail connections.

FOOD AND DRINK Sherry from Jerez, accompanied by olives and tapas (snacks). Fish, including fresh anchovies; *jamón de Jabugo* (ham); gazpacho (chilled soup).

onto courtyards and gardens planted with orange and lemon trees. And down along the river you can still see the huge cigarette factory where Carmen, the tragic gypsy heroine of Bizet's opera, supposedly once worked.

A Final Flowering

By 1275, the Moors had retreated to Granada 160 miles (250 km) southeast of Seville, in the vastness of the Sierra Nevada. Granada witnessed the extraordinary last flowering of Moorish culture. If the modern city lacks Seville's vitality, its Moorish monuments more than compensate. Two promontories extend from the Sierra foothills into the city itself, divided by the valley of the Río Darro. On one of these stands the Alhambra, whose red

stone walls and towers glow in the evening sun. Within, the architecture encapsulates all the symmetry and grace of Islamic design. At the foot of the steep path to the imposing Gate of Justice is a grove of elms planted by the Duke of Wellington during the Peninsular Wars. Archways lead through arcaded courtyards and pavilions of the Nasrid Palaces, built almost entirely of wood and stucco and decorated with exquisite arabesque patterns and calligraphic inscriptions from the Koran. Symmetry, order, and water are the keynote themes: pools and fountains in enclosed paradise gardens offer relief from the dusty olive groves and dry Mediterranean landscape of the surrounding countryside. The complex is set amid terraced rose gardens looking out over plains toward the

Córdoba Cathedral was built around the main mosque of western Islam after the city was captured by the Christians in 1236.

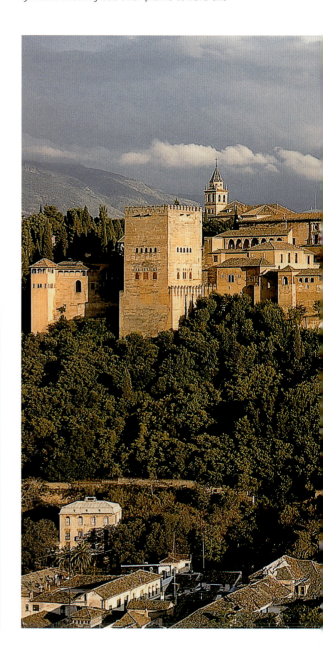

-> The Moor's Last Sigh

Heading southeast from Granada into the Sierras, you reach the pass known as El Ultimo Suspiro del Moro—the Moor's Last Sigh. Here, Boabdil, last emir of Granada, looked back over his lost kingdom after the city fell to Ferdinand and Isabella in 1492. Boabdil was allowed to retire to the Alpujarras, a mountain range just south of the Sierra Nevada whose valleys the Moors had transformed into a verdant landscape of olives, almonds, and orchards through elaborate irrigation channels (acequias) that still cut through the hills today. Many of Boabdil's subjects followed him, but the Christian monarchs soon broke their agreement and drove him out. With its lush valleys of poplars and willow, forests of holm oak and pine, rivers and rushing torrents, the Alpujarras is one of the most unspoiled corners of Spain. You can trek along ancient mule tracks from one whitewashed village (pueblo blanco) to another for much of the way from Bubión, on the brink of the Poqueira Gorge, to Travélez, the highest village in Spain. Towering over it is Mulhancén, at 1,400 feet (3,482 m) the highest mountain in Spain; from its peak you can see Morocco on a clear day. From Bérchules, with views across the Guadalfeo Valley to the almond- and olive-covered slopes of the Sierra de la Contraviesa, another acequia leads to the convergence of the Chico and Grande rivers.

mountains. At the rocky tip of the promontory is the Alcázar, a semiruined fortress dating from the 11th to the 13th centuries. From its ramparts, you can see one of the most unexpected cityscapes in Europe: the white flat-roofed buildings, the palms and cypresses, and the tall minarets outlined against the sky seem to have been transported from Morocco. This is Albaicín, a settlement founded by Moors driven from Baeza in the 1200s. The western wall of the old Moorish citadel and the city gates with their horseshoe arches still exist. Most of the churches are built on the foundations of mosques, and beside many of the minarets—now bell towers—you can still see the cisterns at which the faithful would wash before entering.

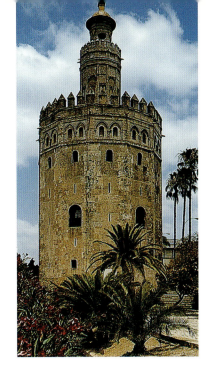

Seville's Torre del Oro was built by the Moors in the 13th century to guard the city's river port.

The Alhambra—the extraordinary culmination of Moorish architecture—sits atop a hill dominating the city of Granada. The name is from the Arabic for "red fort."

THE ESSENCE OF PROVENCE

Provence, once ancient Rome's favored *provincia*, has some of the most evocative remains of antiquity in western Europe, as well as two of its last wildernesses: the Camargue and the Gorge du Verdon.

A *gardian*—a cowboy of the Camargue—on one of the small white horses that are unique to the region.

PROVENCE IS A SENSUOUS LAND of strong colors, aromatic scents, and dramatic landscapes. It embraces the windswept flatness of the Camargue in the west and the rugged limestone canyon of Verdon in the foothills of the Alps.

The quality of light exaggerates the region's rich ochers and dark greens, the fierce yellow of sunflowers, and the purple of cultivated lavender. The hills smell of *herbes de Provence*, and it is no accident that the center of France's perfume trade is the Provençal hill town of Grasse. Craggy hills and gnarled vines shelter medieval towns where old men play boules (bowls) and sip pastis beneath plane trees. Baked by the summer sun and often scoured by the ferocious Mistral wind roaring down the Rhône valley, Provence is a place for people who like their hedonism salted by an awareness of unforgiving nature. The region's wines are less grands vins than rich or fruity brews, its famous dishes—bouillabaisse, ratatouille, salade niçoise—not haute cuisine but earthy fare that tastes of the soil and the sea.

Amazingly, this pungently characterful region still survives relatively close to the great population centers of northwest Europe. Inevitably, it has attracted a great deal of attention—not least from

painters such as Vincent van Gogh, Paul Cézanne, Henri Matisse, and Pablo Picasso—yet despite the books, films, and television programs, the region and its people have resisted being turned into tourist parodies of themselves.

The west of Provence is bound by the 346,000 acres (140,000 ha) of lagoon, salt marsh, dune, and pasture of the Camargue, where the Rhône moves slowly into the sea. It is an eerie landscape of massive skies, shivering waters, and wind-bent reeds. In summer the mud bakes into cracked salt-crusted polygons; in winter it feels as though you've come to the bleak edge of the world. There are pink flamingos, and white horses ridden by the *gardians* (cowboys) who tend the black bulls unique to the area. The best way to discover the Camargue—the least damaging to the area's fragile ecology—is on horseback. Riding tours can be arranged through the tourism office at Saintes-Maries-de-la-Mer.

Classical and Medieval Influences

On the westernmost edge of the Camargue, the medieval village of Aigues-Mortes shelters inside astonishingly well-preserved walls, built by King Louis IX (reigned 1226–1270) to launch his doomed crusade of 1248. In the inland towns of Arles and Avignon, north of the Camargue, classical Rome meets medieval Europe. Arles was once an imperial capital of Rome; today remnants of that era—massive ruins, including an amphitheater (still used for bloodless bullfights in which matadors simply snatch rosettes from the beasts' horns)—loom above the narrow medieval streets of old shuttered houses and traditional cafés.

West of the town are the limestone hills of the Alpilles where white peaks rise starkly above slopes clad with oak and pine. At their northern edge is Saint-Remy de Provence, a gracious little town encircled by 14th-century walls, and full of sidewalk cafés and restaurants. Vincent van Gogh stayed in an asylum near here after cutting off his ear.

Lapped by a sea of sunflowers, the little town of Mornas in the Rhône valley nestles at the foot of a massive limestone cliff, overlooked by a ruined castle.

–> FACT FILE

CLIMATE Mediterranean; July-August 82°F (28°C); snow in inland areas in winter, heavy rains possible everywhere.

TIME TO GO October-June (to avoid the worst crowds).

NEAREST AIRPORTS Marseille and Toulon.

WHAT TO BUY Perfumes, wine, *santons* (Christmas figures), lavender products.

TRANSPORTATION The major towns are connected by rail; buses ply the routes between the smaller centers. For more remote regions, rent a car. Beware local drivers who think nothing of taking mountain hairpins at 70 mph (110 kph).

Lavender fields contribute to Provence's characteristic colors and scents; the distilled essence of the flowers is a vital ingredient in some of France's finest perfumes.

Rome is not far away: just outside the town is the ruined town of Glanum, with triumphal arch and mausoleum, a 60-foot (18-m) high limestone wedding cake commemorating both Emperor Augustus's heir, Caius, and Lucius, who died young.

Popes in exile from Rome held court at Avignon in the 1300s. Today, the town has a disproportionate metropolitan verve because of a large student population and vibrant arts scene. Its international music and theater festival draws performers and visitors from around the world every July and August. The medieval bridge (immortalized by the song *Sur le pont d'Avignon, l'on y dansé*) has only three of its arches left after centuries of flooding. The city center—full of old churches and elegant 17th- and 18th-century houses—is still enclosed by medieval walls and dominated by the huge battlemented Palais des Papes (Papal Palace).

Medieval spirits dominate in Les Baux, a village that has given its name to bauxite (aluminum ore). The mineral lends a shimmering whiteness to the white crag on which the old village sits, enclosed by forbidding medieval walls. It is a brooding, unsettling place, a medieval ghost town where mullioned windows gape at a fierce cobalt sky. From 1000 to 1400 the lords of Les Baux ruled from here with mixed splendor and savagery, patronizing troubadours who sang of courtly love and slinging enemies off the cliff. The present village clings to the lower slopes, among olive groves and scrub, leaving the old part deserted.

The modern town of Orange, 15 miles (24 km) north of Avignon, conceals a distinguished Roman past, complete with triumphal arch. The Roman theater is awe inspiring, with curving banks of seats cut into a steep hill and a stage backed by an enormous sandstone wall with a statue of the

Emperor Augustus in a central niche. Battered by time it may be, but this is no mere ruin, for operas are regularly performed here.

The Heart of Provence

The Lubéron, a 35-mile (56-km) range of beautiful rugged hills, captures the essence of Provence. The lush plateau of the Petit Lubéron is separated from the rugged and higher Grand Lubéron—a superbly scenic national park—by a wooded valley, the Combe de Lourmarin. The northern face of the Lubéron is damp and alpine; the vine-covered southern slopes bask in 300 days of sunshine a year—though the heights get bitterly cold in winter. Here are hiking and riding trails, rivers to canoe, *gîtes* (cottages) to rent, and lives of artists to trace.

The vast palace built by the popes during their medieval exile in Avignon (below) looms over the remaining spans of the Pont St. Bénézet, the "pont d'Avignon" of the French song.

Ocher for artists' paint is extracted from the rocks of Roussillon, a hilltop village north of the Lubéron. Everything about the place is red: sand, stone, stucco, tiles—all surmounted by a red church tower with a rusty wrought-iron belfry. The views are wonderful, though sadly the place has become too popular for its own good. The artist Paul Cézanne was born here in 1839, and his studio is preserved as it was when he died in 1906—complete with a wine glass by his easel—on the north side of town. The distinctive cone of the Montagne Sainte-Victoire, which Cézanne painted over and over again, rises 9 miles (15 km) east of Aix. Today it is an elegant town of fountains, grand avenues lined with 17th- and 18th-century town houses, sculpted doorways, wrought-iron balconies, fine restaurants geared to leisurely lunches, and old cafés.

The Lubéron subsides into the rolling countryside of the Var, and the land rises toward the deeply scarred limestone plateau of upper Provence with stunning panoramas falling away, layer upon layer. Suddenly, the land drops away into the grand canyon of the Gorges du Verdon, a sheer 700 feet (200 m) to the Verdon River. The canyon is impassable by car but can be negotiated on foot or by white-water raft. But once entered at the Point Sublime, there's no way out until the river emerges some 15 miles (24 km) later into Lac de Sainte-Croix. It is possible to drive around the rim of the canyon; there are many hair-raising bends, and the 65-mile (103-km) loop takes the better part of a day.

Europe's largest natural canyon, the wild and rugged Gorges du Verdon, contains many scenic roads winding their way around dizzying hairpin bends.

In the Cours Mirabeau, Aix-en-Provence, cafés spread onto the sidewalks beneath massive plane trees.

TELEFERIQUE FROM CHAMONIX

"One of the most grand and sweeping bits of granite I have ever seen.... The Charmoz glacier on my left sank from the moraine in broken fragments, and swept back under the dark walls of the Charmoz, lost in cloud."–John Ruskin, 1849

WHERE THE BORDERS OF FRANCE, Italy, and Switzerland meet, the earth's surface crumples into a great jumble of splintered rocks thrown up by the cataclysmic impact of two continental plates some 200 million years ago. Rising above it all is the 15,760-foot (4,807-m) ice-capped summit of Europe's highest mountain, Mont Blanc, surrounded by lesser peaks and deeply crevassed glaciers, and ringed by fearsome spears of rock known as *aiguilles* (needles).

The nearest town to Mont Blanc, and the obvious base from which to explore this savage and exhilarating landscape, is Chamonix, nestling in the green valley of the River Arve, where the wooded hillsides and lush meadows–carpeted with wild flowers in the summer–form a lyrical contrast to the sheer mountains that rise on either side. It is no longer the little mountain village from which Dr. Paccard and Jacques Balmat set out to climb Mount Blanc for the first time in 1786, and to which Ruskin returned year after year, but a large and lively town full of hotels, restaurants, and bars catering to tourists, climbers, and skiers.

Chamonix (left) has been a mountaineering center since Paccard and Balmat first climbed Mont Blanc (right) in 1786. This view shows the sharp profiles of the appropriately named Aiguille ("needles") du Midi in the middle distance.

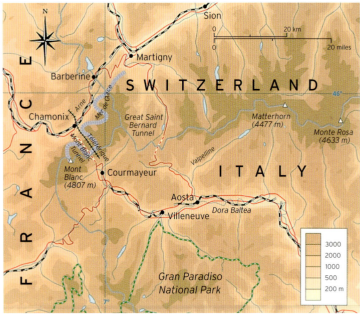

But the landscape, with its constantly shifting effects of light and weather, remains as magical as ever. Sometimes the *aiguilles*, struck by the rays of the setting sun, glow like fiery stalactites. Sometimes the mountains are completely obscured by cloud, and you look out onto a gentle landscape of green meadows and dark wood–until the mist evaporates and suddenly the mountains appear so close you could reach out and touch them, their glistening snow faces and dark screes picked out with unearthly clarity.

From Chamonix, you can take a rack and pinion railway up to the Mer de Glace, a vast tongue of ice 9 miles (14 km) long, ¾ mile (1,200 m) wide, and up to 1,300 feet (400 m) deep in places. If you're feeling fit you can take a hike up–there are several trails. Close up, the glacier seems less beautiful and more powerful, no longer a white glimmering sheet but a threatening mass, striated into great folds and dirty with the rock it has scoured from its path. Once at the top, you look out across the ice and snow to the pyramid-shaped Grands Charmoz and

the Aiguille du Dru—looking for all the world like a fearsome stake that has just this moment burst upward through the surface of the planet. Whatever you do, don't venture out onto the glacier without a guide—deep crevasses often lurk beneath a thin covering of snow and ice, ready to swallow the unwary walker. You can take a short cable-car ride right down through the tunnel carved into the depths of the glacier. It is an eerie experience—the light gleams greenly through the ice, and you hear strange creaking and cracking noises as the glacier inches its way down the mountainside. Because of this movement, the tunnel has to be remade every spring.

A Vertiginous Ascent

One of the best views of Mont Blanc can be obtained by taking the téléférique from Chamonix to the top of the 12,600-foot (3,842-m) spike of granite known as the Aiguille du Midi. Set out early, by 9 A.M. at the latest, because it gets very crowded after then, and the summit is often clouded by midday. Be sure to dress warmly: even in summer it can be well below freezing at the top. The 2-mile (3-km) ascent is one of the highest and steepest in the world, and it must be said that swaying in a little cage of metal and glass over an awesome 1,800-foot (600-m) abyss is definitely not for vertigo sufferers. After a stop to change cars at Plan de l'Aiguille, the téléférique climbs to the lower of the Aiguille du Midi's twin peaks, the Piton Nord, where the cable car station and a restaurant perch precariously over the void.

From here, a bridge leads to the higher Piton Central, crowned by a telecommunications tower: there's an elevator to the top. The views across snowfields, glaciers, sheer rock faces, and splintered crags to the summit of Mont Blanc is utterly awe inspiring. Rank upon rank of snow-topped mountains recede into the distance; far away to the east—if the weather conditions are favorable—you can see Monte Rosa in Italy and the distinctive jagged barb of Switzerland's Matterhorn.

From the téléférique station on Piton Nord, you can take a series of cable car rides over the snowy Vallée Blanche, via the Pointe Helbronner—right on the Italian border—and down the Italian face of the mountains to the village of La Palud. It is an unforgettable half-hour journey, crossing an international frontier by swinging from peak to peak through some of the wildest and most spectacular alpine scenery without setting foot on the ground. From La Palud, a bus will take you the 10 miles (16 km) back to Chamonix through the Mont Blanc tunnel

A Taste of Italy

It is well worth making a more extended foray into Italy; the tunnel—a terrific feat of engineering opened in 1965—takes you through into the Valle d'Aost, one of northern Italy's loveliest regions. Its main town, Aosta, is just 30 miles (48 km) by road from Chamonix. Now a busy town on the main route from France to Turin, Aosta—the name derives from "Augusta"—was once an alpine outpost of Rome. The town center is a lively and stylish place with a distinctly Italian feel, elegant tree-lined boulevards, and an impressive Roman triumphal arch, all framed by a wonderful backdrop of mountains.

Aosta is also the gateway to the Gran Paradiso 12 miles (20 km) to the south. Dominated by the mountain of the same name, Italy's oldest national park encompasses 175,000 acres (70,000 ha) of glorious wilderness—high mountain valleys under perpetual snow, bleak hillsides to which a few wind-twisted firs cling, sparkling brooks, mountain tarns, and lush lower valleys. Wooded slopes give way to meadows full of wildflowers. Once the hunting preserve of King Vittorio Emanuele II (ruled 1849-1878), the park now provides a refuge for endangered species such as ibex and chamois. And if by now you've had enough of cable cars and the paraphernalia of skiing, these southern valleys are ideal hiking country, threaded by mountain trails, with refuges positioned at convenient spots.

There is some fine walking in the summer months among alpine meadows such as this one near Chamonix.

The heart-stopping cable-car journey passes spectacular ice-fields on the flanks of Mont Blanc, including the stunning Mer de Glace.

–> FACT FILE

CURRENCY Euro.

CLIMATE Alpine; even in the summer, temperatures can fall below freezing on the peaks.

TIME TO GO December–March for skiing; May–September for hiking.

NEAREST AIRPORTS Lyons, Geneva, Turin.

WHAT TO TAKE Sunglasses, sunblock creams, good boots, warm windproof clothing, binoculars.

MORE INFORMATION Tourist Office, 85 place du Triangle-de-l'Amitié, Chamonix, France; Tel: +33 (0)4-5053-0024; web: www.tourisme.fr/office-de-tourisme/chamonix-mont-blanc.htm.
Piazza Chanoux 8, Aosta, Italy; Tel: +39 (0)1-1523-6627; web: www.regione.vda.it/turismo.

RENAISSANCE ITALY

Renaissance Italy was a land of raw umber and burnt sienna, of rolling meadows and the dark flames of cypress trees; an artist's paradise, a cultural heartland, and a gourmet's delight.

Exploring the regional wines–including Chianti and Brunello di Montalcino–and food such as the sweet *panforte*, is an essential part of the Italian experience.

CYPRESSES AND PARASOL PINES stand out dark against a sky baked eggshell blue. An old farm turned into a holiday villa rests calmly beneath its red-tiled roof in the curve of a valley, its swimming pool glinting a bright blue. In the distance the towers of a miniature city rise between vineyards and olive groves. The landscape of Tuscany and Umbria, patiently molded by thousands of years of human cooperation with nature, is so beautiful that it is easy to forget the charming little hilltop or valley towns adorning it once buzzed with an urban dynamist that produced one of the greatest turning points, revolutions even, in human history: the Renaissance.

To grasp the full immensity of this revolution, go to the Uffizi Gallery in Florence and look at Gentile da Fabriano's *Adoration of the Magi* of 1423, with its stately, stiff figures, flat perspective, and lavish use of gold leaf. Then cross the river to the church of Santa Maria del Carmine and contemplate Masaccio's *Expulsion from Paradise* fresco, with its emotive, startlingly modern-looking nudes of Adam and Eve, painted just 4 years later. This was not merely a change of artistic fashion, but a radical shift in the way we look at the world and ourselves. It's no coincidence that "scientific perspective," so fundamental to the way we now see the world, was worked out by two Florentines: Leon Alberti

(1404-1472) and Flippo Brunelleschi (1377-1446), or that it was a Florentine philosopher, Niccolò Machiavelli (1469-1527), who formulated the principles of Realpolitik with such brutal elegance in his book *The Prince*. The modern world started here with the Florentine Renaissance.

Florence stands on the Arno River, between the Chianti hills to the south and those of Fiesole to the north. It began its rise in 1115 when it became a republic. Despite ferocious internal conflicts, it gradually became the region's preeminent city, ruling most of Tuscany. In 1434, the wealthy Medici family seized power, although at first they disguised their autocracy in republican trappings. What the Florentines lost in political liberty they gained in stability–and art. The Medicis were phenomenally enlightened patrons–perhaps the greatest ever–and soon the city's cultural achievements were such that it could boast of being the new Athens. This was no idle boast, for the Medici commissioned works from the most adventurous artists and architects of the time, including Botticelli (1445-1510) and especially Michelangelo (1475-1564), who is buried in the church of Santa Croce.

Stand on a hill overlooking Florence–at Fiesole with its graceful villas, or San Miniato with its Romanesque church–and you will see the city

Tuscany and Umbria are studded with fortified hilltop towns. San Miniato is crowned by the tower of the Rocca, built by the Emperor Frederick II in the 13th century when the town was an outpost of the Holy Roman Empire.

spread before you, looking much as it did 500 years ago to Leonardo da Vinci, another Florentine. The view is dominated by the vast red dome with which Brunelleschi crowned the city's green and white marble gothic Duomo (cathedral) in the 15th century.

Heart of the Renaissance

Florence is a compact city, and all of its main sights can be reached on foot—fortunately, cars are now banned from the narrow streets of the medieval and Renaissance center. Within that small space lies probably the greatest concentration of artistic masterpieces on earth. A short walk south of the Duomo is the Piazza della Signoria, a square bounded on one side by the gothic arcades of the

Siena's main square, the Campo, is dominated by the splendid 14th-century gothic Palazzo Pubblico (town hall), with its vertiginous 320-foot (97-m) bell tower.

Loggia housing the *Perseus* by Benvenuto Cellini (1500–1571) and on the other by the Palazzo Vecchio, a brownstone medieval fortress with a 300-foot (91-m) tower. In front of this stands Michelangelo's heroic statue of David—or it did, until the original was removed to the Academia Gallery to escape pollution and this replica was substituted. The adjoining Uffizi is one of the world's great art galleries, crammed with paintings—such as Botticelli's *Birth of Venus* and *Primavera*—so famous they seem images from your own subconscious. The Uffizi becomes very crowded in high season and visitors are recommended to book tickets well in advance.

A covered walkway runs from the Uffizi across the Ponte Vecchio—the 14th-century bridge that still has its galleries of shops. According to legend, the great poet Dante—another Florentine—glimpsed his beloved Beatrice on this bridge. Standing at dusk on the bridge, with the boats swooping over the waters of the Arno as it flows past the palaces and under the exquisite Renaissance arches of Ponte Santa Trinitá—bombed in World War II but lovingly reassembled—it seems a plausible story. Whatever happens, do not miss Michelangelo's statues in the Medici tombs in the Medici Chapel, which he also designed, adjoining the church of San Lorenzo. These almost nude recumbent figures, symbolizing Morning, Evening, Day, and Night seem too tragically noble just to commemorate minor Medici princelings. After so much high art, try one of the excellent pizzas outside. Florence is justly proud of its cuisine: Tuscan olive oil, greenish black and reputedly the world's best, fresh herbs, and vegetables create distinctive flavors for local dishes. The best local hams come from Tuscan wild boar; pecorino, creamy sheep's cheese, is another treat. Light red Chianti is matched by heavy Vino Nobile di Montepulciano.

A typically idyllic Tuscan landscape of gently undulating hills punctuated by cypress trees in the Val d'Orcia near Bagno Vignoni, to the south of Siena.

FACT FILE ←—

CURRENCY Euro.

CLIMATE Mediterranean; long hot summers and mild winters.

BEST TIME April–June and September–October when the weather is very pleasant and there are fewer tourists.

NEAREST AIRPORTS Amerigo Vespucci Airport in Florence connects the city to other Italian and some European cities. Galileo Galilei Airport, in Pisa, 50 miles (75 km) west of Florence, is used for international flights. Perugia Airport, for domestic flights and some international charter flights in summer, can be reached via Milan International Airport.

WHAT TO BUY Leather, antiques, clothes, jewelry.

FOOD AND DRINK The region is known for its fine cooking, in particular its meat dishes, olive oil, and excellent wine.

MORE INFORMATION Province of Florence Tourist Board, Azienda Promozione Turistica, Via Manzoni 19, I-50121 Firenze; tel: +39 (055) 23320; web: www.firenzeturismo.it. Provinces of Perugia, Assisi, Gubbio, Todi, and Spoleto Tourist Boards, Azienda Promozione Turistica, Via Mazzini 21, I-06100 Perugia; tel: +39 (075) 575951; web: www.umbria-turismo.it.

Florence's great rival, Siena, 35 miles (54 km) to the south, is astonishingly well preserved in its traffic-free center. In Siena even today, city life preserves its medieval form, for it is divided into 17 *contrade* (quarters). Every aspect of civic and social life–births, marriages, employment, deaths–take place within an individual's *contrada*. Rivalry between the two cities is intense, and erupts twice a year in the Palio, a horse race held on July 2 and August 16 in the town's main square.

Known as the Campo, this huge cobbled oval flanked by venerable brick buildings is dominated by the gothic Palazzo Pubblico (town hall), built in the 14th century and surmounted by its vertiginous 320-foot (97-m) tower. Narrow streets radiate from the Campo. In the 14th century, the city planned to double the size of its Duomo, bizarrely striped in white and dark green marble like licorice, by building a new nave. But before it could be

completed, Siena's fortune waned, and the unfinished arcades stand open to the sky like the skeleton of a beached whale.

Hilltop Towns of Umbria

Although there is a slow train between Florence and Siena, it is easier to explore the countryside by car. Amid olive groves west of Siena, San Gimignano bristles with medieval towers. To the east lies Umbria, a region with even more rural beauty than Tuscany. To the southwest is Assisi, home of St. Francis, recently devastated by an earthquake.

Traveling east, the landscape becomes more mountainous toward the Apennines, where wild boar still forage. Deep snows often make mountain villages inaccessible in winter; heavy spring and autumn rains keep the tourist at bay. The town of Gubbio clings tenaciously to its windswept crag as it clung for centuries to its freedom. Narrow lanes climb steeply between somber palazzi to the main square where the 14th-century crenellated town hall juts out over a dizzying drop. Some 25 miles (40 km) north of Gubbio, the little town of Urbino crowns a hill. Above a cluster of magnificent Renaissance churches loom the twin towers of the Palazzo Ducale, seat of the Montefeltro dynasty, an untouched early Renaissance gem, where the great painter Raphael (1483-1520) grew up. Here one of the most brilliant Renaissance courts flourished in the 15th century, and the town today retains much of its 16th-century character. Around 1476, Piero della Francesca painted the twin portraits of Duke Federigo da Montefeltro and his wife (which are now in the Uffizi in Florence). The tough, shrewd politician and his duchess contemplate each other through the picture frames; in the background, hills and plains stretch sublimely away.

The Ponte Vecchio, spanning the River Arno at Florence, was built in 1345, although the jewelers' shops that crowd its arcades date from the 1500s. You can still cross the bridge via the secret passage constructed for the city's powerful Medici rulers.

VENICE, QUEEN OF THE SEAS

See Venice, as Goethe suggested—"with artist's eyes"—to appreciate the translucency of light, the reflections and shadows of the waters, the colors and movement on canals and in the piazzas.

The Carnival at the end of Lent is one of the city's oldest traditions; it was ruled by commedia dell' arte characters such as Harlequin.

VENICE OWES ITS EXISTENCE TO THE SEA—to experience the full truth of this statement, take a boat out to the islands of the lagoon around it and watch the city recede into the wide expanse of water and sky, becoming a mirage of domes, pinnacles, towers, and palaces. Like many of the world's most evocative cities—Istanbul, St. Petersburg, New York—Venice is untypical of the country to which it belongs, but nowhere else is really like Venice at all. Whether sweltering beneath the summer sun or swathed in winter fogs, the city is literally unique.

Venice is built on a collection of islands, seahorse shaped, and crisscrossed by more than 150 canals and 400 bridges, which were settled in the 5th century by refugees from the mainland. The republic they established lasted more than a thousand years, growing fabulously rich on trade with the East, extending its rule over islands and cities. Such mixed Eastern influences, and especially such wealth, are reflected in Venetian art and architecture—often fantastically rich and ornate—but

not noticeably in its food, where seafood is the chief allure. *Vongole* (small clams) are a local delicacy, caught in the lagoon and fried live in olive oil and garlic.

In Venice you either walk—or go by water. To see Venice the very first time (assuming you are not coming from the airport by water taxi), take a *vaporetto* (water bus) from the railroad or the (only) parking lot in Piazzale Roma. On the slow journey down the Canal Grande, you see palace after palace rise from the waters, some gothic in style such as the fanciful 15th-century Ca' d'Oro, some Renaissance such as the massive somber Ca' Grande, but almost nothing seems to have changed in the two centuries since Canaletto painted it all.

After chugging under the bridge of the Rialto, once the city's commercial center, the vaporetto reaches the Piazza San Marco (St. Mark's Square). This immense square, though often crowded, remains the heart of Venice, with Renaissance arcades on three sides housing famous cafés such as Florian's or Quadri, once Richard Wagner's favorite. Napoleon called it the "finest drawing room in Europe," and orchestras still play here every evening. Be warned: these cafés are not cheap! On the piazza's fourth side rises Venice's cathedral: St. Mark's Basilica, a five-domed Byzantine church overlaid by an extraordinary fantasy of pinnacles and gold stars on an azure background. On its front stand four ancient Roman bronze horses looted from the Hippodrome at Byzantium (Istanbul)—but the ones you see now are reproductions; the originals are inside to protect them from pollution. The tall *campanile* (bell tower) beside the basilica is also a replica, the original having collapsed with minimal damage to surrounding buildings in 1902. To the right is the Palazzo Ducale (Ducal Palace) with its gothic arcades and red and white diamond-patterned facade. The republic was ruled from here, and from here prisoners were led over the Bridge of Sighs to

Overlooked by the exotic splendor of St. Mark's Basilica, the Piazza San Marco is one of the world's classic café locations.

A gondola glides beneath the Ponte della Paglia in front of the 15th-century Palazzo Ducale, where the most secret machinations of the Venetian state were once conducted.

the prison. Casanova, most famous of its prisoners, escaped over the roof of the palace, the only captive ever to do so.

Almost any turning in Venice will bring you face to face with some architectural marvel or a gallery full of world-class paintings. Among the many churches that give the Venetian skyline its air of elegant fantasy are the Renaissance Santa Maria dei Miracoli, the baroque Santa Maria della Salute (with paintings by Titian and Tintoretto), and on the island of the same name, San Giorgio Maggiore, by the Renaissance genius Palladio, whose pale dome is one of the city's landmarks. The Accademia Gallery houses masterpieces of Venetian art down the centuries, but for a more modern note try the Peggy Guggenheim Foundation in the half-built

Palazzo Venier, noted for its surrealist art.

Sooner or later everyone gets lost in the labyrinth of canalside pathways that is Venice away from the crowds. Despite being one of the world's most touristed cities, you need only take a wrong turn to find yourself in a narrow alley beside walls punctuated only by barred windows, before you emerge into some square basking in the afternoon sun. Then, footsore and hot, is the time to take to the water. Gondolas, the obvious first choice, are as fantastic as anything in Venice—fantastically impractical and expensive, but very romantic if you don't object to bobbing around in the wakes of the motorboats. If you want to gondola cheaply, take a *traghetto*—communal gondolas that cross the Canal Grande at various fixed points.

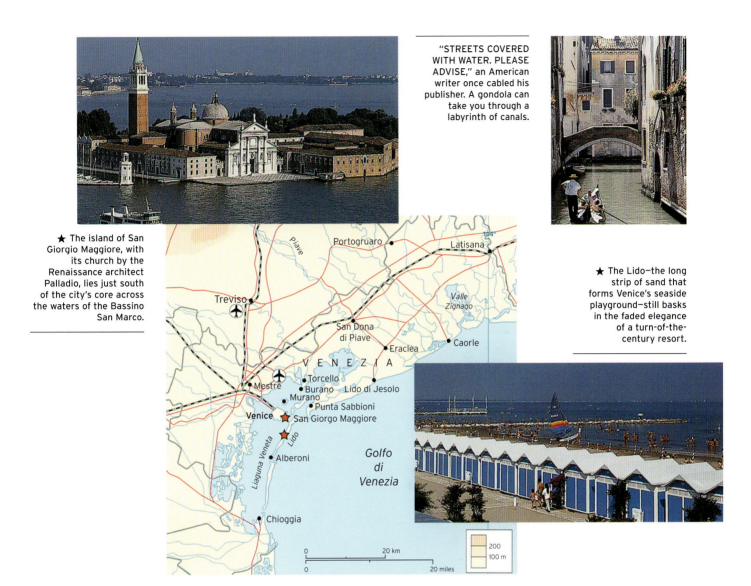

★ The island of San Giorgio Maggiore, with its church by the Renaissance architect Palladio, lies just south of the city's core across the waters of the Bassino San Marco.

"STREETS COVERED WITH WATER. PLEASE ADVISE," an American writer once cabled his publisher. A gondola can take you through a labyrinth of canals.

★ The Lido—the long strip of sand that forms Venice's seaside playground—still basks in the faded elegance of a turn-of-the-century resort.

The Lagoon and Islands

The mouth of the Grand Canal (left) is dominated by the domes of Santa Maria della Salute. Begun in the 1630s in thanksgiving for the city's deliverance from the plague, the church took 50 years to complete.

When you tire of the city, take another vaporetto to the lagoon and islands. The vaporetto from Fondamente Nuove chugs along through the (normally) placid lagoon, pulling up at wayside halls lying scarcely above the water. The island of Murano is crowded with glassmakers' workshops; the craft has been practiced here for centuries, and if the products are often kitsch, there's undeniable satisfaction in taking home something you have seen created with such skill. Burano, bright with colored houses, is famed for its fishing and lacemaking, and again you can watch its lacemakers practice their traditional calling. Torcello, the furthest of these scattered islands, was among the first to be settled; some of the houses on the Rialto were moved stone by stone from here when the island became malarial and was abandoned. Today it is a lonely, evocative place, with little besides its imposingly plain cathedral standing amid overgrown fields. If you enjoy solitude (like Ernest Hemingway who wrote *Across the River* and *Into the Trees* here) you can stay at one of Torcello's simple guesthouses, but you'll be stranded on the island after the last vaporetto leaves in the early evening.

Biggest by far of all these islands, the one that shelters the lagoon from the sea, is the 9-mile (14-km)-long Lido. The poet Byron, when he lived in Venice in 1816-1819, used to ride along the then-deserted beach under the pine trees, but for the last century it has been Venice's seaside resort. Grand hotels line the wide beach, and none is grander than the Grand Hotel des Bains, a luxurious fin de siécle building where the German novelist Thomas Mann wrote *Death in Venice* in 1911 and where, 60 years later, Luchino Visconti made the movie of the book. But more typically Venetian in its ornate fantasy is the Moorish-style Hotel Excelsior. Even if you don't want to swim or sunbathe, the Lido is worth a visit.

THE METEORA

Pinnacles of rock with monasteries perched precariously on their summits form a dramatic gateway to the backbone of Greece.

Skulls of former head monks in the chantry of the Great Meteoron greet today's tourists.

THE GIANT, ELEPHANTINE STUMPS of the Meteora erupt suddenly with dizzying verticality from the completely flat plain of Thessaly. They are an extraordinary and unexpected geological formation contained in a tiny 25 square miles (65 sq km) at the innermost point of the plain, standing like natural monoliths marking the gateway to the Pindhos mountains, the backbone of mainland Greece. The mountains beyond them stutter to a halt in these great splinters of blue-gray rock, soaring hundreds of feet into the air above the fertile valley floor, fissured and scarred by the prehistoric seas that once covered the region.

Such a landscape is surreal in itself, but stranger still are the Greek Orthodox monasteries that perch on its almost inaccessible peaks. Hermits first began to seek solitude in which to commune with God on these pinnacles in the 9th century. It is extraordinary to contemplate exactly how they scaled the sheer rock faces, which climbers rate among the toughest in Europe–St. Athanasios, who founded the Great Meteoron in the 1300s, is said to have flown up on the back of an eagle. Until stairs were hewn into the rocks in the 1920s, all access was by means of ladders or a net winched up by rope. One traveler, asking how often the rope was replaced, was given the reassuring answer, "When the good Lord permits it to break."

The area was long a lawless border country, part of the Serbian empire created by Stephan Dushan

The mighty Pindhos mountains, the backbone of mainland Greece, provide unspoiled walking country.

in the 14th century, later the refuge of Greek rebels against Ottoman rule, and then the stronghold of Greek partisans in the Second World War and communist fighters in the grim civil war that followed. At its peak in the 1500s, the Meteora–the name literally means "suspended in air"–including 13 monasteries and some 20 dependencies, drew revenue from estates as far off as the Danube valley. Decline set in during the 1700s, when the least accessible monasteries began to be abandoned, and by the middle of the present century there was just a handful of monks and nuns struggling to maintain the disintegrating buildings. They were saved from complete ruin only by the construction of the road that made the monasteries accessible to tourism. If the Meteora's sense of solitude has diminished, at least the survival of the monasteries has been assured.

Working Monasteries

Many people "do" the Meteora in a day or a weekend. Better to explore on foot the high meadows with, in spring, the wildflowers for which

–> FACT FILE

CURRENCY Euro.

CLIMATE Wet and cool November–March, hot in summer.

TIME TO GO Late January, early February for Greece's "halcyon days," a spell of fair weather in midwinter, and April, to avoid the crowds, catch spring sun, flowers, and Greek Easter.

WHAT TO TAKE Respectable clothes (skirts for women); walking gear.

NEAREST AIRPORT Thessaloniki, but Athens has far more flights.

PUBLIC TRANSPORTATION There are regular buses to Kalambaka from Loannina, Trikala, Thessaloniki, and Athens, and trains from Thessaloniki or Athens, changing at Stavros.

ACCOMMODATION There are about seven campgrounds around Kastriki, various small hotels, as well as rooms to rent in tavernas and private homes. More information is available at www.meteora-greece.com.

Materials to build the precariously positioned monasteries were hauled to the summits by rope ladders and pulleys.

Greece is justly famed, and the secret clefts and strange turbulent rock formations between the monasteries. You will also discover abandoned troglodytic dwellings and monasteries, and trace the fly-on-the-wall progress of climbers up the awesome cliff faces. Six monasteries are still functioning. Perched at the top of a massive, 1,750-foot (533-m) spur known as the Platys Lithos (broad stone) is the highest of them, the Great Meteoron. Its high-domed Church of the Transfiguration was built in the 1500s on the traditional Byzantine square cross plan. The interior is surprisingly light and airy, displaying the well-preserved frescos to advantage. The 1557 refectory, with its round stone table and vaulted roof supported by five pillars, was rescued from dereliction in 1960 and converted into a museum in which many fine icons and other monastic treasures are displayed. The views from the Great Meteoran across to the neighboring pinnacles and the tantalizing ring of mountains are an incentive to stay longer and explore the area at leisure.

The monastery of St. Stephen (Hagios Stefanos), though the furthest from Kalambaka by road, is the only monastery visible from the village. It is also the most accessible, since it can be reached from the main mass of Kuklioli hill by drawbridge. A cobbled path climbs through a dark vaulted entrance passage into the sunlit courtyard flanked by wooden galleries. There are two churches: the plain late 18th-century Church of St. Charalambos, and the dark somewhat somber St. Stephen's built in the 1300s. Rousanou, also known as Hagia Varvara, is a small monastery now occupied by nuns. It sits tightly on a sharp spire of rock close to the main mountain face, to which it is now connected by an iron footbridge. There is scarcely an inch of ground to spare, and the wooden upper stories are built out over the vertiginous abyss.

Each of the inhabited monasteries at Meteora charges a small admission fee. Orthodox standards of dress are strictly enforced. Sleeveless clothing and shorts are prohibited, and women must wear skirts. Some monasteries provide shawls and skirts at the entrance, but don't rely on this. Monasteries may be visited all year round, but from July to October they are crowded, and in May every child in Greece seems to come here on a school trip. There are hotels in the village of Kastraki; from here monasteries can be reached on foot. But there is more choice—and a fine 13th-century Byzantine cathedral—in Kalambaka, about a mile down the road. The old walled town of Trikkala—once the capital of Serbian emperors, just 13 miles (22 km) away—is connected to Kalambaka by a regular bus service.

If you want to avoid the crowds, go from November through April. Though the weather will be cool and often damp, you may be rewarded by days of crystal-clear winter sunshine, the "halcyon days" between January and mid-February. Then you can look across to long-abandoned inaccessible

The honeycombed rock faces were once inhabited by troglodytes and made into chapels, whose ruins remain.

From the hidden valleys and high meadows of the Meteora are breathtaking views of the Thessaly Plain and the Pindhos mountains.

monasteries, unvisited for centuries except by the Egyptian vultures and red kites that nest there. And if you're really lucky you may even see a golden eagle, like the one that bore St. Athanasios to the peak of the Great Meteoron, riding a thermal far below you.

Deep into the Backbone of Greece

The main E92 road is one of the most spectacular mountain routes in a country full of them, and the only pass over the Pindhos that remains open all year. It takes you into virgin Greece, the source of five of the country's major rivers, where deep limestone ravines are clad in forests of beech, oak, chestnut, and fir. Away from the main towns, the most aggressive sign of tourism is the occasional hiker, where physical isolation has preserved regional dialects and traditions from outside influences—including Turkish domination. Metsovo, some 37 miles (60 km) beyond the Meteora (and on the bus route), has bowed to the pressures of commercial tourism, but is perched on two sides of a ravine looking over splendid mountains to the south and east.

WHERE EAST MEETS WEST

"It is more like some enchanted city out of 'The Thousand and One Nights' than like any real town built of bricks, stones, and mortar."–Demetrius Coufopoulos, 1895

The imperial hall of the harem in the Topkapi Palace where the man of the house lived with his wives. The word "harem" is Arabic for "forbidden," but increasing numbers of rooms are being opened to the public.

THIS ANCIENT CITY AT THE MEETING POINT of Europe and Asia has had three names in its long history: Byzantium, Constantinople, and Istanbul. Today it is filled with the staggering legacy of the two empires that made it their capital: the Byzantine Greeks and Ottoman Turks. Still Turkey's greatest city, marvelously sited on a peninsula, it is among the most colorful, noisy, and fascinating places in the world, a mecca for shoppers, gourmets (Turkish cuisine is rightly renowned), and travelers.

The double Theodosian walls—named for the 5th-century Byzantine emperor who had them built—stretch 4 miles (6.4 km) across the neck of the peninsula and are still wonderfully intact. With the area they enclose, they have been designated a UNESCO World Heritage Site. Modern Istanbul sprawls far beyond the walls, but within them old Istanbul forms a complete contrast to the manicured historic sites of western Europe. Here antiquity–just–survives cheek by jowl with the

present: the homeless squat in the towers of Roman walls, antique capitals serve as bird baths in a muddy yard, an auto repair shop turns out to be part of an Ottoman building, and football is played in a filled-in Byzantine reservoir. As you admire thousand-year-old monuments, the modern city's traffic roars past inches away. Such chaotic intermingling of past and present reflects the city's mixed ancestry.

Looking for a new capital, Roman emperor Constantine (reigned 306-337 A.D.) chose the Greek city of Byzantium, defensibly sited, which then became Constantinople, city of Constantine. After the fall of the West Roman Empire in 476, Constantinople continued to rule the slowly declining East Roman or Byzantine Empire for a thousand years until it fell to the Ottoman Turks in 1453. The city's conqueror Sultan Mehmet II (reigned 1451-1481) made it capital of the Ottoman Empire, which it remained until Turkey became a republic in 1922 with its capital at Ankara.

Today, if you stand in the heart of the old city on the site of the former Byzantine hippodrome—now

just a grassy park—your eye will be drawn to two majestic domes. The older and smaller is that of the great Byzantine cathedral of Hagia Sophia—the name means Holy Wisdom—which was built by Emperor Justinian in 533-539. Its shallow dome, rising 180 feet (55 m) above the ground and spanning 100 feet (31 m), is now flanked by four minarets added by the Ottomans after it was converted into a mosque, but the interior preserves much of its original appearance, a vast, airy space

The Golden Horn divides Istanbul in two, with the old imperial center on one side, and more recent cultural and business development on the other.

Shoe shine is just one of the many trades enacted throughout the old city.

POPULATION 10 million.

CURRENCY Turkish lira.

CLIMATE Mixed maritime/continental; often hot June–August, it may snow in winter.

TIME TO GO Any time, but spring is most pleasant.

NEAREST AIRPORT Ataturk International Airport is 15 miles (24 km) from the city with a bus service into the center.

WHAT TO BUY Carpets, jewelry, leather goods.

WHAT TO TAKE A money belt to deter pickpockets, warm clothes in winter.

CITY ACCOMMODATION Normally plentiful, from the cheap, including the youth hostel situated right opposite Hagia Sophia, to the luxurious, including the faded splendor of the old Pera Palace Hotel, once a haven for travelers on the Orient Express.

with columned gallery, glittering mosaics, and multicolored marble brought from every part of the empire. On the walls angels and other Byzantine icons can still just be seen. Hagia Sophia is now a museum.

The Byzantines themselves never surpassed Hagia Sophia and came to regard its construction as almost miraculous, but the Ottomans finally did so with the other great dome that dominates Istanbul's skyline: the six-minaret Sultan Ammet Mosque. Built between 1609 and 1616 by the architect Mehmet, it is often known as the Blue Mosque on account of the blue and white Iznik tiles

that give the interior its cool elegance. It is still a working mosque.

At the tip of the peninsula is Topkapi Palace, a graceful complex of courtyards, apartments, pavilions, and gardens overlooking the waters of the Golden Horn and Bosphorus. Construction started in 1466, and for centuries this was the residence of the sultans from which the vast Ottoman empire was governed; by the 1800s some 5,000 officials, courtiers, and servants lived within its walls. Opened to the public in 1924, it is now the world's largest palace museum, displaying 86,000 historic artifacts including costumes, jewelry,

Over 20,000 Iznik-ware tiles decorate the interior of the Blue Mosque (above), and gave it its name. On the outside, however, its dome and six minarets are the impressive features.

furniture, and a marvelous display of calligraphy. The gardens of Topkapi now make a welcome oasis of quiet in a city notably lacking green spaces—and you can look out across the busy maritime traffic of the Bosphorus to the shores of Asia.

The Grandest Bazaar

Istanbul is an exciting city for shoppers, especially those who are good at haggling. The Kapali Carsi, or Covered Bazaar, the world's largest, dates back to early Ottoman times. The labyrinth of streets and passages houses more than 4,000 shops selling Turkish crafts: carpets, hand-painted ceramics, gold jewelry, copper and brassware, meerschaum pipes, and leather goods. Beware of buying anything that could be classed as an antique—in the unlikely event of it turning out to be genuine, you'd be liable to a prison sentence if you tried to take it out of the country without a license. Behind the Yeni Mosque at Eminönü is the Misir Carsisi (Egyptian or spice bazaar), where the air is laden with the scents of caraway, cinnamon, mint, saffron, and thyme.

Turkish food is considered one of the three great classic cuisines of the world—along with the French and Chinese—though vegetarians should beware that many innocuous-looking dishes of chickpeas, okra, or other vegetables are made with beef stock and may contain a small cube of meat for good measure. Fish in particular is excellent in Istanbul—the catch is landed directly on the waterfront from the teeming waters of the Bosphorus, where you can buy it freshly grilled over charcoal and served between slices of bread. For a more leisurely meal, there is a cluster of good fish restaurants around

One of the charms of Istanbul is the mingling of past and present, as in the football field lying beneath ancient city walls built to defend against Attila the Hun's forces.

Hagia Sophia, originally a Christian church, then a mosque from 1453, and now a museum, is renowned for its beautiful mosaic decoration.

Kumkapi. Turkish beer, notably Efes, and wine are good, too.

The sea is never far away—as you turn down an alley between ramshackle wooden houses you may catch sight of its glittering waters, and at night you can hear the foghorns of the great tankers laboring through the Bosphorus. Some of the best excursions from the city are by boat. A 2-hour ferry ride from the Sirceki Pier will take you to the Princes Islands. Once a place of exile for out-of-favor Byzantine royalty, these islands in the Sea of Marmara are covered in pine forest and wild lilac, dotted with fine old wooden mansions and Greek Orthodox monasteries, and remain entirely free of motor traffic. From Eminönü you can take a 2-hour boat trip up the Bosphorus to the Black Sea. Trees spill down to the water's edge as you pass the Dolmabahce Palace, once the residence of sultans, old villages such as Arnavutköy with their little Greek tavernas and excellent fish restaurants, and the Belgrade forest with its elaborate system of Ottoman aqueducts.

CRUSADER CASTLES OF SYRIA

Built to withstand all enemies including time, the massive crusader castles still dominate the valleys and mountains of western Syria seven centuries after they were abandoned.

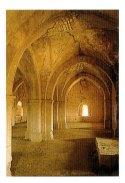

The fortress of Safita reflects the infiltration of northern Europe's gothic style in the Middle East.

IN 1909, A YOUNG OXFORD STUDENT set out through Palestine and Syria to visit as many of the crusaders' castles as he could. Fired with the romance of history, he traveled more than 1,000 miles (1,600 km) on foot in the heat of summer, enduring many hardships. His observations were eventually published in 1936 as *Crusader Castles*. By then, however, its author, T. E. Lawrence, had acquired a very different fame as Lawrence of Arabia.

Nowadays you can visit the main castles in much greater comfort, as specialist operators run tours with expert guides. Even if you want to forge your own path, you won't need to walk: buses ply the routes from the main centers of Damascus, Homs,

Hama, and Latakia. For maximum independence, your best option is to rent a car in the capital, Damascus. Though no castle is more than a day's round trip from a town with accommodation, each is sufficiently remote to make your journey an adventure and voyage of discovery.

Guardians in the Landscape

The castles are situated on the edge of Syria's fertile plains between the Jebel al-Ansariye mountains and the Mediterranean coast. The countryside is unexpectedly pretty, very different from the harsh desert of the interior. Provided you do not travel in midsummer, you pass through

Krak des Chevaliers is one of the best-preserved medieval castles in the world, a testimony to the determination of the crusader monks who built it.

The height from the depths of the moat to the uppermost ramparts of the main keep at Qalaat Saladin is an impressive deterrent to invaders.

Marqab Castle stands on a volcanic peak, from which the basalt of its walls was quarried.

grassy hills covered with wild anemones in spring, citrus orchards, olive groves, and stands of oak and pine, often with high mountains visible to the east and the Mediterranean Sea to the west.

Traveling 40 miles (65 km) east from the industrial city of Homs is the greatest of all crusader castles, Krak des Chevaliers (Qalat al-Husn), incredibly well preserved. As you approach through rolling landscape, massive walls loom up ahead from a 2,200-foot (670-m) hill. Lawrence described it as "the finest castle in the world." However, this is no romantic ruin, but military architecture that means business, all smooth, sweeping planes designed to leave an attacker exposed to merciless defensive fire. First occupied by crusaders in 1110, Krak des Chevaliers was given in 1142 to the Knights Hospitaller. An order of "fighting monks" that grew up during the Crusades, the Hospitallers were responsible for much of the existing fortifications. Protected by two concentric rings of walls and towers, with a rock-cut moat between, the castle resisted the great Sultan

Saladin's attempt to capture it in 1188, only falling in 1271. Inside the inner ring the gothic chapel and Great Hall, with its intricately carved portico, offer some relief from the military severity of the defenses.

From the ramparts of Krak (if the weather isn't too hazy), you can see the tall white keep of Chastel Blanc, 15 miles (24 km) to the northwest. Set on a hill amid orchards and olive groves, the castle was established in 1112, but most of what survives was built by the Templars, another order of fighting monks, in the early 13th century. The outer walls have almost disappeared, and today the village of Safita straggles right up to the keep itself. This is a pretty and relaxing place—its altitude keeps it fairly cool even in the summer—with old stone houses built around courtyard gardens.

The Crusaders' Last Stand

From Safita it is 18 miles (30 km) to Tartus, an attractive if tacky old port on the Mediterranean coast, whose streets of low stone houses have changed little since the Crusades, when it was called Tortosa. Locals stroll along the waterfront in the evening while men play backgammon and smoke *margules* (pipes) in the many coffee shops. Some comfortable hotels make Tartus a good place to spend the night.

The crusaders' keep can still be seen on the shore, but the main relic of their era is the Cathedral of Our Lady. First built in 1123, it was restored by the Templars after Saladin sacked it. The dour, fortresslike exterior conceals a gothic interior that might grace a French city. Just offshore is Arwad Island, the crusaders' last outpost, where they clung on until 1302, 11 years after the mainland had fallen. There are plenty of boats making the short crossing, and amid the winding lanes full of cafés and net menders are the remains of two citadels, one Templar, one Muslim.

About 24 miles (38 km) north of Tartus, not long before you reach the town of Baniyas, rises the grim bulk of an extinct volcano, with spectacular views across the Mediterranean. On it stands the gigantic and somber crusaders' fortress of Margat (Qalaat Marqab), built from black basalt quarried from the mountain itself. The triangular curtain wall and round keep were built by the Hospitalers after they took over the castles in 1186. The Great Hall is now in a ruin, though the chapel, with its graceful gothic arches, survives intact.

Some 35 miles (56 km) to the north, a steep road zigzags through dramatic gorges to where the crusader castle of Saone perches atop a narrow ridge between two ravines. It has been known since 1957 as Qalaat Saladin in honor of its conqueror. Originally built by the Byzantine Greeks, whose ruins can still be seen, Saone was occupied around 1120 by the crusaders, who vastly strengthened the fortifications. The castle is divided into two parts, a lower ward and a more fiercely defended upper ward dominated by a squat, powerful keep. The moat is cut out of solid rock: one of the castle's most remarkable features is the tall needle of stone 90 feet (28 m) high rising out of the moat to support a drawbridge. Qalaat Saladin is best reached by taxi from Latakia, Syria's main port and a major holiday resort, which makes a good base for exploring the area. In Roman times it was called Laodicea ad Mare, and a triumphal arch and a ruined Temple of Bacchus survive from the era.

To gain an idea of the power and brilliance of the crusaders' Islamic opponents, you could finish off your trip with a stay in Aleppo (Halab), 100 miles (160 km) to the north. In crusader times it was one of the great cities of the Muslim world; today it is Syria's biggest commercial and industrial center. Its massive citadel, mostly built by Saladin's son Ghazi, is one of the most impressive examples of Islamic military architecture in Syria. The old quarter of the city contains more than enough to make a stopover worthwhile, including many historic mosques, well-preserved *hamams* (bathhouses), and ancient *khans*

Aleppo's 13th-century citadel (below) is one of the most brilliant examples of Islamic military architecture, combining formidable defenses with structural elegance.

FACT FILE<-

LANGUAGES Arabic is the official language, but French and English are widely spoken.

CURRENCY Syrian pound.

CLIMATE Summer is very hot, 85°F (29°C); midwinter can be cool and wet, 50°F (10°C).

TIME TO GO Spring, for the flowers, and autumn.

NEAREST AIRPORTS Damascus and Aleppo.

WHAT TO BUY Carpets, jewelry, brass, copper.

WHAT TO TAKE A flashlight for exploring ruins; insect repellent.

IMPORTANT NOTE Travelers with an Israeli visa in their passport will not be admitted to Syria. Those who intend to visit both countries usually arrange to carry two passports. Remember to check the political stability in this volatile region before traveling.

(hostels). Most absorbing of all perhaps is the souk, some 10 miles (16 km) of narrow winding passageways lined with stalls and bustling with trade, where you can display your skills at haggling. When tired, you can try some of the tiny restaurants serving local olives and kebabs, perhaps washed down by *oud*, an aniseed-flavored liquor resembling Pernod. The local beer is also drinkable, but few people praise the wine.

The crusaders believed passionately that they were liberating historic Christian territory—with churches like that of St. Simeon, near Aleppo—from the "infidel."

DUBROVNIK, PEARL OF THE ADRIATIC

"...rising from the rocky coast like an Adriatic Camelot."–David DeVoss

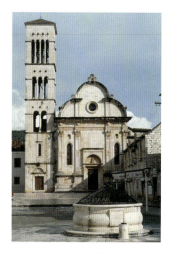

The lovely curves of the baroque cathedral of St. Stjepan in Havr, one of the prettiest towns on the Adriatic.

DUBROVNIK SITS MAJESTICALLY on one of the most beautiful harbors of the Adriatic Sea. Elegant buildings of pale stone, neat red roofs, and baroque spires peer above the iconic walls, which have protected the city for more than 400 years. Proud, independent, and wealthy for much of its 1,300-year history, this jewel of a city has suffered invasions and sieges, and was virtually razed during a massive earthquake in 1667.

Most recently, heavy bombardment during the Yugoslav conflict left two thirds of the city in ruins when war ended in 1992. Shell holes still scar its churches and the new red tiles that cap the rooftops have yet to weather, but, thanks to the hard work of its citizens, Dubrovnik has once more earned Byron's famous epithet–"the pearl of the Adriatic."

Dubrovnik

St. Blaise, the city's patron, guards the Pile Gate, the main entrance to the historic kernel of the Old City (Stari Grad). From here, the showcase Avenue Placa (also called Stradun) begins its grand sweep, flanked on one side by Onofrio's Fountain, and on the other by the semi-ruined Franciscan Monastery. Both were virtually destroyed in the 1667 earthquake, but the monastery's enchanting late-Romanesque cloister survived. Nearby, Europe's oldest apothecary, founded in 1317, continues to administer remedies.

Placa's polished cobbles lead inexorably to the heart of the city, the lovely Luža Square, where cafés cluster under canopies. It is also known as St. Blaise's Square, after the frothy baroque church dedicated to the city's patron saint. At Orlando's

Sailing is very popular along the Dalmatian coast, and almost every town has a marina.

Balustrades and terraces at the exquisite gardens of the Trsteno Arboretum offer sublime sea views.

Column, in the center, new laws were declared and wrongdoers punished during the Ragusan Republic, which lasted from the 14th century until Napoleon's arrival in 1808. The nominal head of this republic, elected monthly and virtually imprisoned for the duration of his tenure, lived in the Rector's Palace, a grandiose hodgepodge of architectural styles that is now a museum. The jewel of the square is the splendid Sponza Palace, topped by a bell tower, its glorious swirls and colonnades among the only reminders of Dubrovnik's Renaissance beauty before the calamitous earthquake.

The streets north of Placa are steep, stepped, and full of flowers. Žudioska, or Jew's Street, is home to one of Europe's oldest synagogues, founded by a Jewish community expelled from Spain in 1492.

The city walls, punctuated by massive towers and fortresses, offer breathtaking views over the old city. Perhaps the best are from the Minčeta Tower, a crenellated giant on the northern flank. By the colorful old port, with its fishing boats and pleasure cruisers, the Dominican Monastery did double duty as fortress and place of prayer, and it contains another delightful cloister set around a garden of palms and orange trees.

Dubrovnik's charms are not only architectural. It's always worth rummaging around the morning market on Gundulićeva Poljana, where you will find pungent cheeses and the local firewater, *rakija*, or stroll down Od Puča to explore the interesting array of galleries and craft shops.

Around Dubrovnik

Ferries leave regularly from the old port for Lokrum Island, which sits just offshore in a thick coat of pine forest, trimmed with sandy beaches. A French-built fortress offers more beautiful views—the ruins of an 11th-century Dominican monastery deteriorate picturesquely, and families can picnic on the shores of the Mrtvo More (Dead Sea) and float on the clear salty waters. Little remains of the lavish country retreat built by Archduke Maximilian Ferdinand von Habsburg in the 1860s, but you can explore the charmingly neglected botanic gardens.

The finest gardens in the region are in Trsteno,

FACT FILE <—

CURRENCY Croatian kuna.

LANGUAGES Croatian. English and German are also widely spoken except in rural areas.

BEST TIME TO GO The crowds descend in droves during July and August, when prices rise and accommodation can be hard to find. Dubrovnik's Summer Festival, which is a prestigious festival of the performing arts, may be some recompense. Choose May or late September, when it is usually warm enough to swim, to avoid the worst of the crowds.

CLIMATE A typical Mediterranean climate with mild winters and hot, sunny summers.

FOOD AND DRINK Cured hams and pungent cheeses, slabs of grilled meat, just-caught fish and chunky seafood stews characterize the Dalmation Coast's fresh and simple cuisine. Try Dubrovnik's typical dessert, *rozata*, which is a kind of crème caramel.

WHAT TO BUY Embroidered and crocheted textiles, olive oil, wines.

AIRPORT Dubrovnik.

ACCOMMODATION There is very little accommodation available in the old town (although there are several luxury hotels in nearby Ploce). Check out self-catering apartments and private rooms if all the old city hotels are fully booked.

A bird's-eye view of one of Dubrovnik's handsome baroque streets, with its charming huddle of red-tiled rooftops.

An elegant summer retreat for more than a century, Cavtat overlooks a tranquil bay.

just north of Dubrovnik. Established by a 15th-century aristocrat and expanded through the centuries by his heirs, these beautiful gardens spill in gentle terraces to the sea. They were opened to the public as the Trsteno Arboretum in 1948 and, despite extensive damage suffered during the Yugoslav conflict, they remain a tranquil, perfumed testimony to Renaissance ideals.

Cavtat, 14 miles (22 km) south of Dubrovnik, huddles prettily around a delightful bay. This fishing village-cum-aristocratic-watering-hole retains much of its delicate baroque architecture, along with a regal Renaissance palace, which is now an excellent museum. The 19th-century Croatian painter, Vlaho Bukovac, was born here, and his home now displays an extensive collection of his work.

The Elafiti Islands, a trio of drowsy islets just west of Dubrovnik, have long been a summer retreat for wealthy city dwellers. The most visited is Lopud, which long provided the Ragusan Republic with sea captains and admirals, whose wealth is evident in the elegant stone buildings that dot the tiny port. Nowadays, the walking paths and palm-fringed beaches are the draw, offering a verdant retreat from the hustle and bustle of the city. On the largest island, Šipan, olive groves and vines stretch between the two main villages, where fishing boats come and go, largely oblivious to the waves of day-tripping tourists. The smallest island

is Koločep, less than 1.5 miles (2.5 km) long, with stone villages strung around palm-fringed bays.

One of the most beautiful of the thousands of islands scattered along the Croatian coast is Mljet, which is a one-and-a-half-hour ferry ride from Dubrovnik. According to legend, this was Homer's Ogygia, where amorous Calypso held Odysseus captive for 7 years. The Uvala Jama caves on its southern coast are said to be where the sea nymph seduced the hero, and it was here she apparently died of grief after his departure. The island has been inhabited since ancient times, and important Roman ruins survive in Polače, still one of the Mljet's largest settlements, along with an early Christian basilica. Part of this 20-mile (32-km) sliver has been designated a national park, where idyllic forest converges around two azure lakes.

At the center of the Great Lake (Veliko Jezero), a tiny islet is topped with the romantic remnants of a monastery and a 12th-century church. The lake is connected to its little sister, Malo Jezero, by beautiful forest paths. From the heights of Mount Montokuc, extraordinary views stretch across the turquoise sea, seductively framed by aromatic pine fronds.

123

NORTHERN EUROPE

"I have wandered all my life, and I have also traveled; the difference between the two being this, that we wander for distraction, but we travel for fulfilment."
HILAIRE BELLOC, FRENCH-BORN ENGLISH WRITER, 1870-1953

WESTERN ISLES OF SCOTLAND

Beyond the windswept shores of this wild and sparsely populated archipelago, there is nothing but the Atlantic Ocean until America.

Neist Point Lighthouse stands guard on high forbidding cliffs south of Loch Dunvegan on the island of Skye.

ASTONISHINGLY, EVEN A COUNTRY as densely populated as Britain contains one of the world's remotest, wildest regions. In the Outer Hebrides—a 130-mile (208-km)-long arc in the North Atlantic, separated from the Scottish mainland by a turbulent channel called the Minch—you are geographically as far from London as Geneva or Frankfurt, culturally perhaps even further, for the ancient Gaelic tongue is still spoken here.

You can stay in a remote croft (farm cottage) and experience profound solitude. Walking for miles on deserted beaches in the lucid light of endless summer evenings, there is nothing to be heard but the cries of seabirds and the barking of seals. On a cloudy, moonless night it is so dark you can't see your hand in front of your face; when it clears, the sky blazes stars, and you may see the northern lights (aurora borealis) perform their ghostly dance across the heavens.

Ferry across the Minch

The main departure port for the Western Isles is Ullapool in Ross and Cromarty. This picturesque old fishing port, built in the 1700s, lies on an inlet called Loch Broom, ringed by heather-clad hills.

Don't be surprised if you see notices in Russian around the town—Russian factory ships come here to buy fish from local trawlermen. There are decent hotels, excellent seafood restaurants, and cheerful pubs (bars). Enjoy these while you can—the landscape of the Western Isles is stunningly beautiful, but the towns and villages are dour functional places. The puritanical morality of the dominant Free Church of Scotland means pubs are few and everything closes on Sundays.

As the car ferry chugs out of Ullapool on the crossing to Stornoway (Steornabhagh), gulls and kittiwakes scream and wheel above the Minch. Stornoway is on the east coast of the largest and northernmost Outer Hebrides, the "Long Islands," which is divided into two: Lewis (Leodhas) and Harris (Na Hearadh). With a population of 8,000, it is the largest town in the Western Isles. The occasional old hotel lends a flourish of Victorian grandeur; more unexpected are Stornoway's tandoori restaurants—there's a small Gaelic-speaking Pakistani population here. Otherwise, gastronomic pleasures are restricted to seafood, usually excellent and very fresh, or the Lewis speciality: boiled gannet (seabird) with potatoes.

All of the islands are connected by causeways or short ferry crossings. Don't expect the going to be fast though; bus services are infrequent, and even if you rent a car in Stornoway, the deeply indented coastline makes any journey a circuitous one. From Stornoway, it is about 25 miles (40 km) across barren peat moors to the island's northernmost tip—the rocky, storm-battered cliffs of Butt of Lewis, a familiar name to anyone who listens to BBC Radio's shipping forecasts.

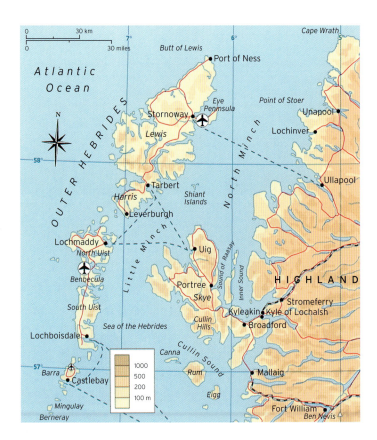

Fishing on the island of Skye—the largest island of the Inner Hebrides.

South along the coast road, one of Europe's most awe-inspiring prehistoric monuments, the Ring of Callanish, overlooks a loch (lake). This neolithic circle consists of some 50 stones, erected between 3000 and 1500 B.C. for unknown religious purposes. At their center is a chambered tomb, probably added centuries—if not millennia—later by a chieftain for his own grave. Around it stand the 13 tallest stones, their gray gneiss as deeply veined and twisted as driftwood. Harris starts where Loch Seaforth—a fjord of Scandinavian grandeur—cuts deep into the island from the east. The land beyond, North Harris, is mountainous and bleak. A narrow isthmus with the main port, Tarbert, connects it to South Harris, almost another island. Its interior is boulder-strewn and uninhabited, but the east coast

FACT FILE<—

POPULATION 26,000 in the Western Isles.

CURRENCY British pound sterling.

CLIMATE Maritime; it seldom freezes at sea level, but expect rain, fog, and very strong winds all year round.

TIME TO GO Spring-autumn; autumn colors are amazing.

NEAREST AIRPORTS Glasgow, Stornoway. There are also flights from Glasgow to both Bebecula and Barra.

WHAT TO TAKE Insect repellent, waterproof clothing, sturdy footwear.

WHAT TO BUY Harris tweed, island malt (Scotch) whisky.

ACCOMMODATION Bed and breakfasts, which offer simple but comfortable beds and very full Scottish breakfasts, including bacon, eggs, and kippers, are usually reasonably priced and comfortable.

shelters small fishing villages such as Kyles Stockinish (Caolas Stocinis) and Ardvey (Aird Mhighe). Deep inlets make the east coast road so convoluted that you may have to stay overnight at one of these places. On the west coast of South Harris, it is possible to walk all day without meeting a soul, along sandy beaches buffeted by Atlantic winds and backed by grassy duneland known as *machair*. In summer this terrain blazes with wildflowers, their scent so strong that ships at sea used to take their bearings by it.

Gateway to the South

From Tarbert or Leverburgh in the south of Harris, a ferry takes you the short hop to the island of North Uist, gateway to the southern reaches of the Hebridean chain. Wildly beautiful and sparsely populated, North Uist, Benbecula, South Uist, and Berneray are connected by a causeway. Between the long shell beaches on the Atlantic side and the labyrinth of rocks, cliffs, islands, and inlets of the eastern coast of these islands, rise spectacular peaks such as South Uist's Beinn Mhor.

Ullapool is the main starting point for a ferry tour of the Western Isles.

Beyond South Uist, take the ferry again to Barra, a *machair*-covered island just 8 miles (13 km) long, its wild beauty somewhat impaired by tourism and a small airport on the beach. The old port at Castlebay (Bagh a Chaisteil) in the south of Barra is the gateway to the archipelago's southernmost and wildest islands, among them Mingulay, Berneray, and Pabbay, which belongs to the National Trust. Uninhabited, these are mere wave-pounded outcrops in the tempestuous Atlantic, where guillemots, kittiwakes, and puffins wheel around the massive cliffs, nesting in every rock face crevice.

"Island of Cloud"

There are also ferries from Tarbert in Harris or Lochmaddy on North Uist back across the Minch to Skye, largest of the Inner Hebrides. Skye—"Island of Cloud" in Old Norse—is a place of magical contrasts, veiled in mists that suddenly clear to reveal heather-clad moorland, lush green valleys, and spectacular peaks. Though the island is just 60 miles (100 km) long, its coastline is so deeply gashed by sea lochs that you would have to cover almost 1,000 miles (1,600 km) to walk around it. Porpoises, basking sharks, and killer whales swim in its waters; sea eagles patrol the skies.

Whether you come from Tarbert or Lochmaddy, the ultimate destination is Uig, a small port ringed by dramatic cliffs on Skye's northeastern peninsula, the Trotternish. This is dominated by spectacular basalt pinnacles called the Storr—a primordial chaos of giant crystals of solidified lava that seem to have just burst through the earth's crust. The highest, the Old Man of Storr, soars 160 feet (50 m)—so formidable it remained unscaled until 1955. At the far end of the peninsula, another cluster of basalt spires, the Quiraing, looms from the mist and sea spray.

Fishing is a way of life in the Outer Hebrides; the fresh lobster may well be on its way to one of the excellent seafood restaurants in Ullapool.

Portree, the only town of any size on Skye, shelters beneath a steep cliff where the Trotternish Peninsula joins the main body of the island. An attractive 18th-century port with a harbor full of brightly painted fishing boats, its many hotels and bed and breakfasts make it a good base for exploring the island. From here the road runs south to Broadford and the Cuillins, the mountains that dominate the south of the island. As you travel west, the red Cuillins, a range of granite hills, give way to the higher and more spectacular black Cuillins. These great black ramparts, their peaks often dusted with snow, rise to more than 3,000 feet (900 m), forming a massive ring around fjordlike Loch Coruisk.

From Broadford, the road continues to the village of Kyleakin, joined to the mainland of Scotland by a controversial new bridge. If that seems an anticlimactic end to your Hebridean odyssey, you can still return by the ferry from Kylerhea, 4 miles (6 km) down the coast.

The scent of wildflowers on the island of Harris is so strong in summer that ships used to take their bearings by it.

THE WEST COAST OF IRELAND

The outermost edges of Europe, where the windswept fingers of Ireland's west coast harbor haunting wildernesses and an ancient culture.

The pre-Christian fortress of Dun Aenghus at Inishmore on the Aran Islands, among farmland where soil is scant and limestone walls are many.

ON THE LAST STRETCH OF LAND before the Atlantic Ocean lies an intoxicating blend of lively towns, old fishing villages, haunting monastic remains, and wild landscapes.

When learning was eclipsed in Europe after the fall of Rome, western Ireland shone like a beacon, drawing scholars and saints to the edge of the known world, where traces of their culture survive today. Along much of this coast, Gaelic (old Irish) is still spoken, cold nights are scented with peat smoke, and impromptu music may start up in a pub at any time.

Grand country houses, built by the old Anglo-Irish gentry, have adapted to the needs of the traveler, and simpler B&B (bed and breakfast) accommodation offers hearty food and a warm welcome. To travel easily, rent a car–buses are infrequent. Driving is a joy; there are few vehicles, no congestion–and often no signposts, so a good map is essential. But the real thrill comes when you take to the sea to visit the wind-lashed islands, and join the gulls and kittiwakes screaming around the wild headlands.

At the southwestern corner of Ireland, in the counties of Cork and Kerry, four rocky peninsulas of

Dunquin Head takes the full force of the Atlantic waves.

130

★ Many traditional stone-built houses like the one above on the Aran Islands offer bed and breakfast accommodation.

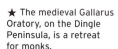

★ County Donegal has a wild coastline with some sheltered inlets, while inland are quiet lakes and dairy farms.

★ The medieval Gallarus Oratory, on the Dingle Peninsula, is a retreat for monks.

red sandstone extend into the Atlantic. The best base for exploring them is Killarney, a small but tourist-conscious town crammed with pubs, restaurants, and B&Bs. Its setting amid lakes and mountains is glorious, but for wilderness head for the southernmost promontory, Mizen Head, whose cliffs look out to the lighthouse rock of Fastnet. The Beara Peninsula, to the north across Bantry Bay, is a magical place. Along its spine runs the mist-shrouded ridge of the Caha and Slieve Mickish mountains, a land of boulder-strewn moorland and plummeting waterfalls. At Ballaghboy, overlooking Dursey Sound at the western tip of the peninsula, take a hair-raising ride in a swinging cable car from the sheer cliffs to wind-blasted Dursey Island. The largest peninsula is Iveragh, whose mountains are the highest in Ireland, rising to almost 3,500 feet (1,066 m) in Macgillicuddy's Reeks, ringed by the Ring of Kerry, a 75-mile (120-km) circuit of roads. Beyond the peninsula's tip, the rocky island of

Skellig Micheal rises 700 feet (213 m) from the waves. Clustered around the ruined church of St. Michael are the beehive stone cells of the monks who lived here in the Middle Ages.

The northernmost finger, the 30-mile (48-km)-long Dingle Peninsula, was also a place of retreat for early monks: the corbeled stone Gallarus Oratory, built between the 9th and 12th centuries, is astonishingly well preserved. From this, the westernmost point of Europe, in the 6th century, St. Brendan—whose shrine still stands on Brandon Mountain—set off on the Atlantic voyage that reputedly took him to America. Dingle is a large fishing village of brightly painted houses, with lively music in its pubs. From here, a ferry crosses to the hump-backed Blasket Islands. The ruined village on Great Blasket sadly recalls the fishing community whose last members were evacuated to the mainland in 1953.

To the north, across the Shannon estuary in County Clare, the cliffs of Moher form a sheer wall of shale and sandstone stretching for 5 miles (8 km) and rising 660 feet (200 m) above raging seas. In the shadow of the cliffs nestles the little village of Doolin, a great center of traditional music. In summer, musicians play in the bars practically every night of the week. Inland rises the Burren, a huge bleak limestone plateau covering 100 square miles (260 sq km). But every crevice is alive with mixed alpine, arctic, and Mediterranean flora. The Burren is also riddled with ancient monuments, like organic outgrowths of its strange rock formations: Stone Age tombs, Iron Age forts, round towers, medieval churches, and four fine 12th-century crosses.

Strong colors in a misty land: a County Kerry fish restaurant advertises its wares.

Ancient Traditions

To the north, Galway Bay cuts 30 miles (48 km) inland. On its northern shore, at the mouth of River Corrib, maritime Galway city is a splendid old town with its medieval church of St. Nicholas and a magnificent 1400s town house, Lynch's Castle, its stone facade decorated with gargoyles.

The city is nowadays renowned for its annual arts festival, held in July. From Rossaveal, an hour's drive south of the city, ferries make the rough 1-hour crossing to the Aran Islands, which look like fragments broken from the Burren—with limestone pavements, wildflowers, and prehistoric remains—scattered across the bay.

The largest Island, Inishmore, is an 8-mile (13-km)-long sliver of rock. Perched above its 300-foot (90-m) cliffs is the prehistoric fort of Dun Aenghus, three concentric semicircles of gray stone walls. The playwright J. M. Synge (1871–1909) recorded the islanders' traditions in the 1800s when they were already disappearing. Many still live by fishing, Gaelic is still widely spoken, and the old ballads of the islands are still sung in the pubs.

Beyond the graceful town of Westport in County Mayo, planned by the architect James Wyatt

(1747–1813), lies mountainous Curraun Peninsula. A bridge connects it to Achill, at 14 by 12 miles (22 by 20 km) the largest island off the coast. It's a wild place, with long golden beaches, mysterious caves, and old fishing hamlets, where salmon fishermen's *currachs* (boats) are moored. The island rises to its western extremity, where the 2,192-foot (668-m) Croaghaun drops sheer to the sea, with cliffs sculpted by the elements.

The Northernmost County

Sligo's subtly beautiful landscape of wild wooded glens and glistening silver lakes has become inseparably associated with Ireland's best known poet, W. B. Yeats (1865–1939), who spent his early years here and is buried in the churchyard at the

foot of the bare stone mountain of Ben Bulben. Sligo's other big peak, Knocknarea, is crowded by a massive prehistoric cairn, which is said to be the last resting place of the legendary Queen Maeve.

Beyond Donegal Bay lies the republic's northernmost county, and its most unspoiled: Donegal is a mosaic of purples, russets, greens, and blacks, of *loughs* (lakes), rivers, and moorland with white-walled houses isolated against bare hillsides. Scattered along the 200-mile (320-km) coastline are small uncommercialized fishing towns, little changed since the 1800s, and long sandy beaches.

Standing at the head of the bay and overlooked by a castle ruin, Donegal Town is a fine old market town where Gaelic is still spoken. Letterkenny, on the shores of Lough Swilly to the north, draws

musicians from over the world to its August folk festival. At the county's westernmost point, the boiling Atlantic is framed by the mighty Slieve League cliffs, at 2,000 feet (608 m) the highest in Europe.

To the north, at Malin Head, Ireland's west coast ends as it began, in a defiant crag. A signal tower and lonely pub look out to the automated lighthouse that guides shipping through terrifying seas, where whirlpools suck at jagged teeth of rock. Cut into the rock face is a monk's tiny cell, the "Wee House of Malin," the harshest imaginable place in which to commune with God.

A quieter face of the Dingle Peninsula on a fine day, showing its sandy beaches and verdant, unspoiled countryside.

-> FACT FILE

POPULATION 3.9 million (Republic of Ireland).

CURRENCY Euro.

CLIMATE Maritime; very wet all year, but temperatures seldom fall below 38°F (4°C).

LANGUAGE Gaelic (Irish) and English are the two official languages.

TIME TO GO March–October.

NEAREST AIRPORTS Cork, Galway, Shannon, Knock.

WHAT TO TAKE Warm, waterproof clothes, insect repellent, good shoes, good road maps, flashlight.

WHAT TO BUY Aran sweaters, Donegal tweed.

FOOD AND DRINK Guinness and Irish whiskey (with an e) are the most famous drinks in the many pubs. Irish coffee (black coffee with sugar, whiskey, and cream) is popular. Seafood, especially oysters and mussels, is excellent, as is the meat.

ALONG THE COAST OF NORWAY

Travel up the coast by ship from Bergen, see the fjords, cross the Arctic Circle to the Lofoten Islands, and glimpse at last the midnight sun shining at the world's northernmost edge.

The eerie northern lights, or aurora borealis, are produced by electrons from the solar wind bombarding the earth's atmosphere.

Stunningly located at the mouth of the Storfjord, the fishing port of Alesund was rebuilt in grand art nouveau style after a fire in 1904.

THE LAST GREAT EPIC JOURNEY in western Europe is the "north way," from which Norway gets its name. This long stretch of water between the fjord-gashed Atlantic coast of Scandinavia and the chain of islands that run alongside is warmed by the Gulf Stream, which allows ice-free ports and habitable land far north of the Arctic Circle. The north way has been a favored shipping route since the Vikings sailed it 1,000 years ago and their route can be traced today by boats and ferries that ply the 1,450 miles (2,334 km) from Bergen to Norway's northeastern-most town, Kirkenes. They take you through ruggedly spectacular scenery to where the midnight sun shines in chilly splendor over an enormous subarctic wilderness, whose vastness is both daunting and exhilarating.

The starting point is Bergen, Norway's second largest (and most rainy) city. Clinging to the coast beneath steep wooded hills, it is a proper, salty old port. Once the northernmost outpost of the medieval Hanseatic League, its atmospheric old warehouse quarter, known as Bryggen, is full of tall, steeply gabled old merchants' houses. Two excellent museums use old furniture and costumes to recreate the feel of the medieval trading port. Bergen is an enjoyable, welcoming city full of attractive shops and bars and a good choice of hotels.

Ice-Carved Fjords

Before you set out for the far north, explore some of the fjords near Bergen. Although they emerge at the coast, they reach way inland—and, because of the varying cutting action of the glacial ice that formed them, their deepest and most spectacular stretches are often far from the sea.

The fjords are probably the most familiar image of Norway, but nothing prepares you for the reality of these immense gashes in the rocky, wooded landscape. From Myrdal (2 hours by train from Bergen) the mountain railway descends a dizzying 3,000 feet (900 m), past waterfalls and sheer rock faces to Flåm, a pretty village amid meadows and orchards on the edge of the Aurlandsfjord. Return by ferry to Bergen along unbelievably narrow canyons whose sheer rock sides exclude the sun except at midday in summer. The effect is unsettling—the sky seems like a thin ribbon of blue far above you, as if you were looking down to a river.

You can travel north from Bergen by the coastal ship *Hurtigrute* (Rapid Route), an 11-day round trip. These ships, which double as car ferries, stop at small fishing villages to take on local passengers and goods. Cabins are available (though you can sleep in the lounges), and there's food on board. It's possible to buy a ticket for part of the journey and then pick up a bus or train (though the latter go no further north than Fauske), rejoining the boat later.

Two days out of Bergen, the *Hurtigrute* docks at Trondheim, one of the few towns in Norway resembling a historic European city. It was a major

Aurlandsfjord was carved into its steep-sided magnificence by the massive force of a glacier.

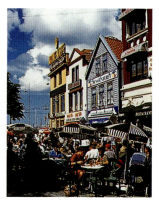

★ A fishing boat undergoes repairs in the harbor at Flakstad, one of the southernmost—and most beautiful—of the Lofoten Islands.

★ The railway from Myrdal to Flåm on the shore of Aurlandsfjord is one of the steepest and most spectacular train journeys in the world.

★ Holberg Square, the center of Bergen's atmospheric merchant quarter, the *Bryggen*. Many of the tall gabled houses date back to the era when Bergen was the northern outpost of the mighty Hanseatic League of trading cities.

pilgrimage site in the Middle Ages, with a cathedral that was, and still is, considered the most beautiful church in the country, the Nidaros Domkirke. Its towering west front is covered in tall gothic niches filled with statues. Above the main portal is an enormous rose window; in the morning, the sun pours through its stained glass to set the shadowy interior ablaze. Down by the Old Town Bridge is an area of old gabled wooden warehouses, many converted into shops and restaurants.

The morning after leaving Trondheim, you cross the Arctic Circle on the way to Bodø some 460 miles (740 km) to the north. Until now the coast, seldom out of sight, has remained remarkably green and fertile for such northerly latitudes; but now, as the boat threads its way past countless small islands, it becomes harsher and more mountainous. Inland is mostly uninhabited moorland; in clear weather you can glimpse the gleaming of the enormous Svartisen glacier.

A Green Archipelago

If this seems chilling, there's a pleasant surprise in store. Beyond Bodø, you land at Stamsund in the Lofotens, a rocky archipelago some 70 miles (112

km) long about 40 miles (64 km) offshore. Behind their jagged gray-green cliffs, the Lofotens are a welcoming place, where patches of gentle farmland nestle between fjords and crags. The climate is astonishingly mild for so far north. In the old fishing villages, you can stay a few days in the *rorbuer*, brightly painted fishermen's huts. The islands are of particular interest to bird-watchers, with large colonies of puffins and other marine birds.

Beyond the Lofotens are the lower-lying Vesterålen Islands. The steamer passes though the narrow channel Raftsunde that separates the two groups. In summer, the boat then makes a brief scenic detour between the sheer blank rock walls of the sinister Trollfjord. Further north still, the *Hurtigrute* calls at Tromsø, the largest town in northern Norway and the world's northernmost university. Apart from the main square, with its 19th-century wooden cathedral, it is a bland modern town, but the sight of a well-lit bar full of students is strangely reassuring after so much natural vastness. Check in to a restaurant and dig into a reindeer steak and a few beers from the world's northernmost brewery.

Almost a full day's voyage from here, around a bleak fjord-gashed coastline, is the fishing village of

Bergen's harbor, with its tall ships and old waterfront buildings, nestles beneath steep pine-clad hills.

Honningsvåg, sheltering on the landward side of the barren island of Magerøya. A bus journeys the final 20 miles (32 km) to Nordkapp. Since this bare and wind-lashed cliff top was dubbed the North Cape in 1553 by an English sailor, Richard Chancellor, it has been recognized as the northernmost point of Europe. Despite the presence of a visitors' center and the touching idealism of the big round bronze roundels with designs by children from all over the world, there is an awesome sense of being at the end of the world as you stare out at the Arctic Ocean.

By now, you have rounded the top of the Scandinavian peninsula and will be traveling not from south to north, but from west to east. The scenery—bare cliffs and tundra—is monotonous but compelling and hypnotic. As you sail up the Varangerfjord, the sight of Kirkenes—the last port for the *Hurtigrute*—could scarcely seem more welcoming. It is just 10 miles (16 km) from the Russian border, though even in these post-Cold War days, the crossing is off limits.

–> **The Midnight Sun**

"The northern sun, creeping at midnight along the horizon, and the immeasurable ocean in apparent contact with the skies, form the grand outlines of the sublime picture presented to the astonished spectator," wrote the Italian traveler Giuseppe Acerbi in 1802. It is precisely the midnight sun that gives any Arctic voyage in summer an air of unreality. The Arctic Circle is the line north of which the sun never dips below the horizon at the summer solstice—though you get a midnight twilight some way further south. The further north you go, the longer the phenomenon lasts: in Bodø, the midnight sun is visible from the first week of June to early July; and at Nordkapp from early May to late July. When planning to travel, bear in mind the opposite effect, the polar night—in these latitudes it remains dark for months on either side of the winter solstice.

ELEGANT CITIES OF MIDDLE EUROPE

Travel to the heart of the old Hapsburg empire to experience the café society and high art of Vienna, and the baroque cityscapes and lively countercultures of Prague, Kraków, and Budapest.

Viennese artists and architects were at the forefront of the art nouveau and art deco movements, and their work is evident in many of the city's buildings.

THERE IS A LAND IN THE HEART OF EUROPE whose borders do not appear on any map. It has been described as a lost continent sunk by the tides of history, whose peaks today break the surface as scattered islands. If you visit four of those islands today—the old Hapsburg cities of Vienna, Prague, Kraków, and Budapest—you will discover that Mitteleuropa (Middle Europe) still exists as a way of thinking, living, and feeling. There is something easygoing about it, always very sharp intellectually but humorously aware of life's difficulties and delights.

The region has taken almost everything this century could throw at it, but the joyously elegant architecture of these cities remains remarkably intact. Four or five days spent in each will reveal how much

of their old spirit survives as well. Since the fall of the Iron Curtain, travel between these cities has become easy again. Though you can fly into Vienna or Prague, the train journey beween the two makes you realize how close they are, both geographically and in spirit. This 150-mile (240-km) journey takes about 6 hours; from Prague to Kraków is only 240 miles (380 km) further, and from Vienna to Budapest just 152 miles (245 km).

The place to start is the old imperial capital itself, Vienna. The city's historic center—the Innere Stadt—is surrounded by the Ringstrasse, a wide sweeping boulevard flanked by grand 19th-century buildings and elegant coffeehouses. Directly in the center is the Stefansplatz, dominated by St. Stephen's

The world's best known Lipizzaner horses, a breed that specializes in high-stepping dressage, are those trained at the Spanish Riding School in Vienna.

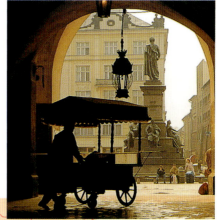

★ Prague's picturesque Malá district is dominated by the green dome of the 17th-century baroque church of St. Nicholas.

★ Kraków marketplace has been the scene of markets since medieval times.

★ In the heart of Vienna stands the gothic cathedral of St. Stephen.

Cathedral, whose spire—which the Viennese affectionately call Steffl (Little Stephen)—and steep roof of glazed tiles dominate the city skyline.

Southwest of the center is Schönbrunn Palace, built under Emperor Leopold I between 1696 and 1730 and extended in the mid-1700s to become Empress Maria Theresa's main palace. The long yellow facade has a restrained baroque elegance, but the state rooms inside are a riot of rococo swirls in wood and plaster. North of the city center, across the Danube canal, the Prater, a big park, extends to the banks of the Danube itself. Here is the amusement park with the giant Ferris wheel, where Orson Welles made his memorable appearance in *The Third Man*.

As befits the former capital of a great empire, there are world-class classical concerts at the Musikverein and opera at the Vienna Staatsoper; you can watch the elaborate dressage of the Lipizzaner horses in the Spanish Riding School or hear the Vienna Boys' Choir sing in the Hofburgkapelle. You can window-shop at the jewelers on the streets of Graben and Kohlmarkt, or if you're in Vienna at Christmas, buy decorations and spiced biscuits at the markets while sipping *Glühwein* (mulled wine) against the cold.

There are many fine restaurants, as well as humbler taverns serving hearty Austrian fare. The cosmopolitan empire influenced Austria's cuisine—Hungarian goulash and Czech dumplings are on almost every menu; even Wiener schnitzel actually

came from Milan. An unmissable Vienna experience is to sit in one of the city's marvelous coffeehouses and watch the world go by. They are decked out with chandeliers, gilt mirrors, and red velvet seats; old ladies take *Kaffee und Kuchen* (coffee and cakes), students play chess, and whiskered gentlemen scan the newspapers while the rich smell of coffee pervades the air.

A Fairy-Tale City

Where Vienna is sedate, Prague is lively, irreverent—and as pretty as a city in a fairy tale. The entire city center is a jumble of gothic turrets and baroque domes, winding cobbled streets, and mysterious passageways. Much of it has now been spruced up in pink, green, and ocher, but backstreets often lead to haunting old courtyards still unrestored. Every corner has its lively bar, where you can sample famous Czech beers. In summer the place is packed with visitors; in autumn and winter it is shrouded in mists, the night air sharp with the sulfurous smell of coal fires

Prague straddles the Vltava River. The western bank rises steeply to the Hradcany, the castle, whose forbidding walls enclose the seat of the Czech government and the cathedral of St. Vitus, with its soaring gothic towers. Standing in one of the cobbled lanes below the castle, you sense its looming presence, and reflect that the great Prague writer Franz Kafka once lived in a tiny cottage here on Zlatá Ulicka (Golden Lane).

The colonnaded pavilion known as the Gloriette, on a hilltop in the grounds of the Schönbrunn Palace, commands splendid views across Vienna.

The neighboring district of Malá Strana is a richly atmospheric place. Its central square, Malostranské Námestí, is overshadowed by the towering walls and green dome of the baroque church of St. Nicholas. Around the edges of the cobbled square, arcades house atmospheric bars and jazz clubs. Narrow streets wind their way past aristocratic palaces and gardens of the 1700s down to the Charles Bridge, lined with gesticulating statues and thronged in summer with crowds, street musicians, and gnats.

On the east side of the river is the traffic-free Staré Mesto. Here lies Staromestské Námestí (Old Town Square), overlooked by the twin towers of Tyn Church and surrounded by pavement cafés and bright painted houses of the 1500s with fantastic carvings. In the passageways leading off are old bookshops and cellar restaurants. In the northern part of Staré Mesto is Josefov, the old Jewish quarter, an eloquent reminder of the rich Jewish culture of Middle Europe destroyed in the Holocaust, and a place of pilgrimage for Jewish visitors from all over the world. The Old-New Synagogue, dating from 1270, is one of the oldest surviving in Europe; the cemetery with its richly carved tombstones leaning at all angles is a haunting memorial.

Youth Capital

East of the Sudeten Mountains, Kraków, capital of Poland, is today coming to rival Prague as the youth capital of Europe. There's a buzz about the place, with its lively student population and glorious old town packed with bars, restaurants, and cafés oozing old Middle European charm. You can dine on Polish specialties such as mountain trout in the stately surroundings of Wierzynek Mansion, Kraków's oldest restaurant, going back to 1364.

Miraculously, the old town survived the Second World War with little physical damage, and now is listed by UNESCO as one the world's 12 most significant historic sites. It centers on the Ryneck Glówny, a vast flagstoned square—the largest medieval square in Europe—flanked by the long arcades of the Sukiennice, the city's 1500s cloth hall, with its scrollwork parapet topped by grotesque faces. The Mariacki Church (St. Mary's) on the east side is topped by a bizarre cluster of pinnacles. Once, goes the legend, a watchman on its tower saw a Tartar raiding party approaching, and he blew the alarm on his trumpet, only to be cut short by an arrow. Every hour, a lone trumpeter still plays the plaintive melody, stopping abruptly at the point the watchman was hit.

Towering above is Wawel Hill, a rocky crag overlooking the River Vistula. Right on the top is the castle, with its splendid Renaissance courtyard and red brick cathedral with gothic turrets and baroque cupolas. This was the traditional burial place of the kings of Poland, and their elaborate tombs—in every style from medieval to the 1700s—line the interior.

Not far south from Wawel Hill is another reminder of the rich Jewish heritage of Central Europe—the old ghetto of Kazimierz. If these narrow medieval streets, with their white painted houses with round doorways and deep-set windows, look familiar, it may be because *Schindler's List* was filmed here. The grandest of the six surviving Kazimierz synagogues is the Old Synagogue, completed in 1557. The main facade has an imposing Renaissance portico and is a museum devoted to Kraków Jewry's history. Kazimierz, however, now has a bright and lively air with restaurants and cafés.

Budapest: Pearl of the Danube

Budapest, elegantly straddling Europe's most evocative river, oozes *fin-de-siècle* romance. The huge public parks and gardens, broad avenues shaded with plane trees, flamboyant secessionist villas, and opulent bathhouses have changed little since the end of the 19th century. Two world wars and four decades of communist rule may have intervened since Budapest's glory days, but the city's languid, even sensual, charms survive undiminished.

Buda, on the right (west) bank of the Danube, and Pest, on the left (east), were joined only in 1873, and each retains a distinct atmosphere. Buda, with its castle and cobbles, dreams quietly on a hilltop; the elegant avenues of Pest fan out smartly on the other side of the great river. Castle Hill, in Buda, is the spiritual heart of the capital, home to the Royal Palace and the theatrical spikes of the Matthias Church. Abandon the map and get lost in the maze of crooked streets, with their pretty pastel-painted houses, clattering cobbles, and charming squares.

Across the river, Pest has existed since at least the 12th century, but almost nothing has survived of the medieval city. A stroll along the waterfront at Dunakorzó (between Chain Bridge and Liberty Bridge) skirts the oldest part of the city and offers beautiful views up to Castle Hill. Pest's heyday was the 19th century, and its showcase promenade is Andrassy Út, a handsome avenue lined with splendid buildings like the Opera House. This impressive ensemble has been awarded UNESCO World Heritage status but retains its lively, relaxed atmosphere, full of crowds eating, shopping, strolling, and drinking. South of Andrassy Út, the old Jewish Quarter boasts a sumptuous Great Synagogue, built in the 1850s and still the second largest in the world.

CURRENCIES Austria: euro; Czech Republic: Czech koruna; Poland: zloty; Hungary: forint (the euro will be introduced in 2009).

CLIMATE All four cities have a fairly continental climate; warm in summer (especially noticeable because of high humidity) with temperatures in the low 80°s F (c. 28°C); they can be very cold in winter and autumn, and heavy snow is common.

TIME TO GO Spring and autumn to avoid the crowds and extremes of weather; Christmas is a particularly good time to be in Vienna.

AIRPORTS Vienna, Prague, Kraków, Budapest.

FOOD AND DRINK In Vienna, Wiener schnitzel (veal coated in bread crumbs) is a national institution, accompanied by some of the local Riesling wines. In Prague you should drink beer to accompany the *knedliky*, dumplings. In Kraków, sample the national Polish dish of *bigos* made with sauerkraut, fresh cabbage, onions, and leftover meat, washed down by Polish vodka, of which there are many flavored varieties. In Budapest, try classic warming stews and thick soups such as *pörkölt*, *paprikás*, or *gulyás* and don't miss the excellent local wines.

The Charles Bridge that links the two halves of Prague is lined with baroque statues added in the 17th and 18th centuries.

ICELAND

A country teeming with hot springs and legends of hidden people.

The powerful Strokkur geyser erupts every 10 minutes or so, to the delight and awe of the gathered crowd.

ICELAND IS A STRANGE, THRILLING LAND, where the titanic struggle between fire and ice is still being played out. The island is a geological hot spot, sitting on the mid-Atlantic ridge, where the Eurasian and North American plate boundaries jostle and collide. Hot springs smolder, mud pools bubble, and geysers vent, a constant reminder of the intense geological activity just beneath the earth's crust. The air is unimaginably pure, intensifying colors and rendering distances hard to judge. Iceland was only settled a thousand years ago, and remains sparsely populated: its remote waterfalls and canyons, hot springs, and lava fields form one of the most unique and beautiful landscapes in the world.

Reykjavik and the "Golden Circle"

Reykjavik is Europe's most northerly capital, sprawled along much of the Seltjarnarnes Peninsula on the southeast tip of the island. It's a trim, low-key city of whitewashed wooden buildings and modest iron churches, multicolored shops, and grassy parks. The heart of Reykjavik is the Old Town, where a clutch of museums, including

the National Museum and the National Center of Cultural Heritage, offer a fascinating insight into Iceland's history and culture. It's the nightlife that has gained Reykjavik a heady international reputation in recent years, although for hip urbanites from other capitals the much-vaunted bars and clubs may come as a disappointment, except during the long white nights of summer.

But the great Icelandic tradition of bathing in thermal pools is guaranteed to please even the most jaded city dweller: most famous is the spectacular Blue Lagoon, which bubbles up from surreal lava fields on the outskirts of the city. The capital is also a great place to try typical Icelandic cuisine, Þorramatur, which is traditionally eaten during the ancient Nordic month of Þorri (January and February). These pungent dishes—among them sour ram's testicles, rotten shark, and sheep's head jam—reputedly all taste better than they smell.

A trio of natural wonders and historical sites lie south of Reykjavik. Dubbed the "Golden Circle," this is easily the most popular excursion from the capital, and the tour includes Iceland's grandest

Reykjavik, the most northerly capital in the world, is famous for the white nights of summer when darkness never falls.

geyser, largest waterfall, and one of the world's oldest parliaments. At Geysir, the great spouting hot spring that gave the world a name for this dramatic natural phenomenon has been dormant for decades, but nearby Strokkur ("the churn") can be relied on to spurt a searing jet of sulphurous water roughly every 10 minutes. Walking paths meander through swirling multicolored mud formations, pockmarked with steaming vents.

In 930 A.D., Iceland's first parliamentary assembly, the Althing (Alþingi), gathered by the shores of Lake Þingvallavatn, where it continued to convene until 1798. It was here in 1944 that the independent Republic of Iceland was declared, and this national shrine is now protected as the Thingvellir (Þingvellir) National Park. Eerie lava fields give way to rifts and canyons, the fault lines of the great Eurasian and North American plate boundaries that run beneath Iceland. Waterfalls dot the entire island, but none is as dramatic as that

of Gullfoss, which thunders powerfully in two tiers over polished black lava cliffs as rainbows glimmer in the mist.

The Wild North

The gateway to the wild north is Akureyri, a vibrant little town (population 15,000) on Iceland's longest fjord, Eyjafjörður (Eyjafjordur). Lofty mountains give way to lush farmland, where the stocky, shaggy Icelandic ponies are still used to round up the sheep every autumn. The region offers the best skiing in Iceland at Hliðarfjall (Hlidarfjall), where—with luck— the northern lights will be whirling through the sky as you descend the slopes. To the east, another of Iceland's beautiful waterfalls cascades in a pair of perfect arcs.

According to legend, a local chieftain threw his pagan images into the Godafoss ("Waterfall of the Gods") when the Icelanders converted to Christianity a thousand years ago. Húsavík, on

The eerie, other-worldly landscapes of Iceland have given rise to legends of elfs, trolls, and "hidden people."

143

Come in summer to
see the eerie glow of
Iceland's "Midnight Sun,"
particularly in the far
north of the island.

Skjálfandi Bay about an hour's drive from Akureyri,
is Iceland's main whale-watching center, with
astonishingly high sighting rates. Several of the
whale species found here are endangered, including
the gigantic blue whale, which is the largest
mammal ever to inhabit the earth. When this whale
blows, the water spurts 40 to 50 feet (12-15 m) in
the air and can be seen and heard for miles.

The approach to the natural paradise of Lake
Mývatn, 30 miles (50 km) south of Húsavik, drifts
through green, gentle farmland that gradually
gives way to a seething, otherworldly panorama
of volcanic hills and lava fields. The deep blue
lake is vast, speckled with leafy islands and islets,
and backed by an undulating skyline of forbidding
craters. Despite its tranquil beauty, Mývatn's
unpoetic name—"Midge Lake"—is well deserved.
Yet these annoying little flies provide food for an
astonishing variety of bird life, including 15 species
of duck alone.

The little community of Reykjahlið (Reykjahlid)
sits on the northeastern shores of the lake in the
shadow of the Hverfell crater and provides a good
base for exploring the unearthly lunar landscape
that creeps out from the lake. At Dimmuborgir
(which means "black castles"), strange lava pillars
and cliffs have been frozen into hauntingly beautiful
shapes, unlike anything else ever found on earth.

Few of Iceland's
magnificent natural
landscapes can compare
with the remote,
unearthly beauty of
the Jökulsárgljúfur
National Park.

The stark, desolate lava field of Eldhraun was used
as a training ground for moonwalks by the Apollo
11 crew in the 1960s. West of the lake, a dirt track
leads to Hveravellir, a hot spring plain caught
between two glaciers, where excellent hiking trails
wind across the bubbling terrain.

North of Lake Mývatn, the Jökulsá á Fjöllum
glacial river cuts a powerful swath through
mountains, creating spectacular canyons fed by
countless waterfalls. The western bank is protected
in the Jökulsárgljúfur National Park, a gloriously
remote region of spellbinding beauty. At the
southern end of the park is the mighty Dettifoss
waterfall, one of the most powerful in Europe.

–> FACT FILE

POPULATION 300,000.

AREA 64,400 square miles (103,000 sq km).

CURRENCY The króna. Traveler checks, credit and debit cards are all widely accepted throughout the island.

LANGUAGES Icelandic. English is widely spoken.

BEST TIME TO GO Summer is the most convenient time to go, with endless summer days (Iceland is just south of the Arctic Circle so it doesn't experience a genuine midnight sun) and the best range of accommodation and transport. In winter, winter sports and the sight of the northern lights may compensate for reduced services. Hiking trails, campsites, and many interior roads are closed (or simply unfeasible to use) in winter.

CLIMATE Iceland enjoys a temperate ocean climate, with cool summers and cold winters. The weather is notoriously changeable, and rain squalls rapidly.

WHAT TO TAKE Layers of warm, waterproof clothing, insect repellent.

AIRPORTS Reykjavik is the main international airport, with 7 daily flights to Akureyri.

TIPPING Service charges and taxes are almost always included in the bill, although excellent service might deserve a token amount.

ACCOMMODATION Accommodation is expensive throughout the island. Book well ahead for Reykjavik and Lake Mývatn during peak periods.

The Selfoss waterfall, 6 miles (10 km) upstream, is only 33 feet (10 m) high, but the silvery threads of scores of cataracts make it one of the most magical in Iceland. The heart of the national park is the mighty Jökulsárgljúfur canyon, stretching through lava-scarred cliffs for 15 miles (25 km). Heading north, the canyon widens into a valley, greener but no less dramatic: the cliffs are riddled with caves, particularly at Hljóðarklettar (Hlódarklettar), which literally means "rock of echoes." This is wonderful hiking or horse-riding territory, and the park authorities provide simple campsites.

–> The Hidden People

About half the population of Iceland (considerably more, according to some polls!) believe in *huldufolk* ("hidden people")–the elves, fairies, trolls, gnomes, and other supernatural beings that are said to inhabit the land. There's even an Elf School, run by the brother of a prominent politician. Mediums are often involved in local engineering projects to ensure that the *huldufolk* are left in peace, and major highways have been rerouted and shopping malls shifted to avoid disturbing their homes.

NORTHERN ASIA

"A good traveler has no fixed plans and is not intent on arriving."
HILAIRE BELLOC, FRENCH-BORN ENGLISH WRITER, 1870-1953

THE TRANS-SIBERIAN RAILROAD

Crossing continents and time zones, stretching almost halfway across the planet, the Trans-Siberian Railroad remains one of the world's classic train journeys.

A *babushka* (old woman or grandmother) tends her reindeer near Tyumen in Siberia.

NOT ONLY TRAIN BUFFS KNOW of the Trans-Siberian Railroad, the world's longest train journey that links the Baltic Sea to the Pacific Ocean. It runs through the heart of old Russia, tracing the route of the Russian peoples eastward in the 16th and 17th centuries—a corridor of opportunity and exploration through the lands of middle Volga, the southern Urals Mountains, between the taiga and mountains of southern Siberia, until finally reaching the Pacific Ocean at Vladivostok. The journey is a world classic, and offers a literally unique opportunity to appreciate the enormity of the Russian landscape and the indomitable character of its people.

Under the communists (1917-1991) the rail route was changed to run from Moscow, but the true starting point is St. Petersburg, the "window on the West" founded in 1703 by Czar Peter the Great as his new capital. Built on 100 islands and linked by 300 bridges, the "Venice of the North" glitters with gold-domed palaces, towers, and churches. At the end of Nevsky Prospect, the principal street lined with cafés, shops, and theaters, lies the Hermitage, housing what is considered by many to be the world's grandest collection of Western painting. The decor inside is so ornate—high ceilings inlaid with gold leaf, marble floors, and columns—that it can distract you from the pictures (by Leonardo, Rembrandt, Breughel, El Greco, Cézanne, Picasso, among many others). After a day spent trekking around literally miles of galleries, your feet and neck will tell you it is time to go.

The Pushkin Palace on the outskirts of St. Petersburg is named for the great Russian poet who spent his formative years in the area; it is part of the Grand Catherine Palace.

Leaving St. Petersburg, the journey to Moscow through fields and forests takes less than a day—the fastest part of the whole trip. Moscow, the Russian capital, concentrates its sights around Red Square: the Kremlin, St. Basil's Cathedral, and today McDonald's and Pizza Hut. You can see them in a day before boarding the train that will take you to the far ends of the earth, for Moscow lies at the epicenter of the huge Russian rail network.

Once the Trans-Siberian Express leaves Moscow, it stops only to change locomotives, take on food and water, or take on and let off passengers. Getting off the train at these stops is no problem. You can stretch your legs, try some local food, or just try to chat with the Russians. The length of the stopovers varies from just a few minutes to more than half an hour. Your carriage conductor, called a *provodnik* (male) or *provodnitsa* (female), will tell you how long each stop is and keep an eye out for you if the train starts to leave. As most trains travel the same route, it is possible to break your journey and stay a few days in, for example, Ekaterinburg, where the last Czar and his family were murdered by the Bolsheviks, Irkutsk on Lake Baikal, or Novosibirsk (New Siberia), the largest city in Siberia.

–> FACT FILE

LANGUAGE Russian. Very little English spoken anywhere.

MONEY Roubles and (preferably) U.S. dollars. The rouble devalues often.

TIME The Trans-Siberian crosses eight time zones between St. Petersburg and Vladivostok, but all trains run on Moscow time. It can sometimes be confusing.

WHEN TO GO Trains run all year round, but summer and Christmas are the most popular times to go, so are best avoided. Temperatures in summer vary from 50°F to 96°F (10° to 35°C), and in winter they go down as far as -40°F (-40°C).

TRAINS The true Trans-Siberian Express is the Rossiya (Train #1 and #2), which goes all the way between Moscow and Vladivostok. The journey time is 7 nights/8 days. You need a separate train to go to/from St. Petersburg. There are numerous trains to destinations in between plus trains to Ulaanbaatar in Mongolia and Beijing in China.

DISTANCES Moscow–Vladivostok 5,776 miles (9,297 km); Moscow–Beijing 5,592 miles (9,001 km).

WHAT TO TAKE A vacuum flask (boiling water is available from the samovar at the end of each carriage), penknife, flashlight, deck of cards, tea, coffee, toilet paper, a large mug, snacks, chocolate, dried fruit.

The 16th-century St. Basil's Cathedral in Moscow is a confection of nine churches in one.

There are more than 800 stations between Moscow and Vladivostok, most very small and simple, but each with a personality of its own. At every station there are roving food sellers. Little old ladies (*babushkas* or grannies) sell homemade salami-type sausages and boiled potatoes covered with chopped salad onions. Others sell ice cream, bread, fish, cookies, beer, soft drinks, and the national drink, vodka. Pot noodles and other subsistence items are available from small kiosks on the platforms.

Into Siberia

Siberia is generally flat and covered in taiga, but traditional houses and small villages fill gaps in the forest, and there are huge swaths of purple and blue wildflowers in spring and summer. Winter is perhaps the most atmospheric time to travel, when the land is covered in a sparkling blanket of white and the locals travel in horse-drawn sleighs. The train at times rumbles over long bridges over the immense rivers of the Irtysh, the Ob, and the Angara.

Perhaps the high point of the journey comes when the train runs around the steep forested shores of Lake Baikal. This is the world's deepest freshwater lake at 5,372 feet (1,637 m), holding about one fifth of the world's reserves of fresh water. The water is so clear that you can see a white 8-inch (20-cm) disk down to 130 feet (40 m). It is also the world's oldest lake, formed around 20 million years ago, and has been reckoned to support 50 species of fish, 500 species of animals, including the world's only species of freshwater seal, and 1,200 plant species, of which two thirds are endemic to the region. However, the lake has become severely polluted and is shrinking rapidly. Strangely, 338 rivers flow into Lake Baikal, but only one flows out. Before the Trans-Siberian Railroad was completed, trains and passengers were transported across the lake by ship. The British-built ship, the *Angara*, is now a floating museum in Irkutsk, Siberia's capital. Listvyanka is the main town at the southern end of the lake; its primary industry is fishing and it is a delightful base for exploring the region. You can go trekking in the nearby Baikal National Park, but in summer the mosquitoes and blackflies are a nuisance.

Siberia used to be a name of dread—the place where Russia sent its troublesome misfits, criminals, political dissenters, and often totally innocent people to work in the mines of its coldest, most desolate parts. Deportees were often sent for life and lost all civil rights. If they survived their penal term, they might be permitted to settle somewhere in Siberia, but could seldom return to European Russia. But now Siberia is more interested in travelers than deportees.

The chapel at Novosibirsk is reputed to be at the geographical center of the old Russian Empire.

The Alexander Column towers over Palace Square, St. Petersburg, a top tourist spot now, and the starting point for the revolutions of 1905 and 1917.

There are about 20 carriages plus a dining car on all the Trans-Siberian trains. They are comfortable if basic, with bunk beds and bedding, though they feel a little cramped with four in a cabin in second class. First class has two berths. You'll probably have to wait your turn for the two bathrooms, particularly early in the morning. At the end of each carriage is a boiler called a samovar, which provides plenty of boiling water 24 hours a day. The food in the dining car sometimes leaves a lot to be desired, being pretty tasteless, but it is not too expensive.

Crossing the largest and deepest river of its route—the Ob at Novosibirsk—presented one of the greatest obstacles in the building of the Trans-Siberian Railroad. The city is a cultural gem—the result of highly educated deportees who ended up settling there.

Lake Baikal (below) holds a volume of water equivalent to that of all five of North America's Great Lakes.

THE GREAT WALL OF CHINA

China's Great Wall has always inspired superlatives—unsurprisingly, for it is one of the greatest building enterprises in the history of the world.

A pageant at the Great Wall exemplifies how it is used for many aspects of Chinese life, including tourism, education, commercial enterprise, and entertainment.

Tiantan—"The Temple of Heaven"—in Beijing is set in its own park.

THE WALL TODAY is much as it was when Lord Macartney, heading the first British embassy to China, which was also the first-ever Western embassy to China, saw it in 1783—fortified walls "carried along the ridges of hills, over the tops of the highest mountains, descending into the deepest valleys, crossing upon arches over rivers." For foreigners it was then a legendary wonder and inconceivably remote. Built to mark the barrier between the highly cultivated lands of China to the south and the open steppes to the north, the wall runs for the most part through mountainous territory, making maximum use of every cliff or precipice to increase its defenses—and also its grandeur. Its westernmost section marches out into the Gobi Desert, a region of sandblasted, almost lunar landscapes, feared by garrison troops more for its bitter winters and baking summers than any barbarians; its eastern end expires amid the factories and farms of the densely populated marshy coastlands of the Yellow Sea.

Today, the wall's great ramparts can be seen snaking like a viaduct across China's barren northern hills by any visitor to Beijing (Peking) willing to ride in a bus or a taxi for an hour. Millions do it every year, catching tour buses in Tiananmen Square—the world's largest square, covering 100 acres (40 ha) at the very center of imperial Beijing— or from the rail station, or arranging trips through their hotels. In addition, trains run to the wall from Beijing's main station, on their way northwest. Most visitors see little more than the 27-foot (8-m) high section at Badaling, 40 miles (70 km) outside the capital. At this solidly restored bastion, which guarded a hilly pass to the northeast, tourists can take a cable car to the 20-foot (6-m)-wide rampart, buy T-shirts, and take snapshots. Another popular section is Mutianyu, 55 miles (90 km) north of Beijing. On the way back from the wall, you can easily make a detour to visit the Valley of the Ming Tombs, where 13 of the 16 Ming emperors lie in state in impressive mausoleums.

Across Switchback Hills

Unless you are willing to venture into areas without any tourist facilities—where you really need to speak Chinese—the best place to see the wall in pristine form, and without too many tourists, is Simatai, 70

Beijing's Forbidden City is made up of a complex of gates, halls, and temples.

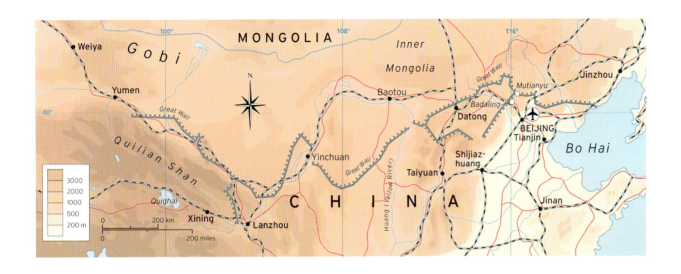

miles (110 km) northeast. Here an 11-mile (19-km) section over switchback hills displays 135 watchtowers, which overlook slopes so steep they can only be scaled on all fours. It is easy to imagine the time when this was frontier territory, where conscripts stared down at armies of nomadic barbarians from Mongolia or Manchuria.

The wall stretches for some 4,530 miles (7,000 km), though estimates vary because it is not a single entity and no complete archaeological maps have been published. In some places two or three walls were built, and new stretches are still being found.

Myths and Facts

The Great Wall is as much myth as fact. Among the myths: that today's wall is more than 2,000 years old. In fact, the Great Wall, or its surviving sections, represent the last and greatest of dozens. Wall building was a constant theme throughout Chinese history from the 3rd century B.C. onward, inspired by the constant need to keep at bay the hordes of restless and acquisitive nomads to the north. For two millennia, Chinese rulers experimented with different ways of dealing with the "nomad problem," trading, intermarrying,

FACT FILE <—

BEST TIME TO VISIT Spring and summer. It is very cold in winter.

LANGUAGE AND NAMES Confusion is rife. Chinese signs and names are often transliterated, but not always. Transliteration officially uses the Pinyin system; but the older Wade-Giles system may be more familiar to some westerners. In addition, many Chinese place names have changed, and minority languages often have their own names for places—which may also be transliterated. If in doubt, ask.

HEALTH NOTES Avoid unbottled or unboiled water, salads, uncooked vegetables, and peeled fruits. Rabies is common, so avoid animals.

VISAS Compulsory, but easy to get at embassies.

MOST VITAL ACCESSORY Business card.

CURRENCY Renminbi, or RMB. U.S. dollars are acceptable, but credit cards are rarely accepted.

attacking, conquering—and, only as a last resort, building walls to keep them out. Nothing worked. In the 13th century, the Mongols easily bypassed the Great Wall's early sections to establish their own Chinese dynasty.

The emperors of the Mongols' successors, the Ming (1368-1644), decided on a more lasting solution: a new Great Wall, which was mainly built in the second half of the 1400s, replacing and joining up previous walls. These earlier versions were partly built of mud, which eroded quickly. The present Great Wall was made of brick and stone and

The wall rambles from the far west past Beijing, where it is at its most picturesque (below). As the ancient guardian of Chinese territory, it is honored by soldiers in traditional Manchu dress (left).

built by force labor. The crenellated rampart was constructed to take five horsemen riding abreast—it was always as much a military highway as barrier— and towers punctuate it every few hundred yards. These were both bases for garrisons and used for signaling, to track the mercurial nomads in their perpetual gallops in search of weak points. Building started in the west. Then, in response to Mongol attacks, it snaked eastward, creating barriers along the southern edge of Mongol territory, cutting north of Beijing, and finally heading east to the Yellow Sea coast. Despite its grandeur, it was as useless as its predecessors—a century after it was finished, China fell to the Manchus of the northeast, and the wall ceased to mark any frontier. The grasslands that were once regarded as barbarian borderlands soon became an integral part of China.

Though much of the wall has crumbled and whole sections are isolated, the most visited parts have been carefully restored as the result of a policy decision in the 1980s. Premier Deng Xiaoping initiated the campaign, which had as its slogan "Let us love our country and restore our Great Wall!" As a result, after centuries of ill treatment, the wall has undergone a renaissance along much of its length, and so remains a symbol of China itself to the Chinese. They refer to it by the name of its most ancient predecessor—"the 10,000-li wall," a li being 0.3 mile (0.5 km). Many legends and myths, which indiscriminately mix fact and fiction, old walls and new, ensure that it remains a bastion of culture in Chinese minds and hearts—as well as in awe-inspiring fact.

-> Believe It or Not? Not!

Once, did-you-know items in magazines used to say that the Great Wall was the only human structure visible from the moon. The notion, originating at the turn of the century, was widely believed after it appeared in Robert Ripley's *Believe It or Not*, a best seller in the 1930s. No one, of course, could check until men first walked on the moon in 1969. In fact, from there it is hard to spot China, let alone the wall, which is hardly visible to the naked eye even from earth orbit. But to stretch a point, something of the Great Wall became visible in orbit in the 1990s—it is the name taken by China for its satellite-launching company.

THE FLAMING CLIFFS OF THE GOBI DESERT

Virtually unvisited for decades, the Flaming Cliffs of Mongolia have long been renowned for dinosaur fossils. Now this scientific mecca can be seen by anyone in search of true wilderness.

Though arid, the Gobi is home to a scattering of herdsmen. This one is part of a family group on a summer migration to mountains west of the Flaming Cliffs.

"ONE GREAT SCULPTURED WALL we named the 'Flaming Cliffs,' for when seen in early morning or late afternoon sunlight it seemed to be a mass of glowing fire." So wrote the American explorer and scientist Roy Chapman Andrews on his first fossil-hunting expedition in the Gobi in 1922.

It is a sight many at the time yearned to see, but few succeeded. For the next 70 years, Mongolia's backcountry, like the country itself, was locked away in the heart of the Soviet empire. Now access is there for the asking. Outside the southern Gobi town of Dalanzadgad, two desert camps cater for tourists (mainly Japanese, to whom the Gobi's vast open spaces have a particular appeal). Buses and cars are available for the 50-mile (80-km) run to the

Flaming Cliffs. There are no proper roads—the whole country has only 1,500 miles (2,400 km) of paved road—but the desert's gravely surface is crisscrossed with tracks that are well known to locals.

A trip to the red sandstone cliffs, known locally as Bayan Zag, provides a chance to see other little-known sites nearby. The cliffs lie just north of a new national park, the Three Beauties, named for the three mountain ranges it contains. This knotty oval of peaks, canyons, high pastures, sand, and gravel is the most easterly of the ranges and outcrops of the Gobi Altai. Its 8,100 square miles (20,979 sq km) ranks Three Beauties with the 10 largest parks in the world. The badlands, dunes, and mountains contain a surprising range of flora and fauna—

Shapes in a barren landscape recall the form of the dinosaurs that once roamed here; beyond them, plains give way to the distant Altai Mountains of the western Gobi.

including snow leopards and wolves. There has even been a report of the very rare Gobi bear, of which a mere 30 are thought to exist.

One destination is the Vulture's Gorge. On the northern edge of the mountains, a track leads into a steep-sided gorge where ground squirrels dart away into burrows and the strong, sweet scent of juniper trees drifts down from the lower slopes. The gorge is choked by ice, dirty with mud and gravel. A marker shows the thickness of ice built up during the winter: 30 feet (9 m). This bulk, combined with the overshadowing peaks, ensures that most years the ice lasts right through the summer.

About 100 miles (160 km) west towers a narrow line of sand. Dunes are rare in the Gobi, and these are the highest—up to 800 feet (242 m). The dunes, created as the prevailing wind funnels along a corridor between two mountain chains, have a peculiarity: they "sing." This ghostly phenomenon, which supposedly used to draw travelers to their doom, is made when winds from the right direction move the silica-covered grains, creating an electrostatic charge that gives off a deep hum.

Revolutionary Discoveries

But the region's greatest treasure is the Flaming Cliffs themselves. They became famous as the focal point of a great scientific enterprise, after the

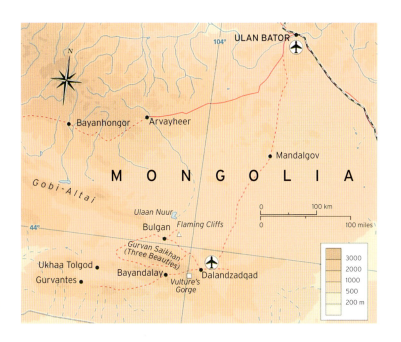

Mongolians sport national costume for their National Day, whether in the capital or in distant outposts of the Gobi Desert.

157

FACT FILE <−

ACCESS Flights into the Mongolian capital, Ulaanbaatar, via Beijing, Moscow, and the Kazakhstan capital of Almaty. There are several flights a week in summer to the southern Gobi town of Dalanzadgad.

ACCOMMODATION Gobi-Juulchin Camp, Tovshin Camp, or one of the basic hotels in Dalanzadgad. Arrangements can be made through Mongolian tour operators, and/or via the main hotels in Ulaanbaatar.

SUMMER CLIMATE Often up to 100°F (38°C), and very dry. If you travel in a car or bus, the heat is not too unpleasant.

TIME TO AVOID Winter, when temperatures reach −40°F (−40°C).

WHEN TO GO June–September.

DRESS Sun hat, good shoes, and sturdy jacket−winds can be vicious.

LANGUAGE Mongolian and Russian, but English and Japanese are coming up fast.

The Flaming Cliffs are in a place known as Bayan Zag−"rich in Saxauls" to the Mongolians. It is still rich in dinosaur fossils, and now legally protected.

discoveries made there in the 1920s transformed awareness of early life on earth. The mastermind behind the discovery, Roy Chapman Andrews, on whom movie director Steven Spielberg based his character of Indiana Jones, was a genius at organizing fieldwork. Chapman Andrews's ambitions lay in the Gobi, largely because his chief at the New York Museum of Natural History, Henry Fairfield Osborn, predicted that Asia would yield the key to human origins. Scientifically, this was almost virgin territory. The major problem was one of logistics. Previous explorers had relied on camels, yaks, and horses, and expeditions were slow, small, and unable to bring back many specimens. Andrews and his team used cars, with supplies of fuel carried in advance by camels. This combination allowed the dozen scientists to compress 10 years' work into 5 summer months. His five central Asiatic expeditions between 1922 and 1930 revolutionized paleontology.

In 1922, after a generally successful but unsurprising summer's exploration, the major find came almost by chance. The expedition's photographer, J. B. Shackelford, found himself on the edge of a sandstone basin that looked ideal for fossils. He climbed down the steep slope of soft rock, and at once saw a tiny skull. Within minutes, other finds followed. That evening, as the sun spotlighted the red cliffs, Andrews christened the gullies and peaks.

The "Flaming Cliffs": the name proved a masterstroke of public relations when the expedition returned triumphant with 2,000 fossils. Moreover, Andrews had found a missing link of a sort–a reptilian one. The tiny skull provided an ancestry for a group represented by Triceratops, well known in North America. Scientists named the sheep-sized creature, with its parrot beak and neck shield, *Protoceratops andrewsi*–"Andrews's first horned face." The following year, Andrews returned to the Flaming Cliffs, with more astonishing results.

Among the new finds was a flat-footed predator, *Velociraptor*, now famous as the smart and vengeful antihero of the book and film *Jurassic Park*. And finally came the find for which the expedition was best remembered: dinosaur eggs. Suddenly, dinosaurs acquired new features, appearing less the monstrous clodhopping reptiles of the popular imagination than almost charming, maternal creatures. When Andrews arrived home, he was mobbed, and acquired the status of a Hollywood star.

The following year, the largest expedition so far set off for Mongolia: 40 men, 8 vehicles, 125 camels, 4,000 gallons of fuel, many tons of food. In May, back at the Flaming Cliffs, more new discoveries emerged, this time evidence of human presence from 12,000 to 7,000 years ago. Finally, Andrews found fossils of 11 ratlike mammals, which showed that already in dinosaur times the mammals were well established. In the Flaming Cliffs lay some of life's deepest roots.

For the next 70 years, with Mongolia firmly inside the Soviet empire, the only scientists who could follow in Andrews's footsteps were from the Eastern bloc. One site, the Nemegt Valley at the far western end of the Three Beauties, proved itself a second wonderland for fossils. Then, after 1990 and the end of the Soviet Union, came a series of expeditions to the Nemegt, which produced a flood of new material, again revising ideas about the origins of mammals and birds.

Living in these harsh regions is not easy. But this and surrounding areas rank as some of the most significant and most rewarding, as well as the least known, of destinations.

Camel herders in the Gobi climb a dune on their way across one of the rare stretches of sand in a gravel and rock wilderness.

Mongolian snow leopards are normally mountain creatures but commute across open desert to colonize isolated ranges; they are rarely glimpsed in the wild.

CENTRAL ASIA

"A journey is a person in itself; no two are alike."
JOHN STEINBECK, AMERICAN WRITER, 1902–1968

TO THE ROOF OF THE WORLD

Traveling through the valleys and passes that traverse the world's highest mountains can be tough, but the cultural and spiritual experience more than compensates for any discomfort.

A sadhu in Kathmandu, with dreadlocked hair to represent the many-tributaried Ganges, and smeared with ashes to represent the god Shiva's role as destroyer.

THE AWARENESS OF BEING in the highest part of the whole earth and the splendor of the Himalayan Mountains on a clear blue day is an experience that, as the Irish travel writer Dervla Murphy wrote, should not be "trapped in mere words." You can walk, bus, or fly by helicopter or small plane from Kathmandu to Lukla, to join the steady stream of trekkers, sherpas, and porters on the Everest trail—the main commercial route, but in reality no more than a yak path—to the market town of Namche Bazar and beyond to Base Camp. The flight along the rim of the Himalayas, a dazzling frieze of white peaks along the edge of the world, is a fitting overture to what lies ahead. Beneath lies rural Nepal: russet and gold foothills—though such a term seems inadequate for the giant sculpted folds and valleys dark with depth—remarkably carved into a thousand terraces, with barely a sign of modern civilization.

Or you can submit to the lure of Tibet as well, and take what must rank as one of the world's most unforgettable bus journeys, from Kathmandu to Lhasa, a return trip that takes 10 days. Visa and permit requirements for Tibet are notoriously confusing and change frequently, so it is wise to get

Prayer wheels line monastery walls. They are spun in a clockwise direction to spread spiritual blessings.

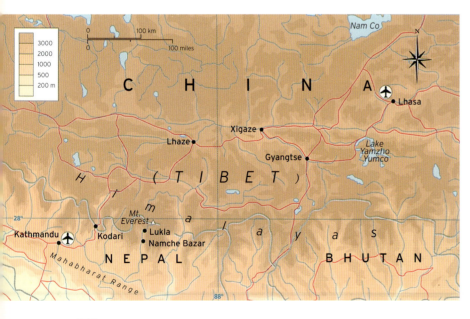

up-to-date information from Chinese embassies. A word of warning: this trip is not for the faint-hearted or unfit. Preparation, in mind, body, and equipment, is essential.

After the riots and reprisals of 1987 and 1989, Tibet was virtually closed to foreigners. It has been the focus for three great empires' ambitions—British, Russian, and, most recently, Chinese. Its geographical isolation behind the highest mountains and its political isolation after China's invasion in 1951 have combined with a reputation for spirituality and magic, heightened in recent years by the Dalai Lama's high profile in the West. Together, these elements give Tibet a romantic quality. Nowadays, visitors can fly in from Beijing, Chengdu, or Kathmandu, though flights to and from Nepal are subject to delay and cancellation. It is also possible to negotiate taking private vehicles in from Nepal.

-> FACT FILE

CURRENCY Nepalese rupee, Chinese renminbi. U.S. dollars are universally accepted.

CLIMATE Impassable in winter. Even in summer, nights can be near freezing.

BEST TIME TO TRAVEL The trip is only possible in summer.

DRESS Down jackets, good sleeping bags.

AIRPORTS Kathmandu in Nepal and, less useful, Lhasa.

FOUR MAIN DANGERS Mountain sickness related to oxygen deficiency at altitude, stomach disorders, extreme dehydration, fierce dogs.

MEDICATION Consult your doctor for remedies to counter mountain sickness and intestinal infections. Diamox is recommended to help combat altitude sickness.

MOST VITAL PIECE OF EQUIPMENT Water bottle(s).

MOST VITAL "DON'T" Don't drink unboiled water.

SPECIAL NOTE Visa and permit requirements for Tibet are confusing and change frequently. Get up-to-date information from Chinese embassies. Check the political stability in this volatile region before traveling.

A sight of Everest—or Chomo Lungama ("Mother goddess of the world"), as it is more descriptively called by the Sherpa people—brings with it an awe-inspiring awareness of being near the top of the world.

The Tibetan Trail

Bus journeys are generally in the hands of two companies, one Nepalese, the other Chinese, with a transfer at the border, although some direct buses are coming into operation, and there is a new rail link from Quinghai in China to Lhasa. Though Nepalese buses are ramshackle, the journey into the high Himalayas from Kathmandu to the Chinese border is only about half a day.

At the Nepalese border post of Kodari, passengers must either walk or transfer to a truck, which carries them the 6 miles (10 km) across no-

man's-land to the Chinese border at Zhangmu: called "Khasa" in the Nepalese language, these days this is one of the most important entry points for visitors to Tibet, and it has a bank, post office, and a number of small stores. It can take up to 2 hours to complete the crossing formalities, before resuming the journey in a Chinese bus to the first night's hotel (which may well provide only very basic accommodation). From here the road leads over undulating barren plateaus, with occasional steep drops and climbs. The vegetation is so sparse as to seem virtually nonexistent, exposing the gritty

This roof detail from the Potala shows the striking colors characteristic of Tibetan architecture.

North of the Himalayas, the vast Tibetan plateau stretches for miles, much of it uninhabited.

ground. On the highest desert, well protected from monsoon rains by the mountains, the going is sometimes tortuous but mostly merely uneven.

On the second day, the road climbs up to 18,000 feet (5,500 m), over the stunningly beautiful Lublungla Pass, which is at a high enough altitude to leave the unacclimatized gasping. There are few facilities here, but any adversities are rewarded: to the southeast, blocking the horizon, is a line of mountains from which looms one glorious, familiar pyramid: Everest, 50 miles (80 km) away, a sight stirring enough to carry passengers through the 12 long hours of journey to the small town of Lhaze.

Favorite Destinations

Next stop is Tibet's second largest city, Shigatse, with better hotels and restaurants, and famous for the monastery that is the seat of the Panchen Lama, who ranks just below the Dalai Lama. His 15th-century monastery, Tashilunpo, houses some 600 monks, has a 90-foot (27-m) statue of the Maitreya Buddha, and the gold-encrusted tomb of the fourth Panchen Lama. Its many dark chapels, with their gilded statues, are rank with the smell of yak-fat candles and sculptures made of butter, which are eventually fed to dogs. On a hilltop are the ruins of a fortress shattered when China occupied Tibet in 1959.

For travelers, Shigatse offers the first sight of Tibetans en masse. They are unbelievably poor by Western standards, and running water is a rarity. But visitors find that this material poverty is balanced by an open hospitality and a winning curiosity. Tibetan ways and poverty contrast starkly with the unnerving presence of Chinese troops and the relative wealth displayed by Chinese immigrants, who receive financial inducements to move to these remote and bitter parts.

Gyantse, the fourth stopover point, is only a small town, but it too has a better class of hotel, with hot showers. The 15th-century Palkhor Monastery has a pilgrim circuit covering 108 chapels and 9 levels, and a hilltop fort overlooking the countryside. From here, it is one more day's ride to Lhasa, over the 16,000-foot (4,990-m) Kampala Pass. There is a superb view of Yamdrok Yomtso Lake, a vast mirror for the sky framed by snow-capped mountains. Traditionally, it was here the lamas came when they wished to receive guidance in finding new incarnations.

Lhasa (whose name means "City of the Sun") is dominated by the sweeping wall of the Potala Palace and is divided between Chinese and Tibetan sections. Chinese apartment buildings are modern, charmless, and spartan. Since a spate of anti-Chinese violence in the late 1980s and subsequent brutal clampdowns, the Chinese military presence has been all pervasive. The central square is often dominated by military parades. By contrast, the Tibetan section, all narrow alleys and potholed roads, at first sight appears squalid but is surging with life. For westerners, however, one advantage of the Chinese occupation is the presence of a few good, and many semi-decent, hotels and shops.

The Potala, the Dalai Lama's gleaming white winter palace that Tibetans simply call "the Peak," looks like a tidal wave of masonry sweeping up the side of the Red Mountain. Dating from the 17th century, this was once the seat of government and is now a museum. Its two palaces form a maze of thousands of rooms and chapels, with stunning bejeweled tombs of former Dalai Lamas. Many of the rooms are gloomy and lit by flickering candles, but the living quarters of the Dalai Lama at the top are full of light.

The Potala is the greatest monumental structure in Tibet, rising 560 feet (170 m) from its position above the Lhasa valley.

HANOI AND THE RED RIVER DELTA

A colorful and tranquil land of lakes, legends, temples, and tradition.

The Red River Delta has long been an important rice cultivation region, and most farmers still use the traditional methods.

Local women in traditional conical hats welcome visitors to Hanoi market.

HANOI HAS BEEN VIETNAM'S CAPITAL for a thousand years. Ha Noi means "between rivers," but the city's original name was the poetic Thang Long, "ascending dragon," which is still used by some locals. The modern city is a tumult of noise and color: ancient alleys and serene temples give way to pockets of neon and concrete, and the roads are clogged with motorbikes and *ciclos* (bicycle rickshaws).

The capital sits at the apex of the Red River Delta, a spidery mesh of rivers and canals that extends for 1,864 square miles (3,000 sq km). This region is the ancestral home of the ethnic Vietnamese, most of whom still live in traditional communities amid the rice paddy fields.

Hanoi

Hanoi is built around several silvery lakes, including Ho Hoan Kiem, the "Lake of the Restored Sword," whose name recalls the legend of a sacred sword dredged up by a fisherman and used to overthrow Chinese invaders. Beyond the lake stretches the labyrinthine Old Quarter, Hanoi's traditional artisan district. The 36 ancient guild streets remain named for the products they made and sold—such as Lantern Street, Silk Street, Coffin Street, and Herbal Medicine Street. The street names remain the same, although the goods are changing as old crafts die out and the demands of tourism bring in hostels, Internet cafés, and fast-food outlets.

A lot has changed, from the communist propaganda blaring from loudspeakers to the fashionably dressed city kids toting mobile phones, but much remains the same. Peasant women in their loose clothing and conical, or *no'n ba`i tho*, hats are weighed down by yokes bearing heavy baskets of fruit and flowers, and narrow doorways lead to the curious "tube houses," which evolved to avoid taxes based on the size of storefronts. Battered temples and pagodas, built in honor of the deities that protect each street guild, still adorn the narrow streets. The Bach Ma (White Horse) pagoda on Hang Buom (Sailmaker) street is the oldest in Hanoi: a founding legend recounts that the king saw a white horse emerge from a temple and decided to build the city in its hoofprints, declaring the White Horse to be the city's guardian.

Spreading south of the Hoan Kiem Lake is the

elegant old French Quarter, where the tree-shaded boulevards are lined with smart art galleries, fashionable cafés, and trendy boutiques. The French colonial influence is still felt everywhere in Hanoi—in the graceful villas tucked behind high walls, the opulent grandeur of the Opera House, and the legendary Metropole Hotel or the majestic Presidential Palace, which was once the residence of the governors-general of Indochina. The French-built prison, better known as the "Hanoi Hilton" since the Vietnam War, has largely been demolished and replaced with a hotel, although a small section was preserved and converted into a museum.

Near the shores of Ho Tay (West Lake), Hanoi's largest lake, Ho Chi Minh lies in state in a monolithic Soviet-style mausoleum while queues of Vietnamese wait for admission in reverential silence. The nearby Ho Chi Minh Museum offers an unintentionally kitsch overview of "Uncle Ho's" life and Vietnam's recent history. Far more interesting is the city's Fine Arts Museum, which has an impressive array of paintings, sculptures, and stone carvings dating back to the 9th century.

Close to the mausoleum, the 900-year-old One-Pillar pagoda perches surreally on a (new) concrete base. According to legend, a childless king dreamed that a goddess offered him a son and was soon after blessed with a child. He built this temple in honor of the goddess, and the locals still believe that she can cure fertility problems. A popular attraction is the water puppet theater.

The Red River Delta

At Hanoi, the Red River splits into its two main distributaries, the southern Song Hong (Red River) and the northern Song Duong, which enclose a vast fertile triangle densely covered with paddy fields. The Red River Delta has long been an important rice-producing region, and the landscape has changed little in centuries. Dams, some of which date from the 11th century, still contain the

Hanoi is built around several beautiful lakes, including the serene Truc Bach Lake.

FACT FILE <−

CURRENCY Dong. U.S. dollars are widely, if unofficially, accepted (take small denominations).

BEST TIME TO GO October–December, when the heat and humidity are not excessive.

CLIMATE Vietnam has a tropical monsoon climate. The worst rains hit during the hot, wet summer. Winters are warm and sunny October–December, but slightly cooler January–March.

HEALTH Vaccinations are recommended for hepatitis A and typhoid fever. In some areas, malaria pills should be considered.

WHAT TO TAKE Long-sleeved light cotton clothing, sun hat, comfortable shoes, insect repellent containing DEET, water bottle, sunblock, and medicines.

FOOD AND DRINK Vietnamese cuisine is characterized by pungent spices and seasonings, particularly fish sauce, lemon grass, and lime. *Pho,* similar to chicken soup with noodles, is the typical breakfast. Pork, shrimp, and vegetable dishes are the most common staples. It is unlikely that you will encounter the more unusual delicacies such as dog or snake, although if you venture outside the city you will find a village near Hanoi complete with restaurants serving cobra, Vietnam's true symbol of virility. Avoid unpeeled fruit and salads, and drink purified or bottled water.

WHAT TO BUY Silk, jewelry, lacquer, ceramics.

AIRPORT Hanoi Noiboi.

VISA REQUIREMENTS All foreign nationals are required to have a visa to enter Vietnam.

In northern Vietnam, the new year is marked with peach blossoms. Hanoi's streets are filled with a profusion of pink blossoms, sold from bicycles by local farmers.

A serene junk crosses Ha Long Bay, a magical region that, according to local legend, is home to dragons.

waterways, protecting villages and crops from the continuing danger of floods. Villagers wearing traditional loose cotton clothing, heads shielded with conical hats made from bamboo, are a familiar sight. Although tractors have been introduced in recent years, water buffalo are still commonly used for cultivation, wallowing in mud pools to cool off.

Traditionally, paddy fields were left fallow for some months during the annual rice-growing cycle, when villagers concentrated on a variety of different crafts. Over the years, each village began to specialize in particular goods, such as ceramics, lacquerware, jewelry, or silk, for example. While every province in the Red River Delta has scores of these craft villages, the most accessible are those close to Hanoi. The most famous is the pottery village of Bat Trang, which is a gentle 6-mile (10-km) cycle ride along the riverbank from the capital. Others include Ngu Xa for cast bronze, Van Phuc for silk, and So for delicious noodles.

Ha Long Bay (Vinh Ha Long)
The Song Duong River empties into the Gulf of Tonkin near the busy seaport of Hai Phong. To the north lies Ha Long Bay, a UNESCO World Heritage Site of unparalleled natural beauty. The bay encloses islands of jagged limestone pillars—more than 1,600 of them—created, according to legend, by dragons spitting out jade and jewels. The dragons were sent by the gods to aid the Vietnamese in their struggle against invaders, and chose to stay in this earthly paradise when peace was restored.

Now boats with traditional junk sails float magically across the bay, ferrying passengers to white-sand coves and echoing grottoes studded with stalactites and stalagmites. These can also be explored from kayaks, available for rent, or you can take the restored paddle steamer to enjoy every imaginable luxury.

Cat Ba National Park
Ha Long Bay attracts more than 2 million visitors every year. For more remote islands, make for the Cat Ba National Park about 20 miles (32 km) east of Hai Phong (where the ferries leave from). Located on the largest of a string of islands that link Ha Long Bay and Bai Tu Long Bay, the national park contains the largest area of tropical primeval forests in Vietnam and is home to an extraordinary variety of bird, animal, and plant life. It also boasts beautiful—and virtually empty—beaches and pristine waters.

KYOTO, HEART OF JAPANESE CULTURE

A modern city with a medieval heart, where abundant gardens and temples soothe the mind.

Kyoto's grid of medieval streets, which defines the modern center, is still visible on the map and when looking over the city from Kiyomizu-dera temple.

AMONG KYOTO'S MANY TEMPLES, one in particular commands veneration, and not only from Buddhists. In the 13th-century Hall of the Thirty-Three Bays, stand 1,001 gilt Buddhas, 10 deep in 100 diagonal rows. They were created to save the world from disaster. They certainly helped to do so, for in 1945 Kyoto was one of the cities on which the United States considered dropping the atomic bomb. It was a Japanese-educated art historian, Landon Warner, who vetoed the idea, arguing that Japan's old capital was its cultural treasure house. To destroy Kyoto would be to destroy not simply the country's will to resist but its essence. The essence remains, preserved not only in temples like the Hall of the Thirty-Three Bays, but in its galleries, house, gardens, and traditions.

From its foundation 1,200 years ago to the early 600s, Kyoto was Japan's capital. It was chosen carefully, in accordance with the strict rules of geomancy, on a plain sloping south toward the sea and backed by mountains, like a seat protecting the emperor and his empire. A river flows south and west, and a mountain guards against evil spirits from the northeast. The palace compound was the city's pole, and a grid of streets divided into east-west sectors. Rebuilt several times after fires and wars, Kyoto finally developed its present graceful, peaceful air from aristocratic residents, after power had shifted permanently to Tokyo in 1868.

Zen Gardens and Tea Ceremonies

Beneath its modern concrete carapace, ancient Kyoto still exists in streets dotted with enough attractions to occupy a lifetime. Here, ancient arts and crafts—dancing, music, ceramics, woodblock printing, scroll painting, and calligraphy—thrive. The city has Japan's two most famous schools for teaching the tea ceremonies. The purpose of the ceremony, introduced in the 16th century, is to induce contemplation and harmony, and the teahouse is ideally set in a complementary garden.

Visiting Kyoto's gardens is perhaps the best way to get a feel for the city's rich and complex character. Japanese gardens owe more to human concepts than to nature. Beautiful objects—rocks, plants, trees, and ponds—are revered as homes of spirits and symbols of a wider landscape. The development of Zen Buddhism in the 1400s inspired a new asceticism in which simple elements—rock, raked sand, pebbles—were formed into patterns to assist contemplation.

The Kinkaku-ji, or Temple of the Golden Pavilion, is a new version of the 14th-century original that burned down in 1950. It was regilded in 1988.

Map of Kyoto showing districts and landmarks:

Takaragaike Park
Shugakuin Imperial Villa
Kita-Ku
Kitayama Dori
Washiga-mine
Botanical Garden
Manjuin Garden
Kohoin Garden
Daitoku-ji
Kitaoji Dori
Shishen-Do Garden
Kinkaku-ji Temple (Golden Pavilion)
Kitaoji Dori
Ryoan-ji
Myoken-ji
Sokoku-ji
Sakyo-Ku
Imadegawa Dori
Ginkaku-ji Temple and Garden
Kamigyo-Ku
Kyoto Old Imperial Palace
Honen-in Temple
Myoshin-ji
Heian Shrine
Marutamachi Dori
Okasaki Park
Nanzeni-ji Garden
Nijo Castle
Nakagyo-Ku
Ukyo-Ku
Yasaka Shrine
Maruyama Park
Mibu-dera Temple
Jojuin Garden
Kennin-ji
Kiyomizu-dera
Gojo Dori
Yasaka Pagoda
Shimogyo-Ku
Gojo Dori
Astronomical Observatory
Toji Temple
National Museum
Shichijo Dori
Higashi Hogan-ji Temple
Amidaga-mine
tsura rdens
Tokaido main line
Ruins of Sai-ji
Kujo Dori
Yamashina-Ku
Minami-Ku
Fishimu-Ku

0   100 km
0   100 miles

FACT FILE <—

BEHAVIOR For outsiders, the subtleties of Japanese manners are a life's work. A few guidelines: a deep nod will do instead of a bow. In homes, remove outdoor shoes and put on slippers provided (there are other slippers for use in the toilet). Don't tip. Bring small presents. In dress, be very neat and clean.

THINGS TO BRING Slip-on shoes.

GOOD BUY BEFORE DEPARTURE Japan Rail Pass.

ADDRESSES Western-style house numbering does not exist. Ask, ask, and keep on asking.

BEST TIMES TO VISIT Spring, for the cherry blossoms; autumn for the maples; and (for Nara) late October through early November, when Shoso-in treasures are on display in the Nara National Museum.

Contemplative harmony is the purpose of this Zen garden at Tofuku-ji Temple. Stones set in the raked quartz can be seen as islands in a quiet sea or tips of the conscious emerging from the subconscious.

In Ryoan-ji temple, Kyoto has the oldest surviving *karesansui* (rock and gravel garden). Built around 1500, it was "discovered" in the 1930s, when Western architects began eulogizing about its use of space. The garden is astonishingly austere: a 102 by 50 foot (31 by 15 m) rectangle of raked gravel, surrounded by low stone walls, and set with 15 boulders in five groups. The only plants are the lichens and mosses on the rocks. Are the rocks mountains or dragons? Are they raked pattern waves or lines of rice in a paddy field, or do they represent the subconscious with the rocks emerging as tips of the conscious mind? There is no one way to see it—there are infinite ways.

Cherry Blossom Time

Kyoto's open spaces are gardens of a different kind, stages on which the city's social life plays itself out.

April, cherry blossom time, is a subject dear to Japanese artists and poets. As symbols of life's transient beauty, they are mentioned in countless haiku, the classical 17-syllable verse form, like this one:

> *Fallen petals rise*
> *back to the branch—I watch:*
> *oh...butterflies!*

The blossoms signal the start of a week of drinking and celebration. One place to admire them is the courtly 5-acre (2-ha) garden of the Heian Shrine, built in 1894 to mark Kyoto's 1,100th anniversary. Another is the 1-mile (1.6-km) path that leads away from Nanzen-ji, one of the greatest of Zen temples. The path is actually two paths on either side of the Shishigatani Canal, along which a university professor, Nishida Kitaro, loved to stroll. In the 50

suburbs of Arashiyama and Sagano, where maples and gingkos splash the hills with startling reds, oranges, and golds. Nearby are the informal gardens of Koryu-ji, whose Treasure House (Reihokan) contains one of the most celebrated sculptures of Oriental art, Miroku Bosatsu. The slim and graceful boy in beatific meditation was carved in lustrous red pine, probably in the 6th century by a Korean. Winter is dominated by the New Year celebrations, when almost the entire city descends on the Yasaka Shrine in the Gion district to light tapers from a sacred fire and every temple bell is rung to drive away the evil of the year past. Then people make a point of marking the firsts of the new year—the first visit to a temple or the market, the first cup of tea—and look forward to the first blossoms of spring.

Cherry blossom season is a time for picnics in Kyoto parks. Double-flowered cultivars are sometimes planted as specimen trees in temple gardens.

The Treasures of Nara

Just 30 minutes by train from Kyoto, Nara was Japan's capital for a century in the 700s. Its parks, pagodas, and treasure houses bring the past into the present, without any industrial overlay. Its main glory is Tadai-ji (Eastern Great Temple), which together with its subsidiary temples commemorates the introduction of Buddhism. Opened in 752, it has the world's biggest wooden structure contained by a single roof—suitably imposing for an emerging empire and its new religion. The roof of today's Daibutsu-den (Great Buddha Hall) is 18th century, but the original was even larger—290 by 165 feet (88 by 50 m). It protects its colossal namesake, a 50-foot (15-m), 400-ton metal Buddha.

Prayer plaques proclaim the power of ancient Buddhist beliefs at a Kyoto temple.

years after his death, the Philosopher's Walk along the flanks of the hills hemming Kyoto's eastern edge has become very popular. Its lines of trees, interspersed with tearooms and crafts shops, run past three temples, one with an exquisite sloping garden of raked gravel, sand, moss, and flowering trees. The path ends at Ginkaku-ji, the Temple of the Silver Pavilion, built as an imperial retirement villa.

Summer is festival time. Throughout July, the city celebrates the Gion Matsuri festival, which culminates with the parade of ancient shrine floats. Gion itself, where aging geishas are still to be seen performing in teahouses, is enlivened by food stalls. Residents spray and wash the streets to keep cool, and families hang out their richest possessions—kimonos, screens, scrolls—ostensibly to expel the damp and mold of the rainy season. In autumn, Kyoto's residents like to head northwest to the

INDIA AND SOUTHEAST ASIA

"I travel not to go anywhere, but to go. I travel for travel's sake. The great affair is to move."
ROBERT LOUIS STEVENSON, SCOTTISH WRITER, 1850-1894

KERALA

An earthly paradise, not surprisingly known by its inhabitants as "God's own country."

Young girls in traditional costume greet visitors in Trivandrum with the traditional dish of rice and coconut.

KERALITES CALL THEIR STATE "God's Own Country." This earthly paradise is bounded by the Arabian Sea to the west and the Western Ghats to the east, padded with tropical forest, fringed with golden beaches, and threaded with countless rivers, waterfalls, and lakes. India's cleanest, greenest, and most affluent state, Kerala offers a calm tranquility rarely found elsewhere in this clamorous, colorful nation.

Travelers come not just to enjoy the heavenly natural surroundings, but also to experience Ayurvedic health and beauty treatments, practice yoga, or learn about its local cuisine and performing arts. It's an odd fact that the world's first freely elected communist government was appointed in Kerala in 1957.

Trivandrum: Ancient Capital

The capital of Kerala is Thiruvananthapuram (commonly known by its anglicized name of Trivandrum), which reclines across seven hills and overlooks palm-lined beaches. This 2,000-year-old city has a decidedly 21st-century feel, with ancient buildings rubbing shoulders with modern concrete blocks and a Technopark.

The city's most distinctive landmark is the Sri Padmanabhaswamy temple, in the Fort area to the south. It's dedicated to Lord Padmanabha, the "Snake God," for whom the city was named, and was built two millennia ago, but it remains—like most

These vast elevated fishing nets beautifully frame the entrance to Kochi's harbor.

Colorful festivals are held throughout the year in the Kerala region. This is a folk-dancing performance at the Kavadiattam Festival.

–> FACT FILE

CURRENCY Rupee.

BEST TIME TO GO Kerala is warm and sunny throughout the year, with April and May the hottest months. The southwest monsoon affects the region April–September, and the gentler northwest monsoon peaks during November. The most popular tourist period is December–February.

HEALTH Inoculations are recommended against meningitis, typhoid, and hepatitis A, as are malaria prophylactics.

WHAT TO TAKE Long-sleeved cotton clothing to combat mosquitoes, water-purifying tablets.

FOOD AND DRINK Delicious seafood, including tiger shrimp, red snapper, squid, crabs, and mullet can be on your plate only moments after being in the net on many of Kerala's beaches. A fiery, succulent fish stew called boatman's curry is recommended. The region's pungent spices and ubiquitous coconuts are commonly used as seasonings. There is plenty of excellent vegetarian food, and lamb is the most common meat, wonderfully flavored with the local cardamom and other spices. Favorite snacks are fried plantain or banana. Drink purified water, and avoid unpeeled fruit and salads and reheated foods.

WHAT TO BUY Textiles, spices, jewelry.

AIRPORTS Mumbai (Bombay) is the main international hub, with connecting flights to Kochi (Cochin) and Thiruvananthapuram (Trivandrum).

BEST FESTIVALS Music Festival, Thiruvananthapuram (Trivandrum), January 27–February 3; Thrissur Pooram, Thrissur, April–May; Harvest Festival of Onam, across the region, August–September; Snake Boat Races, Alappuzha (Alleppey), second Saturday in August; Shivaratri, across the region, February–March; Kochi Carnival, Kochi (Cochin), December 25–31; Ramadan, across the region, December.

CUSTOMS Don't eat with your left hand (the left hand is used for cleansing). Dress conservatively when visiting temples, and remove shoes. Be careful about taking any photographs without permission, especially those of deities and the interiors of temples. Cover up, except while on the beach. Topless sunbathing is officially illegal. Conserve water and electricity where possible.

VISAS All foreign visitors require a visa for travel to India.

Boats ply the intricate network of rivers and canals that form Kerala's famous backwaters.

of Kerala's Hindu temples–closed to non-Hindus.

The popular seaside resort of Kovalam, just 10 miles (15 km) from the capital, is still splendidly set around heavenly beaches, but mass tourism has taken a heavy toll. Plush hotels with private beaches dot the coast south of here; Varkala, just north of the capital, is quieter and a little less developed.

The Cardamom Hills
Spice plantations spread extensively over the Cardamom Hills, where the mingled scents of cardamom, pepper, cloves, tea, and coffee delicately perfume the air. Deep in steamy tropical forest, the Periyar Wildlife Sanctuary and Tiger Reserve are home to elephants, sambar, bison, antelope, and several primates, as well as the famously elusive tigers, of which about 40 are thought to live within the park boundaries. Elephants frolic playfully on the shores of the expansive Lake Periyar, which curves around the lush wooded slopes, and boat cruises explore its waters.

Heading north into the Western Ghats, Munnar was once a popular hill station during the time of the British Raj. The town is now rather ramshackle, but the setting is breathtaking, ringed by lofty mountains—including Anamundi, South India's highest peak—with verdant tea plantations carpeting the sloping valleys. The first plantations were established here by Scots in the 1870s, who must have been reminded of home when they first laid eyes on these mist-swathed slopes.

Alleppey and the Backwaters

Alappuzha (still known as Alleppey) is the gateway to Kerala's famous Backwaters, dubbed "the Venice of the East" for its network of emerald lagoons and estuaries. The town itself is a chaotic jumble of wooden huts overlooking murky canals, but it's the starting point for the popular *kettuvallum* ("sewn boats") that negotiate the Backwaters. These elegant wooden boats were once used for transporting heavy cargo, but elaborate domed canopies made of locally produced *coir* (coconut fiber) have transformed them into exquisite and often surprisingly luxurious houseboats for tourists. The boats drift serenely across lakes and narrow canals, where the only sounds are often the plop of fishermen's nets or the giggles of women soaking coconut husks to make coir. In August, Alappuzha celebrates the Nehru Cup Snake Boat Race, when gorgeously decorated boats with a rearing stern in the shape of a cobra compete to the delight of thousands of spectators.

In the heart of the Backwaters, Kumarakom is poised languidly on the shores of the vast Vembanad Lake, with distant forested peaks forming a serene backdrop. Life is slow in this lush, gentle paradise, and it's a popular destination for Ayurvedic and yoga holidays, as well as offering walking, fishing, boating, and bird-watching, particularly in the Kumarakom bird sanctuary.

Coconut fibers are dried in the sun and turned into coir, used to make the canopies of the *kettuvallum* boats.

Cochin

Kerala's most captivating city is Kochi (Cochin), which is curled around a broad natural harbor studded with islands. Arabic and Chinese sea merchants in search of spices traded in Kochi long before Vasco da Gama landed here in 1498. The Portuguese went on to establish India's first European colony, which fell to the Dutch a century later, and then to the British in 1795. Each foreign power, like the merchants who preceded them, left their imprint on the city, from trim English-style village greens to the gigantic Chinese fishing nets still poised over the harbor.

There are three main neighborhoods: the historic areas of Fort Kochi (Cochin) and Mattancherry, which occupy a peninsula jutting into the bay, and the modern sprawl of Ernakulam on the mainland. Ferries and bridges connect the scattered islands caught within the bay. Fort Kochi is the oldest and most atmospheric neighborhood, a tiny labyrinth of narrow lanes and steep-roofed houses. The fort has long gone, but India's oldest Catholic church still survives, and overlooking the sandy strand are the huge Chinese fishing nets, made of bamboo and weighted with rocks, which are said to have been introduced several hundred years ago by the Chinese. Fishermen dip the nets, unloading the catch onto the quays, where stallholders wait to prepare the spectacularly fresh fish. The very oldest section of all is Jew Town, where the still-functioning Paradesi Synagogue ("Foreigners' Synagogue") was built in 1568, and still retains its beautiful floor of hand-painted Chinese tiles and glittering Belgian chandeliers.

Keralan Experiences

Kerala offers some unique experiences. Ayurveda (a Sanskrit word meaning "the science of life") is a comprehensive system of medicine that was once widespread in India until the arrival of a different medical approach with the British Raj. It has undergone a revival, particularly in Kerala, where holistic treatments for health, beauty, and wellness are widely offered. Patients are categorized by body types (*prakriti*), which are determined by the proportions of the three *doshas* of air, fire, and water. When these doshas are imbalanced, illness ensues, and Ayurvedic medicine seeks to redress the imbalance.

Kalaripayattu, the world's oldest martial art, originated in Kerala and incorporates elements of martial dance, which make it spellbinding to watch. Kathakali, an ancient Keralan fusion of dance, drama, music, and ritual, features elaborately costumed performers reenacting stories from the great Hindu epics. Traditionally, performances take place throughout the night, but shorter pieces are regularly performed for tourists, particularly in Kochi (Cochin).

VARANASI, INDIA'S SACRED CITY

Varanasi is one of the greatest shrines on earth. Hindu and Buddhist pilgrims by the millions flock to it, seeking purification and escape from life's suffering in its holy waters.

The old city of Varanasi–a name meaning "the city between two rivers (the Varuna and the Asi)"– stretches back from the west bank of the Ganges.

FOR NON-HINDUS, the first sight of the banks of the Ganges at Varanasi is extraordinary: a 3-mile (4.8-km) crescent of river, lined by long gray *ghats* (steps), to which every day tens of thousands crowd, seeking the blessings conferred by the sacred waters–purification in life, release from the cycles of reincarnation and death. As pilgrims wash themselves in the flowing waters, families tend funeral pyres, sending smoke drifting over the city's huddled streets and temples. In Varanasi the odor of sanctity is all pervasive. For Hindus, the Ganges is the most sacred of their seven sacred rivers, and

Varanasi—the site of the most sacred of temples devoted to Shiva, one of their chief deities—is one of the seven cities with the power to give salvation, a power it has had for millennia. Varanasi is one of the world's most ancient, continuously inhabited sites—in Mark Twain's awed words, "older than history, older than tradition, older even than legend." A city has stood here for 4,000 years. From the earliest days, of Hinduism more than 3,000 years ago, the devout referred to it as Kashi, "the Luminous." Known for two centuries by its anglicized form Benares, the city reverted after Indian independence in 1947 to its ancient name, derived from two Ganges tributaries, the Varuna and the Asi.

The Holy River

Lying in the middle of the intensely cultivated and densely populated Gangetic plain, Varanasi today is a large city teeming with life. But its focal points are

The street sellers are colorful and their wares enticing, but if you buy fruit or vegetables, wash them in sterilized water or peel them before eating.

A little Hindu girl sells votive offerings for pilgrims to lay at the many shrines.

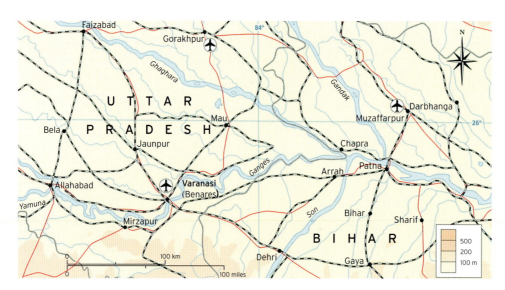

still the ghats, of which there are more than 100, each marked with a lingam, the universal Hindu stone phallus (usually simplified into the inoffensive shape of an inverted test tube). At sunrise, the series of steps, which are exposed and covered as the water rises and falls throughout the year, become a shifting mass of almost naked bathers, priests, yoga adepts, and mourners. Much to the astonishment of visitors arriving from the luxury hotels on the city fringes, Hindus regard the Ganges as the "elixir of life" and immerse themselves in its muddy waters, often rather cautiously at first, despite the ashes of corpses and open sewers that turn the river into a potential health hazard. But such is the special nature of the Ganges waters—a sign of divine blessing according to believers—this hazard seldom produces the epidemics of cholera or typhoid you might expect. Despite this visitors are advised not to bathe in, let alone drink, its waters.

So great is Varanasi's holiness that any Hindu dying within its confines is regarded as being released from the otherwise endless round of reincarnations. The city is therefore a refuge for the aged, who often seek shelter in the temples awaiting death, a pitiable sight to nonbelievers but an inspiration to the devout. Once released from life, their corpses are cremated on the two "burning ghats." One, Jalasi, next to the most sacred of all the ghats (Marnikarnika), is always crowded with funeral parties and the ghat's guardians (but note: photography is forbidden).

Each of the ghats dividing and linking the line of 18th- and 19th-century temples and palaces has its own significance and its own adherents, being the Hindu equivalents of Catholic shrines with their associated saints. The best way to see them is to get up before dawn—except in chilly midwinter this early hour makes the best viewing time anyway—and hire a rowboat with a boatman. You can then view the ghats in sequence as your boat moves

silently along the river, the early morning mist on the waters mingling with the smoke from many pyres before the fierce heat of the Indian sun dissipates it.

Five of the ghats are of special significance, forming the Panchatirthi ("five crossings") at which pilgrims should bathe in sequence, performing rituals at each. One confers particular merit: the Dashashwamedha ("10-horse sacrifice") ghat, named for a sacrifice performed by the god Brahma. Pilgrims can benefit from his perfection simply by bathing there.

Winding Hinterland

The city is more than its riverside. Ranging back from the central ghats is the Old City. Its local name, Vishwanatha ("Lord of All"), derives from its main temple complex, also known as the Golden Temple, from the gold plating on its spire. It is dedicated to Shiva in his manifestation as Lord of the Universe. Visitors find their way to it by edging through a maze of overhung alleys that are crammed with the bedlam and acrid smells of hundreds of shops and stalls. They are rewarded by the sight of a smooth black stone set in a silver plinth. It is a Shivalingam, one of many worshipped at Shiva shrines across the Hindu world. Here, though, it has special import. A short walk north of the Golden Temple is Jnana Vapi ("wisdom well"), where Shiva is said to have cooled his lingam. The waters, considered to be a fount of knowledge, are covered to prevent a rush from the faithful.

The Buddha's Park

Varanasi is also sacred for Buddhists, for Siddhartha Gautama, the Buddha (Enlightened One), gave his first sermons here. The 6th-century B.C. Gazelle Park where Buddha "set in motion the Wheel of the Law" is at Sarnath, just 6 miles (10 km) north of Varanasi, an easy cab or bus ride away. About 1,400 years ago, there were 30 Buddhist monasteries there. After Buddhism's eclipse under the impact of Islam in the 1200s, time and Vandals destroyed almost everything. British archeologists reopened it in the 1800s, and more restorations, amounting almost to rebuilding, followed in the 1920s, partly financed by American Buddhists. Now its immaculate if somewhat sterile ruins draw pilgrims from the world over. Temples and shrines gather as if in obeisance round two stupas—one a mere stump, the other a 100-feet (33-m) tower—both of which are said to mark the exact spot of the Buddha's first sermon.

In Varanasi, the Hindu and Muslim worlds also abut, intermingle, and sometimes clash. The great 17th-century Jnana Vapi mosque was built by the Mogul emperor Aurangzeb—a fanatical Muslim—as a deliberate affront to Varanasi's sanctity as believed by his Hindu subjects. But the mosque takes its name from the Hindu Wisdom Well, which stands a stone's throw away.

-> FACT FILE

AIRPORTS New Delhi international airport, local flights to/from Varanasi.

CURRENCY Indian rupees. U.S. dollars accepted at banks and money exchanges.

LANGUAGE Hindi, but English is widely understood.

WHEN TO GO October–April; December and January can be cool at night; avoid the monsoon July–September.

HEALTH PRECAUTIONS Inoculations against hepatitis A and B, typhoid, cholera, polio, meningitis, and tetanus are essential. Malaria is resistant to chloroquine-based drugs. Drink only bottled or boiled water, avoid uncooked vegetables, salads, peeled fruit, and unboiled milk. Take medication against almost inevitable attacks of diarrhea, plus worm pills, antihistamine pills, and antibiotics.

TIPPING Tip hotel/restaurant staff.

WHAT TO TAKE Padlocks, sink plugs, mosquito repellent, sunblock, hats, sunglasses, tampons.

ACCOMMODATION Plenty of hotels to suit most budgets.

DO NOT Eat food with your left hand (the left hand is reserved in Asia for toilet functions); wear shoes in temples or mosques; wear shorts or go shirtless outside big hotels; swear at Indians no matter what the provocation; assume it is okay to photograph people.

The bathing ghats on the west bank of the Ganges; the most magical time to visit them is early morning.

AUSTRALASIA

"Even disasters—there are always disasters when you travel—can be turned into adventures."
MARILYN FRENCH, AMERICAN WRITER, B. 1929

DREAMTIME IN THE NORTHERN TERRITORY

A seemingly barren landscape harbors Dreamtime spirits
and wind-sculpted mountain islands.

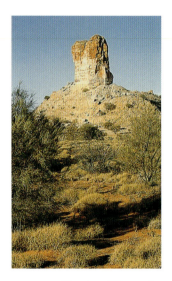

Chambers Pillar, on the
northern edge of the
Simpson Desert, is a
couple of hours' drive
southeast of Alice
Springs. Iron oxide gives
the sandstone its red
coloration.

AS YOU DRIVE SOUTHWEST from Alice Springs
along the Stuart Highway, you enter the untamed
heart of Australia, an ancient, barren landscape
long worn down by wind and water. The monotony
of the outback scrubland is relieved by the raw
umbers, startling reds, and rich golds of its rocks,
by dry riverbeds, tortuously sculpted by rare but
violent rains, and by shimmering expanses of crust-
rimmed, crystalline white salt pans where shallow
lakes have evaporated. An incongruous note is
struck by the Outback Camel Farm at Stuart's Well,
about 55 miles (90 km) south. Australia has the
world's only numerous surviving wild camel herds,
about 15,000 camels in all, descendants of those
imported by the early settlers in the 1800s.

Further inland, make a detour off the Stuart
Highway to the sandstone monolith of Chambers
Pillar, a couple of hours southeast on the fringes of
the Simpson Desert, and to Kings Canyon, some
200 miles (300 km) from Alice Springs. Don't miss
the loop walk, offering breathtaking views from the
canyon's 300-foot (100-m)-high walls, with detours
to the "lost city," a maze of weathered domes, and
the "Garden of Eden," a sunken valley with
permanent waterholes and lush vegetation.

But nothing in the generally arid immensity
compares with your first sight of Uluru/Ayers Rock
(285 miles/460 km from Alice) as it appears
massively above the horizon. It grows until it
appears as large as a mountain on the low-lying
bushland. This is no mountain, but your eyes are
not deceiving you, for the Rock is huge, the world's
largest sandstone monolith, rising abruptly, pitted

with caves and gullies, 1,145 feet (348 m) above
the surrounding flatness of the scrub. The first
European to report seeing the Rock was a surveyor
named Ernest Giles, in 1872. A year later it was
climbed by William Gosse, who described it as
"certainly the most wonderful natural feature I have
ever seen" and named it for Henry Ayers, then
premier of the colony of South Australia. The rock
is now known by its Aboriginal name, Uluru, which
is the name the local Aborigines gave to a rock hole
high up on the monolith. There are many sacred
sites around the oddly deserted base of Uluru, and

Aboriginal rock carvings
near Alice Springs (above).
Uluru, or Ayers Rock
(right), is a key site
associated with the local
Aborigines. Much of this
immense sandstone rock
is submerged beneath
the ground.

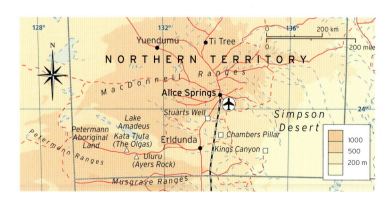

-> FACT FILE

HOW TO GET THERE There are direct flights to the airport near the Ayers Rock Resort from all major Australian airports.

CLIMATE Markedly continental, with hot summers—the temperature can reach 110°F (45°C) between November and March—and surprisingly cold winters, when it can fall below freezing at night, particularly if skies are clear.

WHEN TO GO April-October.

NEAREST TOWN/AIRPORT Ayers Rock Resort, 12 miles (20 km) from the Rock, is the service village for the park. The airport is 3 miles (5 km) outside town and connects with most Australian cities and airlines.

THINGS TO DO Scenic flights over the Rock; a night-sky show relating Anangu legends; watching the Rock change color at dawn and sunset (for cultural and safety reasons, Aborigines request that visitors do not climb the Rock); free ranger-guided tours; visit the Cultural Center. Uluru and Kata Tjuta are UNESCO World Heritage Sites.

THINGS TO BUY Aboriginal artifacts; paintings, batiks (during special exhibitions only), and carvings.

WHAT TO TAKE Sunscreen, hats, water bottles, comfortable clothes.

The monstrous bald heads of Kata Tjuta/the Olgas in Uluru-Kata Tjuta National Park, west of Uluru/Ayers Rock, conceal the eerie Valley of the Winds.

though they are normally fenced off, the park rangers can explain their significance.

Ownership of the Rock was returned to the Aborigines in 1985, but reluctantly accepting the inevitability of tourism, they leased it back to the federal government. It is now administered jointly by its traditional owners and Environment Australia.

The Sunset Color Show

Until the end of the Second World War, only a few intrepid travelers visited Uluru on camels, guided by local cattle drovers; then in 1948 an asphalt road was built. The Ayers Rock Resort has sprung up 12 miles (20 km) away, at the edge of Uluru-Kata Tjuta National Park, to cater for travelers, and is connected by air to Alice Springs.

No photographs or verbal descriptions can fully capture the allure and weird beauty of the Rock. The closer you approach, the more beautiful it grows—grander, rounder, steeper, even softer, as if it were half alive, a prehistoric monster. It has a circumference of 6 miles (9.4 km), and it is thought that some 8,000 feet (2,500 m) of rock lie under the sand, beneath the visible monolith, like a desert iceberg. It is, in fact, an island mountain, technically called an inselberg, which was pushed up by earth movements around 500 million years ago.

The 1-mile (1.6-km) climb takes about 2 hours. There is a chain along the steepest section at the beginning but no fence. The Rock is closed to climbers after 8 A.M. in summer, when temperatures can soar above 100°F (38°C), and also in wet or windy weather. It can be very cold in winter. The climb is not recommended for anyone with heart problems or who suffer from vertigo. Several people have died from falls or heart attacks while climbing the Rock. In fact, the Aborigines now

request that visitors do not climb the Rock at all.

For a short but sensational experience, take your car (you will need a car) to the prominently marked Sunset Viewing Spot to the west. The Rock rapidly changes color from yellow to orange to red to purple and finally flares scarlet, as if giving off heat from deep within it. The color show only lasts for a few minutes before the rock fades to dull brown and then is lost in the swiftly falling night. On the rare occasions when it rains, Uluru takes on an ominous black metallic sheen.

Many Heads and Windy Valleys

The Uluru-Kata Tjuta National Park covers an area of 327,584 acres (132,566 ha). It is a very arid region, with only about 8 inches (200 mm) of rain annually, so the vegetation is mostly sparse bushes. But the sudden showers that occur in summer produce an explosion of wildflowers, including Stuart's Desert Rose, which is the Northern Territory's floral emblem.

Some 20 miles (30 km) west of Uluru rise the Olgas, a clutch of 36 egg-like mountain fragments once submerged in a long-vanished sea. The

Desiccated desert oaks in the Australian outback near Kata Tjuta, west of Uluru. The rare rainfall is the trigger that causes otherwise dormant flowers to bloom.

largest, Mount Olga, was named for a German Queen by Ernest Giles, who described the rocks as like "enormous pink haystacks, all leaning against each other."

The Olgas are now known by the name the Anangu Aboriginal people gave them: Kata Tjuta, meaning "many heads." It is obvious from a distance how the rocks earned their name; they have been worn down over eons into giant deeply creviced bald domes of composite granite and basalt, cemented together with mud and sand. The highest, at 1,790 feet (546 m) above the plain, is some 600 feet (200 m) higher than Uluru. They are an important site in Aboriginal men's law.

A memorable 4-mile (6-km) trail from the northern parking lot leads through Valley of the Winds, and it can be a haunting experience. The shadows play among the rocks, and the winds whistle uncannily even in almost calm weather, though it is almost a green oasis amid the outback, where daisies, mint bushes, and acacias grow. Look out, too, for the rock crevices deep in shade, where rare rainfall may linger just long enough to

-> The Dreamtime

Australian Aborigines believe that ancestral beings moved about the land in the creation time (sometimes known as the Dreamtime), forming its physical features and leaving their mark on the landscape. Many ancestral Dreamtime spirits are connected with the formation of Uluru and Kata Tjuta. Uluru is also an important meeting point of the mythical and sacred pathways that crisscross this area, marking the journeys the ancestors made as they molded Australia's harsh landscape. The Aborigines fear that their laws will be broken and their sacred sites violated if tourists are allowed to intrude into sensitive areas.

germinate an extraordinary range of plants, such as the peachlike quandong, which has waxy blue-green leaves and edible red fruits.

The Rock is an important meeting point of the "dreaming tracks," the crisscrossing mythical and sacred tracks that mark the journeys the ancestors made as they molded Australia's harsh landscape.

THE GREAT BARRIER REEF

To stand on the world's greatest coral reef off the northeastern edge of Australia is like walking on water; all around is ocean as far as the eye can see.

In summer, loggerhead turtles haul themselves ashore to lay their eggs in the sand. The young emerge 4 to 8 weeks later and make a desperate bid to reach the sea without being eaten by predators.

THE GREAT BARRIER REEF, a chain of coral reefs fringing the coast of northeastern Australia, dwarfs every other coral reef on the planet and has the richest submarine ecology in the world.

Rise early to take a tour boat out from the Queensland coast. Dawn breaks to reveal a line of white breakers on the horizon, and you can feel the sea change in mood as it moves over shallower waters approaching the coral shelf. Where the water is shallowest of all, it is possible to stand on the reef (wearing shoes as a guard against the razor-sharp coral). Above the waterline you are surrounded by ocean; look below, where the reef falls away, to see a kaleidoscope of marine life through crystal-clear water. Corals like petrified plants in hues of peach, pink, and white are a home for a richness of marine life that competes for space in the warm, sunlit, oxygenated waters of the reef. You can find sea lilies, sponges, urchins, anemones, sea squirts, clams, and fish, all of which are so brightly colored they look artificially painted—

almost as if each species is trying to outdo the others in brilliance of design to make its mark among the crowds.

Vital Statistics

The Great Barrier Reef, now 8,000 years old, is the world's largest structure made by living organisms and is a UNESCO World Heritage Site. It is a chain of more than 2,900 individual reefs and some 700 islands stretching 1,200 miles (2,000 km) near Fraser Island, just south of the Tropic of Capricorn, to Cape York and Torres Strait, south of Papua New Guinea. At its southern end the reef is about 200 miles (320 km) from the mainland, but in the north it is much closer to the coast and less broken.

Coral reefs are delicate structures built up from the skeletal deposits of living creatures, marine polyps. New generations of polyps attach themselves to the remains of their predecessors, and in their turn die, and so a reef builds up, generation upon generation at a rate of an inch (2.5 cm) or so a year. The skeletons are white, but it is the pinkish, still living, top level of polyps that give the reef its rosy hue.

Coral polyps are fussy creatures, not tolerating water much below 68°F (20°C), which explains the reef's southern limit, or muddy waters like the Fly River estuary in Papua, which accounts for its northern limit. Nor will coral grow beneath a depth of 100 feet (30 m) because it needs sunlight.

The coral itself is a dense submarine jungle of shape and color, with some 400 different species, brain and staghorn coral among them. Near Orpheus Island, for a few nights following a full moon in late spring, you can see the different species of coral spawn simultaneously. The normally

There are 25 island resorts along the coast; Hinchinbrook Island, here viewed from Goold Island, is particularly unspoiled.

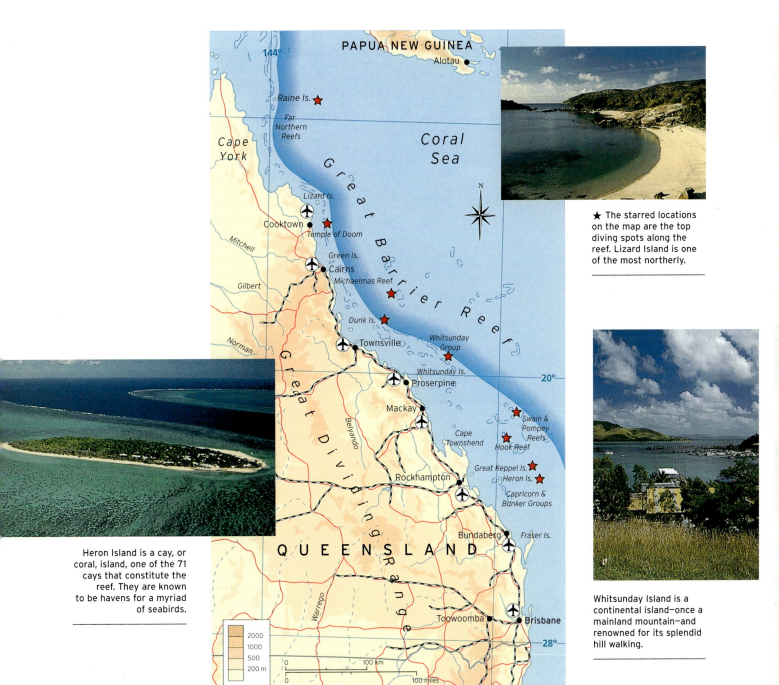

★ The starred locations on the map are the top diving spots along the reef. Lizard Island is one of the most northerly.

Heron Island is a cay, or coral, island, one of the 71 cays that constitute the reef. They are known to be havens for a myriad of seabirds.

Whitsunday Island is a continental island—once a mainland mountain—and renowned for its splendid hill walking.

crystal-clear waters turn into a gigantic underwater snowstorm as myriad tiny bundles of sperm and eggs shoot upward from the reef and burst.

A Balanced Ecology

There are about 1,500 species of fish and 4,000 species of mollusks, and, on a larger scale, the gentle dugong (the sea cow thought to be the origins of the mermaid myth, which is endemic to the reef), green turtles, and humpback whales, which migrate north every winter from Antarctica.

There are less welcome inhabitants, too; in the warmer months (November through April), deadly box jellyfish lurk off the reef's north-facing beaches, hard to detect except in the clearest waters, so don't swim unless the locals have given the okay. Great Keppel Island is normally fine for swimming all year round, but still ask. Saltwater crocodiles may also be a hazard, but more common problems are scorpionfish, with their beautiful but highly poisonous spines, and stonefish, which lie on the bottom looking exactly like stones. Sea snakes can be a problem, but oddly the much-feared shark is not. Despite the area's wealth of marine life, this is a delicately balanced ecology. Some years ago, crown-of-thorns starfish were devouring the reef; the threat seems to have abated for now, but the hordes of human visitors have not. The basic rule for starfish is: look, but don't touch!

View the reef through the base of a glass-bottomed boat, don snorkel and goggles, or take a diving course. For here you can find not only the most rewarding scuba diving in the world, but the cheapest as well, and much of your learning is "on reef." You can dive from most of the coral reef

islands, or cays, which are connected to the mainland by fast catamaran or helicopter. The three mainland bases are Airlie Beach, Townsville, and Cairns. From Cairns—a town of 68,000 people—the reef is only a few miles offshore. A quieter alternative is Great Keppel Island, at the southern end of the reef.

Back on Dry Land

Great Keppel is a continental island, the remnant of a mainland mountain, submerged thousands of years ago when the sea level rose. On islands like this and the Whitsunday group, you can find relief

The Gold Coast claims to have the best surfing in Australia. Inland from Surfers Paradise there is a subtropical rain forest.

-> **FACT FILE**

AIRPORTS Cairns, Brisbane, many smaller airports.

WHEN TO GO Best avoided during the rainy, hot months of January–March. Temperatures never drop below 68°F (20°C) on the coast.

WHAT TO TAKE Sunblock, wide-brimmed hats, flashlight, shoes for walking on coral.

WHAT TO DO Snorkeling, scuba diving, swimming, sightseeing by boat, hiking on Great Keppel and other islands, white-water rafting.

Divers may encounter a giant clam, which can be over 3 feet (90 cm) long and weigh up to 440 pounds (200 kg). On spawning, clams release over a billion eggs.

from the overabundance of sea life in hill walking and exploring the bush and its native wildlife. Or you can head inland through a coastal region lush with sugarcane to one of Queensland's 211 national parks, near Cooktown, where there are superb examples of Aboriginal rock art.

The Tully and North Johnstone rivers, in the mountains between Cairns and Townsville, make for great white-water rafting. The Tully River, though reduced in volume because of the hydroelectric dam on it, has in the past carved out a spectacular gorge, now a national park, through a rain forest-covered plateau that makes a good day's hiking.

A scenic railroad snakes 19 tortuous miles (30 km) from Cairns up to Kuranda. It was built in 1888 at vast expense and has dozens of bridges and tunnels through the mountains. The railroad passes the Barron Gorge, with its waterfall, at its most impressive after the rainy season, before reaching the tiny town (population 750) of Kuranda, a popular resort almost overgrown with palm trees. Here there is Wildlife Noctarium, where you can see native animals in a simulated night, and you can also make other expeditions into the surrounding rain forests.

CRADLE MOUNTAIN, TASMANIA

Spectacular peaks, deep gorges, jewel-like lakes, and wide open moorlands combine to make Cradle Mountain-Lake St. Clair National Park one of the finest walking areas in the world. But its wildness is for serious walkers; it is no place for a casual stroll.

The giant grass tree lends a subtropical air to some parts of the Tasmanian bush.

"THIS MUST BE A NATIONAL PARK FOR ALL TIME. It is magnificent. Everyone should know about it, and come and enjoy it," declared Gustav Weindorfer, an Australian immigrant scientist who fell headlong in love with Cradle Mountain in Tasmania on first seeing it in 1910. His simple but impassioned words echo the sentiments that have led to the preservation of the entire wilderness around it, including Mount Ossa, Tasmania's highest mountain at 5,300 feet (1,617 m), and Lake St. Clair National Park, part of a UNESCO World Heritage area.

Tasmania, Australia's southernmost and only island state, is extremely rich in rugged scenery,

and has a markedly cooler, wetter, windier climate than most of Australia. High cliffs along the southern and southwestern coasts look out toward the not-so-distant Antarctic, and empty moors stretch for miles.

The most impressive location of all is the 325,845-acre (131,921-ha) Cradle Mountain-Lake St. Clair National Park, with its precipitous jagged peaks, deep ice-scoured valleys, lakes and tarns, expanses of wild moorland, and abundant wildlife. Thin soils and scrub and dramatic, shattered rock faces bear witness to the glaciers' swift retreat at the end of the last ice age, for this is one of

Bushland forms the runup to Lake St. Clair, the deepest lake in Australia, seen here in the distance.

Australia's most heavily glaciated areas. But in spring and early summer, the wildflowers are legion, and autumn leaf colors are enhanced by those of Tasmania's only native deciduous species, the tanglefoot beech, with leaves that turn from bright green to gold and red. Despite the park's popularity—in high season more than 100 people set out on the trails every day—the pristine wildness of the area has been kept remarkably intact.

Walking the Wilderness

There are numerous day walks in the area, but the 50-mile (85-km) Overland Track from Cradle Valley to Cynthia Bay at the foot of Lake St. Clair attracts most visitors. The track can be walked in either direction, but most travel north to south, beginning at the Cradle Mountain ranger station and finishing at the ranger station near Derwent Bridge. The track can be walked at an easy pace in 5 to 7 days, but a fuller exploration of the region, including an ascent of Mount Ossa, would require 8 to 10 days. Walkers should sign the logbook at Waldheim Chalet before setting out and on completing their walk. They should also check at the park ranger station before setting out and be sure family or friends know of their

The Acropolis, one of the views from the Overland Track, is aptly named.

FACT FILE ←—

AIRPORTS Burnie, Devonport, Launceston, Hobart.

TRANSPORTATION The park and Overland Track are accessible from Launceston in the north and Hobart in the south by regular bus services.

DISTANCE The Overland Track itself is 50 miles (85 km) and takes 5-7 days to walk depending on pace.

WHEN TO GO November–April when the weather is most stable. March and April are particularly good for walking.

PERMITS Range from 1-day permits to a permit valid for entry to all Tasmania's national parks for 2 months. Rangers check for permits; defaulters incur on-the-spot fines. Walkers must prebook permits for the Overland Track at www.overlandtrack.com.au during high season (November–April).

SPECIAL EQUIPMENT Be prepared for extremes in weather conditions; sleeping mat and good four-season sleeping bag; solid footwear essential.

ACCOMMODATION AND SUPPLIES Huts throughout the park; campsites, lodges, and some cabins at each end of the track. All trekkers must carry a tent because the huts are often full. The park is a "no fire" zone so you must carry a portable stove. Limited supplies are available at either end.

One of the area's many breathtaking waterfalls, seen from behind.

Many trails start from Dove Lake, but one of the most delightful is the 2-hour lake circuit.

whereabouts, so that a search will be triggered if they go missing.

November to April is the best time to walk, though experienced walkers sometimes like to do the track in winter, to see the snow-covered moors and peaks flashing white against a brilliantly deep blue sky, hundreds of miles from any pollution. Even in summer the weather can be unpredictable, with sudden rainstorms and days of dramatic clouds. The track is well marked for its entire length, and there are six unsupervised huts, plus three emergency shelters, along the route that walkers can use for overnight accommodation. Try to start walking early; these huts are often full, being taken on a "first there, first in" basis. The easiest way to walk the Overland Track is in stages of 5 to 6 hours, allowing time to explore some of the other tracks.

Beginning in Cradle Valley, which is scattered with eucalyptus trees—look out for the snow gum—a journey of some 8 miles (13 km) to the Waterfall Valley huts takes a comfortable 5 to 6 hours. From Marion's Lookout, the reflection of Cradle Mountain on the surface of the lake gives a perfect vista of the sharp peak in calm, clear weather. Just past Kitchen Hut is a signposted track to Cradle Mountain summit, an extremely steep, rocky track that takes an hour each way. The panoramic views

from its top are spendid, and a bronze plaque indicates all the surrounding mountains, including Legges Tor, the highest peak of Ben Lomond, at 5,160 feet (1,572 m) Tasmania's second highest mountain, almost 100 miles (160 km) distant. There are a number of superb waterfalls within a few hundred yards of the Overland Track.

From Waterfall Valley to Lake Windemere is another 8 miles (13 km) over a sharp ridge, with extensive views in fine weather, and then across open moor and forest, remarkably similar to parts of the Scottish Highlands, to the shores of Lake Windemere. There is a modern heated hut that sleeps 28 people. By the end of the first day, everyone is usually discussing walkers' favorite topic—food.

The track runs on, always well signposted, through a terrain that varies from eucalyptus forest to marshy plains of buttongrass and finally reaches Cynthia Bay on Lake St. Clair. Gentler alternatives for the less energetic, there are several shorter 1-day walks from Cradle Valley. Call in at the Visitor Center for advice on those best suited to the weather. The 4-mile Dove Lake circuit takes 2 hours and offers magnificent views.

NEW ZEALAND, NORTH ISLAND

Lake Taupo and Tongariro–where spiritual Maori significance meets UNESCO World Heritage.

New Zealand's North Island is one of the most active geothermal regions in the world, seething with hot springs and bubbling pools.

FOR MAORIS, Lake Taupo and the Tongariro National Park in the heart of New Zealand's North Island are the realm of Ruaumoko, god of earthquakes and volcanoes. The region has immense spiritual significance for Maoris, and the Tongariro National Park is one of only two in the world that enjoy UNESCO World Heritage status for both natural and cultural importance.

This vast volcanic plateau continues to smolder, creating steaming hot springs, bubbling mud pools, and spouting geysers. The landscape is endlessly varied, the strange seething earth in geothermal regions contrasting colorfully with myriad rivers and lakes set amid lush forest. Unsurprisingly, this beautiful land attracts huge numbers of visitors, but it's always possible to get off the beaten track.

Lake Taupo

New Zealand's largest lake is cradled in the caldera of a mighty volcano, which last erupted in 181 A.D., spewing forth an immense column of molten matter that shot more than 30 miles (50 km) into the sky. The force was so great that chroniclers as far away

as China and Rome described the unearthly reddening of the sky. The geothermal activity continues to rumble under the earth's thin crust, throwing up geysers and bubbling hot springs, and warming the now-placid lake.

Its still waters, backed by the distant silhouettes of storybook volcanoes, now provide an idyllic setting for fishing, hiking, bathing, sailing, and countless other outdoor pursuits. The lake is huge, almost the size of Singapore, and is fed by more than 40 rivers where the trout fishing–even in a country world famous for the sport–is superlative. Brown trout were introduced in the 19th century and quickly thrived; rainbow trout were added more recently with equal success. Now the lake and rivers teem with so many plump fish that many of the local tour operators are prepared to stick their necks out and guarantee a catch.

It's not all peace and quiet at Taupo, though: for those seeking thrills and spills, there is skydiving, bungee jumping, white-water rafting, and a host of other activities. At Taupo, a pretty township sitting on the northeastern shores of the lake, the hot springs have become smart resorts boasting luxurious spas and beauty centers, as well as water slides and other kids' amusements. To the south, in smaller, quieter Tokaanu, wooden boardwalks crisscross the Tokaanu Thermal Park, where steam hisses from fissures in the swirling rock, and mud pools gurgle ominously. There are more mineral-rich hot springs to soak in here, long considered by the Maoris to have healing properties.

At Wairakei Terraces, a replica Maori village in Taupo, Maoris provide visitors with an introduction to their rich culture and heritage. The original Wairakei Terraces, cascades of silica terraces in startling shades of blue, pink, and white, were destroyed during an earthquake in 1886, but they have been carved again by hand. Boardwalks are splayed across the terraces, leading to more steaming hot pools and spurting geysers. This is a good place to try New Zealand's only authentic native cuisine, *hangi*, which is prepared by covering baskets of food with damp cloths and leaving them to steam. This ingenious cooking method is still used for preparing traditional feasts.

Until comparatively recently, Maori was under threat as a living language and ancient traditions

were dying out. But Maori culture is currently enjoying a renaissance, and the enormous rock carvings at Mine Bay are testimony to a resurgence of Maori pride. These carvings depict the great Maori ancestor Ngatoroirangi and were etched by Matahi Whakataka-Brightwell in the 1980s. The most visited natural attraction are the powerful Huka Falls: the Waikato River narrows suddenly some meters upstream, forcing the waters over the cascade with an earsplitting roar.

Tongariro National Park

The magnificent wilderness of the Tongariro National Park stretches south of Lake Taupo. At its heart is a trio of mighty volcanoes—Tongariro (6,457 feet/1,968 m), Ruapehu (9,176 feet/2,797 m), and Ngauruhoe (7,513 feet/2,290 m)—all of which are *tapu* (sacred) to Maoris. They believe that the mountains around Lake Taupo were once gods and fierce warriors. Of the seven mountains, only one, Pihanga, was female, and the other mountains fought fiercely for her attention. For one night, the entire land shook as the mountains battled violently, but the next morning Tongariro stood next to Pihanga and became the supreme leader. Two mountains—Putauaki and Taranaki—headed north and south, while Tauhara smoldered sadly on the

New Zealand's varied and spectacular landscapes have made it the world's favorite dream destination.

199

lake's northern shores. Taranaki wept so copiously that his tears are said to have formed the great river Whanganui. Ngauruhoe and Ruapehu came to stand next to their new leader, and the trio retain an enduring spiritual importance for the Maori people.

The national park, New Zealand's first, was formed in 1887, when the land was gifted to the government by Maori leaders alarmed by the incursion of European settlers. "Tramping," as hiking is known locally, is the main activity in the national park. The Tongariro Crossing, which crosses the legendary mountain, is justly considered New Zealand's best one-day walk, an exhilarating climb from flower-scented alpine meadows, past twisted lava formations and azure lakes to extraordinary crater views wreathed with wisps of cloud. There are fewer climbers in winter, though the trail may be closed during bad weather. This is just one of a number of trails within the park, which are adapted for all fitness levels. Mount Ruapehu is the most accessible peak, with a chairlift taking most of the strain. From the chairlift station, it's a 90-minute hike to the summit, where the extraordinary Crater Lake—a hot, deep, acidic lake—has special importance to Maoris. Ruapehu is

The storybook outline of Mount Ngauruhoe was used as Mount Doom in *The Lord of the Rings* film trilogy.

According to Maori legend, the North Island was fished up from the sea by the demigod Maui.

the most active volcano of the trio and erupted spectacularly in 1995 and 1998. Its southern slopes are carpeted with ancient native forest, and the mountain is also home to two of New Zealand's largest ski fields at Whakapapa and Turoa. Ngauruhoe, with its sheer black slopes, had a starring role in *The Lord of the Rings* film trilogy, where it was used as the terrifying Mount Doom. Themed tours highlighting the film locations are a popular activity, and among the numerous adventure sports also offered here are white-water rafting, hunting, game fishing, horseback riding, and scenic flights.

The excellent Tongariro National Park Visitor Center is situated at the main gateway to the park and provides a wealth of information. It is open from October through March, 8 A.M.–6 P.M., and from April through September, 8 A.M.–5 P.M.

-> FACT FILE

CURRENCY New Zealand dollar.

BEST TIME TO GO The peak season is December–January. To avoid the crowds, visit October–Christmas or February–April. For skiing and other winter sports, the best time to go is July and August. The fishing season, for which permits are required, is October–June, and some rivers are closed during the spawning season.

CLIMATE Subtropical all year, with temperatures seldom falling much below 20°C (68°F) or rising much above 28°C (82°F). Rain throughout the year.

WHAT TO TAKE Sunblock, sunglasses, sun hat, a sweater for cool evenings, waterproof clothing.

FOOD AND DRINK The trout from Lake Taupo is delicious and widely available. Also try the world's only geothermal shrimp.

WHAT TO BUY Maori handicrafts and textiles.

ACCOMMODATION There is an excellent choice of accommodation, ranging from backpacker hostels to ultraluxurious lodges. It's advisable to book ahead in peak season.

AIRPORTS The nearest international airport is Auckland. There are regular air shuttles to Taupo Airport from Auckland and Wellington.

VISAS Citizens of most European countries, the U.S., Canada, and most Southeast Asian nations do not require visas for a stay of up to 90 days. UK visitors are automatically issued a 6-month permit, and Australians may stay indefinitely.

Powerful plumes of steam shoot into the air in some of the North Island's dramatic geysers.

QUEENSTOWN, ADVENTURE CAPITAL

Queenstown provides a holistic experience, where ley lines and natural wonders meet adventure sports and a cosmopolitan lifestyle.

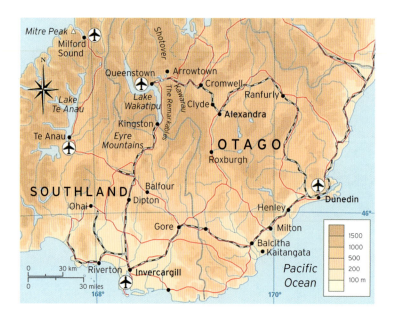

YOU DON'T HAVE TO BE SPORTY to appreciate Queenstown, but it helps. It is the ultimate adventure resort, the reputed home of bungee jumping, and a mecca for antipodean skiers. But in a country that has an excess of sights of outstanding, unpolluted natural beauty, Queenstown is supreme in its combination of natural and human facilities. Quite apart from the carefully cultivated adventure scene, it combines a stunning position between lake and the aptly named Remarkable Mountains, with accessibility (not to be taken for granted in this deeply dissected landscape) and an equable climate. To the west is wet, densely forested, forbidding coastline, where cliffs drop sheer into the sea; south are chill marshlands. But Queenstown is a haven, a "rainshadow zone" sheltered from the heaviest rains and not far from the spot that scores one of the country's highest number of sunny days a year. The spectacular scenery inspired the makers of *The Lord of the Rings* movie trilogy, and thousands of fans visit the stunning locations featured in the films every year. Though the resident population is only around 2,500, there's a cosmopolitan buzz, with international eateries from pizzerias to Japanese teahouses, and a great line in New Zealand seafood specialties such as Bluff oysters, crayfish, South Island whitebait, and Nelson scallops, all brought in fresh daily from the ocean less than 100 miles (160 km) distant.

Queenstown was once a Maori settlement, but the area was deserted when the first westerners arrived in the 1850s. Then in 1862, two sheep shearers discovered gold on the banks of the Shotover River, and within a few years, a classic gold-rush town was born. The streets were laid out and impressive buildings erected to accommodate the thousands of people pouring in to make or spend their fortunes. But the gold ran out, and by 1900 Queenstown was almost a ghost town, the population having dwindled to a couple of hundred.

Natural Advantages

The Remarkables and the Eyre Mountains are, by geological standards, mere youngsters, which explains their vigorous upsurge to almost 10,000 feet (3,000 m) and the gorge-cutting powers of the rivers. But you don't need to be a bungee jumper, a hang glider, a hot-air balloonist, or a heli-glider

Kawarau Bridge, Arthurtown, Queenstown, where you can take the plunge in the home of bungee jumping—or just watch others do it from a viewing platform.

GETTING THERE By air from Auckland, Christchurch, and various local connecting flights; by bus from Christchurch, Dunedin, and Invercargill.

CURRENCY New Zealand dollars. No exchange problems.

WHEN TO GO November–April, lower rainfall, although it rains a lot and sudden storms are common year round. In winter snow can be heavy. Temperatures depend on altitude. New Zealand's vacation season, December–January, is best avoided.

ACCOMMODATION Queenstown has many hotels but they fill up in season, so book in advance.

WHAT TO TAKE Sunglasses and sunblock. The hole in the ozone layer is directly above New Zealand in November. A raincoat and sweater are advisable, and heavy clothing in winter.

You can take a jet-boat ride through the rapids of the Shotover River.

(though there are opportunities for all four activities) to appreciate the stunning mountain, lake, and river panoramas. There are leisurely cruises on Lake Wakatipu, South Island's second largest lake, which elbows its way 100 miles (160 km) through the island's mountainous spine. One's on a coal-burning steamship that was once the region's chief means of transportation and communication with the outside world. Or you can walk above the town to Queenstown Hill, at 3,000 feet (900 m), or take a trip on the skyline gondola (cable car). The town is at its prettiest, say the winter sports enthusiasts, in the winter, when the locals sometimes have to ski to work, and the "après-ski" life is reputedly among the best in New Zealand. The slopes are just snow-covered rock above the low tree line, not at all like the forested runs of Europe. But autumn is a mosaic of golds and russets among the southern beech forests on the lower mountain slopes; this is the time to explore the trails around Arrowtown, which still retains some old gold-rush charm.

Take a good look at the trees and flowers: New Zealand's flora developed in isolation from the rest of the world: and more than 75% of it is found nowhere else. The bird life is similarly distinctive: the kea is a notorious resident of these parts and one of the world's biggest parrots. What it lacks in color—a drab brownish green with a flash of red on the underwing—it makes up for in sassiness. Kea have been seen sliding down rooftops, legs in the air, and are notorious for stealing moldings and windshield wipers from cars to play with.

Thrills with a View

Summer is the time to go upriver for some serious action. This is the area that introduced the world to bungee jumping and the jet boat. Pipeline, on the site of a former water pipeline for gold sluicing, claims to be the highest bungee jump in the world. The drop is 340 feet (102 m), and those who take the plunge are rewarded with a commemorative

Paragliding offers perhaps the most remarkable overview of the Remarkables.

T-shirt. At Kawarau Suspension Bridge 10 miles (16 km) from the town there are observation platforms for vicarious thrills overlooking the 142-foot (43-m) drop from the bungee takeoff point to just above the river below. Hair-raising jet-boat trips hurtle down through the turbulent Shotover and Kawarau rivers, shooting rapids and dodging rocks and right-angle bends in the steep-cliffed gorges. There's pure white-water rafting as well as the local variant on plastic sleds. The rivers are graded from 1 to 6, 6 being unnegotiable; most of the Shotover Canyon is 3 to 5.

Mountain biking among such mountains is for the seriously fit, although it is possible to have your bike ridden up to the highest point, and you just follow the route down. There is unrestricted access across hill tracks. The ultimate experience for trekkers is the 3-day trip to Milford Sound via the 24-mile (39-km) Routeburn Track, with hostels along the way.

Eighth Wonder of the World
From Queenstown's small airfield it is only a short flight to what the English writer Rudyard Kipling (1865-1936) described as "the eighth wonder of the world": Milford Sound on the west coast. The sound is only 9 miles (15 km) long, but it is surrounded by mountain cliffs rising 4,000 feet (1,200 m) vertically and laced with giant waterfalls dropping directly into the sea. A cruise on many of the ships on the sound should be missed by no visitor to South Island, for it allows you to come right up to the spectacular Bowen Falls, and Mitre Peak, rising 5,558 feet (1,694 m) like a pyramid out of the sea. Back on dry land, you can spend the night at Milford Sound, with its rather limited accommodation, or take the road 100 miles (160 km) south to Te Anau on Lake Te Anau, another mountain-encircled lake.

More leisurely activities are possible including cruises on Lake Wakatipu, New Zealand's second largest lake.

THE PACIFIC

"The earth belongs to anyone who stops for a moment, gazes, and goes on his way."
COLETTE, FRENCH WRITER, 1873-1954

HAWAIIAN CONTRASTS

Forged by volcanic fire, molded by the winds and the ocean, the Hawaiian islands are one of the most beautiful archipelagos in the whole Pacific, and among the most varied in the world.

HAWAII'S EIGHT MAIN ISLANDS mean many things to its many visitors: tropical playground, wildlife paradise, geological wonder—the archipelago is a positive geological conveyor belt of volcanoes—and an exotic fusion of many different cultures. "*Aloha*," the pilot says as the plane comes in to land, "welcome to Hawaii," with the authentic catch between the two i's. Hawaii is not only varied, it is a land of extremes—Mount Waialeale of Kauai is the wettest place in the world, with a rainfall of 450 inches (11.43 m), yet the Kau Desert on Hawaii Island is one of the earth's driest spots. But generally, the archipelago has just about the balmiest climate on the planet, thanks to perpetual trade winds that keep it temperate. There is no bad season in Hawaii, which explains its year-round popularity—although there is a peak tourist season from December through March. Tourism brings $20 billion annually.

As you arrive in Honolulu, on the island of Oahu after a long flight—Hawaii is 2,400 miles (3,860 km) from the U.S. mainland—you drop down into the

Deeply wave-cut coves and lush valleys—the one in the photograph is the lost tribe valley of Honopu—make Kauai a prime film location, as well as a destination for off-the-beaten-track travelers.

FACT FILE ←—

CLIMATE Warm all year round, into the high 80°s F (low 30°s C) most days. The mountains have heavy rains December–February, but other parts remain mostly dry.

TOURIST SEASONS December–March best avoided.

SURF SEASON October–April.

SIGNIFICANT HAWAIIAN WORDS *Aloha:* love, welcome. *Hula:* dance. *Lei:* flower garland. *Mana:* spiritual power. *Mu'umu'u:* long loose dress. *Taro:* food plant. *Tsunami:* tidal wave.

FOOD AND DRINK Oriental influences on what is basically American cooking. Special Hawaiian dishes include chicken *luau*, chicken pieces cooked with taro tops and coconut cream. Pineapple also figures prominently.

★ Waikiki Beach, Honolulu's waterfront, is Hawaii at its most exuberant, and most expensive.

★ Waimea Canyon's waterfall is in a state park on Kauai's beautiful and remote west coast.

★ Subtropical vegetation and dramatic cliffs plunge down to sandy Waipio Bay on Hawaii Island.

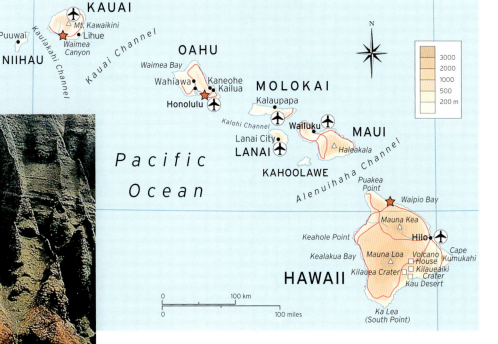

valley that gives the island its butterfly shape. Here you could have a simply terrific vacation without moving from the capital's resort, Waikiki, with its 2 miles (3 km) of sand, skyscrapers, and exuberant beach–and nightlife. The old harbor area has recently been turned into an appealing waterfront development, with shopping plazas, restaurants, and sidewalk entertainers. But Honolulu offers more than just these; it is living history. Downtown, the statue of King Kamehameha (pronounced "ka mia mia") recalls the man who unified Hawaii in 1795. Opposite stands the Lolani Palace, seat of the later monarchs until the last was deposed in 1893, five years before the U.S. annexed the kingdom. (Hawaii finally became the 50th state in 1959.) These are historical fossils embedded among modern buildings, with a population of whites, Japanese, Hawaiians, Chinese, and Koreans making Honolulu probably more cosmopolitan than any other U.S. city.

Land of Extremes

Take a plane trip and the pattern of more than 100 islands, with eight main ones strung over 400 miles (640 km), will open up before you. To the west lies Pearl Harbor. The U.S. first set up base there in 1908 and still mounts guard with 20 nuclear submarines. It was here, on the morning of December 7, 1941, that the Japanese attacked, an event still recalled by the Arizona Memorial.

On Oahu, giant waves–up to 30 feet (9 m) high– roll into Waimea Bay on the north shore to create what some claim is the best, though also some of the riskiest, surfing on earth. Waimea, too, has its historical reminders. One is a *heiau*, or temple of human sacrifice, where fearsome tattooed warriors slew and ate three members of a British expedition in 1792.

A stay on Hawaii itself–the "Big Island"–for which the whole state is named, provides an insight into the archipelago's origins and a unique experience. The entire chain owes its existence to a

-> Pearl Harbor Revisited

Though most of the base is off limits, the battleship *Arizona* still lies where she sank, preserved as a memorial to the 900 men who died on her. At the time, the attack was thought infamous. Now, since many Japanese tourists are drawn here, the commentary on the attack emphasizes its military brilliance.

In the vast harbor that Sunday morning, all was quiet: attended by over 100 cruisers, seven of the fleet's eight battleships lay at their jetties along "Battleship Row" (the eighth was in dry dock across the harbor). The attack caused fearful destruction: four battleships sunk, 188 planes destroyed, some 2,400 men killed. It seemed a masterstroke. In fact, historians agree, the attack was less damaging than it seemed–the dockyard installations and the oil supplies were largely untouched, and two carriers were safely at sea. Even much of the damage done was repairable–six of the eight battleships took part in the war later. More to the point, the attack instantly turned the United States from a nation struggling to stay at peace into a determined belligerent. Pearl Harbor united the nation as no other act could have done. The following day President Roosevelt, announcing war, told a cheering Congress that December 7 was "a date that will live in infamy." Britain declared war on Japan the same day. There would be no rest until the Japanese threat had been removed.

"hot spot" in the earth's crust, which continually vents lava, building new land on the Pacific bedrock, almost 3 miles (5 km) below. But the bedrock, driven by subterranean currents that power continental drift, is moving steadily northwest. No sooner was an island formed than it was cut off from its volcanic source, allowing another island to form. The process has been going on for 70 million years. Indeed, extinct volcanoes, or "seamounts," make a line stretching 3,000 miles (4,800 km) toward the Siberian coast. There are five active volcanoes in Hawaii: three are on the Big Island, which is a mere 6 million years old, with another submerged just off the coast. Contrasting with Honolulu's throngs, the Big Island is sparse and wild–130,000 people in 4,000 square miles (10,000 sq km). The contrast appears at its starkest on a drive along the bleak Saddle Road from Hilo to the extinct volcano of Mauna Kea, climbing through mists over rusty red volcanic rocks to the observatory on the summit.

But another contrast awaits to the south, in Hawaii Volcanoes National Park. Its heart, Kilauea, is still very much alive. This active caldera sits on the flanks of the much larger Mauna Loa, at 13,677 feet (4,103 m) the largest volcano in the world. Kilauea is not explosive: it seeps molten rock that oozes slowly down to the ocean. Here roads and trails cross scenes of lunar desolation, where recent flows have left undulating pillows and fields of lava. Access is monitored, but visitors can often approach steaming newly formed flows of this easy-flowing pasty lava, known by its Hawaiian name, *a'a*.

The Big Island has its own more recent history. On the west coast is Kealakekua Bay, where Captain James Cook met his death in 1779. He had returned to the islands after a grueling journey up America's northwest coast, and been received in style. Too much style, as it turned out. When his ship was forced back into the bay by a storm, the Hawaiians turned resentful. A boat was stolen: there was a scuffle. Cook lost his temper, and fired. The crowd hacked him and four marines to death. A 27-foot (9-m) obelisk, raised in 1884, marks where he died, but only the adventurous see it close up. The road leads to the edge of the bay, but to reach the shore, and the memorial, demands a 4-hour round trip hike down the 500-foot (150-m) cliff that shelters the bay and gives it its name, which means "pathway of the god." A good supply of water should be taken.

CRUISING THE GALAPAGOS

Neither palm trees nor beaches lure visitors to the Galapagos Islands, but the unique chance to see close up the species that helped inspire Darwin's theory of evolution.

Giant tortoises gave the islands their name—"galapagos" means tortoises in Spanish.

THE GALAPAGOS ISLANDS ARE MOSTLY rather ugly, even weird-looking islands of black volcanic rock thinly covered with scrub. They do not have many good beaches, nor particularly marvelous swimming or surfing, and certainly no great food or wine. But they do not need to enter any beauty contest, for they have one tremendous asset: they are in effect natural laboratories, where you can see evolution in action. Unique species have evolved here, which the 19th-century naturalist Charles Darwin described and publicized, and the islands have become one of the world's finest ecotourist sites. Visitors who arrive by plane or boat on the main island of Santa Cruz 500 miles (800 km) from the mainland can still see the famous Galapagos tortoises being reared at the Darwin Research Center just outside the main town Puerto Ayora. The wildlife freely visible elsewhere is even more astounding. Ferries run once or twice a week from Santa Cruz to the other main islands,

San Cristóbal, Floreana (also known as Santa María), and Isabela; private boats take in smaller islands as well, and an air service links Santa Cruz, San Cristóbal, and Isabela.

The most rewarding, as well as the largest island, is Isabela. Although forming over half the group's total area, it is remarkably undeveloped. Its main town, Puerto Villamil, offers little to tourists, but for the adventurous there is a reward. The island has six volcanoes. In sea channels a few minutes' walk from the port, schools of white-tipped sharks swim in and out. The island's own breed of giant tortoises are on view at a Rearing Center. More live in the wild and en masse on Volcan Alcedo, a 4.5-mile (7-km) caldera. But feral goats thrived on the volcano's scrubby slopes, unbalancing the fragile ecosystem, and the site is closed to casual visitors until the goats are eradicated.

Every island—many of which still bear alternative English names, recalling the time when British and American whalers and sailors made casual use of them—has its own character: Bartolomé is a kaleidoscope of red, blue, and black lava fringing shimmering beaches; Española has remarkably tame mocking birds; Santa Cruz possesses one perfect beach of white sand, where you can swim, snorkel, and even swim with marine iguanas and turtles that give the bay its name, Tortuga Bay; Santiago, though assailed by voracious goats inland, has a wealth of marine creatures on its beaches; and Floreana is famous for the tempestuous life and death of three eccentric Germans in the 1930s.

Virgin Isolation

Some 4.5 million years ago, all these islands emerged as lava from a volcanic vent some 500 miles (800 km) off the coast of what is now Ecuador, forming 14 main islands and numerous pinpricks. As the rock cooled, seeds blew in from the mainland, birds blown far from home landed, and animals arrived on driftwood. In this virgin isolation, they evolved into separate species: birds minutely adapted to their own niches, giant tortoises, the world's only seagoing lizards, a local penguin, and masses of sea lions.

Many species became adapted to their own island—a flightless cormorant is found only on Isabela and Fernandina islands—for the main islands

Culpepper Is.

Wenman Is.

Pacific Ocean

Galapagos Islands

South America

Quito

Lima

Pinta Is.

Marchena Is.

Roca Redonda

Genovesa Is.

Albemarle Is.

Equator

Vol. Wolf

-132°

Bahia Banks

San Salvador Is.

Vol. Darwin

Fernandina Is.

Bartolomé Is.

Isabela Is.

Rabida Is.

Baltra Is.

Pinzon Is.

Bahia Isabel

Santa Cruz Is.

San Cristóbal Is.

Vol. Santo Tomas

Santa Rosa

Puerto Ayora

Santo Tomas

Santa Fe Is.

El Progreso

Puerto Villamil

Vol. Cerro Azul

Tortuga Is.

Puerto Baquerizo Moreno

Floreana Is.

Caldwell Is.

Gardner Is.

Española Is.

1000
500
200
100 m

0   50 km
0   50 miles

132°

The endemic creatures of the Galapagos archipelago include the blue-footed booby, which nests on the ground.

Though the main base for tourism, Santa Cruz Island has a rich variety of wilderness areas, like this bay, which can only be reached by boat.

are too far apart for easy travel between them. When Darwin saw them in September 1835, 3 years after they were claimed by Ecuador, his mind began to nurture a new vision of life on earth. Most famously, he was struck by the 13 endemic types of finch, still referred to as "Darwin's finches," including one that uses cactus spines to probe for food. Here, he wrote later, "we seem to be brought somewhat near to that great fact—that mystery of mysteries—the first appearance of living beings on earth."

The result was *The Origin of Species* in 1859, with its premise that species owe their existence to natural processes—changing through time as the "fittest" survive to reproduce—rather than divine creation. The idea of evolution was not new, but never before had it been presented with such overwhelming evidence or with such persuasive power. It unleashed a furor that has never truly subsided.

Even when Darwin was there, pressures on the wildlife were growing. The giant tortoises, which grow up to 550 pounds (250 kg) and last for weeks without water, had long been used for meat by passing sailors. Indeed, the island themselves,

originally called Las Encantadas, the Enchanted Islands, were renamed after the tortoises—Islas de los Galápagos: the Tortoise Islands. Some boats would lift several hundred on board and eat them one by one. Over time, rats and dogs from the ships destroyed their eggs. Goats ate their food plants. Three of the original 14 subspecies are now extinct, and 5 others endangered. But the species as a whole should survive, guaranteed by its scientific importance and popularity.

A National Park

It was these human pressures, and their imported animals, that persuaded Ecuador to declare the islands a national park in 1959. Because the islands are a very popular cruise destination, with a few good hotels, access is strictly controlled, and there is a limit on numbers as well as an $100 entrance fee. Most people come in groups, often in cruise ships that originate in the U.S., but some people fly in from the capital Quito, high in the Andes. Today tourists provide most of the vital funds that allow scientists to preserve the creatures and their

FACT FILE <─

EQUIPMENT Good walking shoes, flashlight.

RECOMMENDED Sunblock, brimmed hat, lightweight raincoat.

TIME TO TRAVEL Year round, but May-June offers the best balance of climate, and preempts the summer rush.

CURRENCY U.S. dollars. Take small bills.

MAINLAND AIRPORTS FOR FLIGHTS Quito, Guyaquil.

ACCOMMODATION Limited and not cheap, so book in advance.

FOOD AND DRINK Avoid peeled fruit and salads as well as the water. Ecuador's national dish is baked guinea pig washed down by its good beer.

environments. Many local guides are wildlife experts.

Other trips can be made to misty bird-rich forests, to odd tunnels of rock lava tubes through which lava once flowed, and to mangrove inlets where turtles swim. Offshore, South Plaza Island has a beach of vociferous sea lions and a desert landscape dominated by prickly pear cacti–the local equivalent of trees.

Many of the smaller islands are hard to reach; but Fernandina, just off Isabela, is worth the effort. It is the most westerly island, the newest, and the most volcanically active (the most recent eruption was in 1995). It is also pristine: rats, goats, and dogs never made it across the narrow straits from Isabela. Visitors are required to keep it that way, in particular so that the hordes of marine iguanas can be left in peace.

Jessica Oil Spill

In January 2001, the cargo ship *Jessica* ran aground off the coast of San Cristobal in the Galapagos Islands. The ship was carrying 160,000 gallons of diesel and 80,000 gallons of bunker fuel, which began to leak only meters from one of the world's most unique and fragile ecosystems. A massive cleanup operation was immediately launched and, almost miraculously, disaster was averted when prevailing winds carried much of the oil leak away from the coast. Nonetheless, the impact of the oil spill on the ecosystem is still being assessed, and it is feared that the long-term damage may be worse than initially thought.

Behind Bartolomé's two beaches, its volcano has produced a barren, cactus-strewn landscape that is a kaleidoscope of red, blue, and black rocks.

The marine iguana, the world's only seagoing lizard, "is a hideous looking creature," wrote Darwin, "of a dirty black color, stupid and sluggish in its movements." Today, most people would be more guarded in their judgments, though no less amazed than Darwin at how the creatures have adapted. They live on shallow-water algae, dive to over 60 feet (20 m), and can hold their breath for an hour.

They are best seen on Fernandina, where a coastal trail leads through their colonies. Hundreds at a time can be seen scrabbling from the waves to bask on the rough lava, absorbing the heat of the sun into their spiny bodies to regain heat lost during underwater feeding, and comically sneezing out salt in powerful little water jets. Though herons and hawks snatch their young, they thrive here because of the lack of predators from outside.

The bizarre marine iguana, unique to the islands, feeds on green algae and can stay underwater for up to an hour.

FROM TAHITI TO EASTER ISLAND

From the lush outgoing islands of French Polynesia to the isolated and enigmatic Easter Island: the two are separated by a vast expanse of ocean, but linked by a common people–and by air.

Enigmatic statues on Easter Island are evidence of a culture that was in its death throes when the Europeans arrived.

A DOT IN A MAP OF THE SOUTH PACIFIC marks the world's loneliest inhabited island and a spectacular and extraordinary archeological sight. On the 10-mile (16-km)-long Easter Island–or *Rapa Nui* (big Rapa)–over 800 vast stone *moai* (statues) stare inland over grassy, treeless landscapes, their backs to precipitous cliffs and shark-infested seas.

Easter Island is a volcanic pimple in the ocean, well over 2,000 miles (3,500 km) from the South American coast, and the Polynesian island of Pitcairn, 2,250 miles (3,622 km) to the northwest. The National Park of Rapa Nui, which covers most of the island, was declared a World Heritage Site by UNESCO in 1995.

The mysterious Stone Age *moai*, carved from the island's dark volcanic rock, are up to 30 feet (10 m) tall, angular of nose, chin, and brow. They hail from a time when the island was covered with rain forests dominated by giant palm trees and settled by a thriving community. The first inhabitants, arriving from Polynesia in the early centuries A.D., made clearings in the forest, planted crops, and

developed a distinctive culture and religion that peaked around the beginning of the 16th century. Though the trees–there is only one species left on the island today–the crops, and all bar 1,000 or so inhabitants have long gone, the tutelary gods built by the Polynesian settlers remain, stark against a barren land.

The island's decline perhaps has alarming lessons for all of humankind. The demands of the population–by A.D. 1500 reaching around 20,000– consumed what was left of the forest. Without trees, there were no more canoes: fishing became impossible; soil erosion set in, and harvests failed. The starving people fought over what remained. The whole culture collapsed and many people died. When the first Europeans arrived in 1722, a mere 2,000 were left, who could provide the merest inkling of their past, leaving many mysteries that still remain to be solved.

Sculptural and Other Challenges

The statues were hewn in the vast Rano Raraku quarry in the crater and some 400 part-finished statues, including the 66-foot (20-m)-tall El Gigante, still lie there today. The completed figures were hauled to the edge of the island and erected on platforms 7 to 33 feet (2-10 m) high, most facing inward to watch over the settlements.

Today's visitors can rent horses or four-wheel drive vehicles to search for shards of volcanic glass (once used as spearheads) among the windswept grass, explore the ceremonial village of Orongo, with its wealth of rock art, perched high on a cliff between the volcanic crater and the coast, and the 1,764-foot (536-m) Rano Kao volcano, with its quarries and crater swamps. And you can trace the awesome route of the young men who each year negotiated a sheer 1,000-foot (300-m) cliff face and swam across shark-infested waters to the islet of Motu Nui to collect the eggs of the sooty tern. The master of the first one back became the chief or "birdman."

The Polynesian Triangle

The historically logical and most rewarding setting-off point for Easter Island is 5-hours' flight away, in French Polynesia. It was from here, 1,000 years ago, that the Polynesians, taking animals and plants in

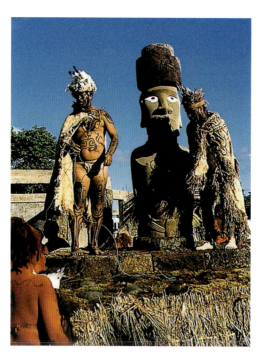

Easter Islanders recall their ancestral culture in an annual festival.

hardy double-hulled canoes, spread to Easter Island and north to Hawaii.

The first time westerners saw Tahiti, they thought they had found a paradise. Palm-fringed beaches, good food, a lush climate, beautiful people, and sex for the asking—no wonder it drew artists (most notably Paul Gauguin) and writers like Herman Melville, Robert Louis Stevenson, and Somerset Maugham. The South Pacific became the stuff of dreams, a musical waiting to be written.

Captain James Cook put Tahiti and its islands on the map in 1767. Westerners changed Tahiti's history forever, for they brought weapons and new diseases, and opened the way for missionaries, whalers, and traders. Paradise was quickly lost and never rediscovered. Tahiti, though the biggest island of French Polynesia, is not typical of the territory's 118 islands. Scattered over 1.5 million square miles (almost 4 million sq km) of ocean, these are extinct volcanoes, circled by coral reefs. In some, the central cone remains; in most it has

eroded away, leaving a halo of coral, an atoll. The 200,000 inhabitants, mostly living on Tahiti, depend on coconuts, pearls, tourists, and, until recently, the salaries of those working on France's nuclear testing program.

Pearl of the Pacific

Of all the Polynesian Islands, Bora-Bora is still the one to die for. This spectacular half-drowned volcano, with its soaring green cliffs and turquoise coral seas, consists of a main island that juts up like a tropical Gibraltar, though about twice the size, and a surrounding reef. There is only one navigable channel, and Bora-Bora is a natural harbor, something that has defined most of the island's recent history. It was the model for James Michener's Bali-h'ai in his *Tales of the South Pacific* (the basis for the Rodgers and Hammerstein musical *South Pacific*). It only achieved such fame, of course, because Michener was there with 6,000 other U.S. servicemen who arrived in 1942 to build a

Bora-Bora has claim to be the most beautiful island in French Polynesia, a romantic stopover for anyone visiting Easter Island.

FACT FILE ←

HOW TO GET THERE There are twice-weekly flights from Tahiti to Easter Island, with additional flights during the high season (December-March). Tahiti has flight connections to Los Angeles, Sydney, and Auckland.

STATUS Chile administers Easter Island as a conservation site; Tahiti is an autonomous French territory.

LANGUAGES On Easter Island, Spanish or English; on Tahiti, Tahitian, French, with English widely understood.

BEST TIME TO VISIT May-October (dry season).

WATER TEMPERATURE About 82°F (28°C) year round at Tahiti.

CURRENCY On Easter Island, Chilean pesos. U.S. dollars are widely accepted, but credit cards are not. On Tahiti, French pacific francs (CFP), fixed to the euro.

HEALTH Care should be taken with drinking water in both places, but there are no major health risks.

PERMITS An admission fee is required for the Parque Nacional Rapu Nui.

WHAT TO BRING Sunscreen, a hat, sunglasses, insect repellent.

FOOD AND DRINK Rather limited on Easter Island, although the seafood is excellent. On Tahiti, French, Chinese, Italian, and Vietnamese restaurants compete. Popular local dishes include smoked breadfruit, mountain bananas, *fafa* (spinach) with young suckling pig, varied seafood.

The dazzling white beaches of Moorea, a 7-minute flight or 45-minute ferry journey from Tahiti, lie beneath volcanic peaks.

stepping-stone toward Japan. When they departed in 1946, they left behind a huge runway that was Tahiti's international airport until 1961. Coastal guns and old radar are still in place.

Planes arrive several times a day from Papeete and other islands, and two ferries make the journey three times a week. Whether they transfer by catamaran from the airport to the main town of Vaitape or arrive by sea, most visitors come for the scuba diving, cruising, and beach life. After a 3-day diving course, a new arrival can swim alongside giant manta rays in the lagoon or encounter moray eels that guard the lagoon's entrance. One excitement for those out picnicking on the dazzling white reef sands is shark feeding. It won't cost you an arm and a leg–the lagoon's sharks are used to free meals and are quite safe. It is also possible to rent four-wheel drive vehicles to explore old Second World War tracks, trips that allow visitors to see ancient *maraes*, coral bases for temples in use before the missionaries came in the 1800s. Game fishers can charter boats of up to 60 feet (18 m). In mid-November, there's the final leg of a 3-day, 72-mile (116-km) canoe race, when 60 or so six-man pirogues pound between four islands, arriving after a 32-mile (52-km) crossing in Bora-Bora to the beat of drums and wild yells from the thousands lining the shallows.

Bora-Bora, like Tahiti, is no pristine wilderness. Even ignoring the scars left by the Second World War, present-day pressures have left their marks. But those volcanic peaks, the cloak of lush green, the dazzling beaches, the iridescent lagoon–they are stuff of reality, as well as dreams.

From the crater of Rano Raraku, Easter Islanders mined the soft volcanic rock that they made into statues.

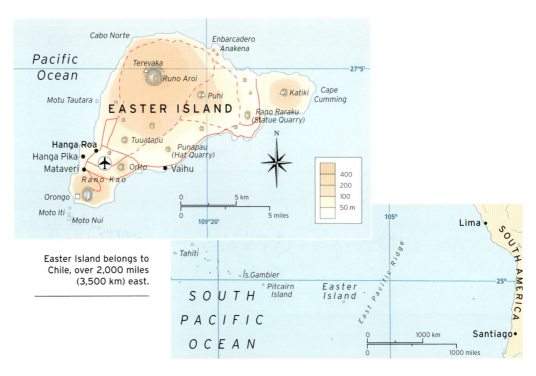

Easter Island belongs to Chile, over 2,000 miles (3,500 km) east.

Directory of useful addresses

NORTH AMERICA

Banff
Alberta Travel
Web: www.banffalberta.ca

Grand Canyon
Grand Canyon National Park, P.O. Box 129,
Grand Canyon, AZ 86023
Tel: +1 (928) 638-7888
Web: www.nps.gov/grca

Yosemite
Visitors' Center, P.O. Box 577,
Yosemite National Park, CA 95389
Tel: +1 (209) 372-0200
Web: www.nps.gov/yose

San Francisco
San Francisco Visitor Information Center
Tel: +1 (415) 391-2000 for information

Adirondacks
Adirondack Park Visitor Interpretive Center
Tel: +1 (518) 327-3000
Web: www.northnet.org/adirondackvic

Vancouver
Vancouver Tourist Center, Plaza Level,
200 Burrard St, Vancouver, Canada V6C 3L6
Tel: +1 (604) 683-2000
Web: www.tourismvancouver.com

CENTRAL AND SOUTH AMERICA

La Ruta Maya
Tourist Office, Amberes 54, Mexico City
Tel: +52 (5) 533-4700

INGUAT, 7a Avenida 1–17, Zona 4,
Centro Civico, Guatemala City, Guatemala
Tel: +502 (2) 331-1333

Costa Rica
Costa Rican Institute of Tourism,
Plaza de la Cultura, Avenida Central, C3/5,
San José, Costa Rica
Tel: +506 223-1733

Inca Trail
Municipal Tourist Office, Portal Mantas 188,
Plaza de Armas, Cuzco, Peru
Tel: +51 (0) 84 263-176

AFRICA

Marrakesh and the Atlas Mountains
Tourist Office, 170 Avenue Mohammed V,
Marrakesh
Tel: +212 4443-6131

The Zambezi and the Okavango
Zambia National Tourist Board
Tel: +260 1 229087
Web: www.zambiatourism.com

Zimbabwe Tourist Authority
Tel: +263 4-752570
Web: www.zimbabwetourism.co.zw

Rift Valley
Kenya Tourist Board
Tel: +254 (2) 2711262
Web: www.kenyatourism.org

MEDITERRANEAN AND NEAR EAST

Moorish Spain
Andalucian Tourism, Calle Compañia,
40-29008 Málaga, Spain
Tel: +34 (951) 299300
Email: info@andalucia.org

Provence
Parc National Regional du Luberon,
60 place Jean-Jaures, BP 122-84404,
Apt Cedex, Provence, France
Tel: +33 (490) 044200

Renaissance Italy
Florence Tourist Office, Via Cavour 1r,
Firenze, Italy
Tel: +39 (0) 55 290 0832

Venice
Italian State Tourist Office (ENIT),
Piazza San Marco, Venice, Italy
Tel: + 39 (41) 529 8711

The Meteora, Greece
National Tourist Office of Greece (EOT),
Tsoha 7 Street, GR-115-21 Athens, Greece
Tel: +30 (01) 322-3111

Istanbul
Touring and Automobile Club of Turkey, 1
Oto Sanayi Sitesi Yani Seyrantepe,
4 Levent, Istanbul
Tel: +90 (212) 282-8140

NORTHERN EUROPE

The Western Isles, Scotland
Scottish Tourist Board, 23 Ravelston
Terrace, Edinburgh EH4 3TP
Tel: +44 (0)131 332-2433

The West Coast of Ireland
Irish Tourist Board, Baggot Street Bridge,
Baggot Street, Dublin 2
Tel: +353 1 602-4000

Cities of Middle Europe
Vienna Tourist Board, A-1025 Wien, Austria
Tel: +43 (0)1 211-140

Prague Information Service, Na prikope 20,
Nove Mesto, Prague 1, Czech Republic
Tel: +420 (2) 124-44

Krakow Tourist Office, ul. Pawia 8, Krakow
Tel: +48 (0)12 422 6091

NORTHERN ASIA

Tran-Siberia
Intourist Office, 13/1 Milyutinsky, Pereulok,
Moscow
Tel: +7 095 956-8844

Great Wall of China
Both the China International Travel Service
(CITS) and the China Travel Service (CTS)
have offices in major capitals.
CITS in Beijing: CITS, Beijing Tourist
Building, 28 Jianguomenwai Avenue
Tel: +86 (010) 651-30828

INDIA AND SOUTHEAST ASIA

India
The Indian government has tourist offices
in Sydney, Ontario, Kuala Lumpur,
Amsterdam, Singapore, Bangkok, London,
Los Angeles, and New York.

AUSTRALIASIA

Uluru/Ayers Rock
Ayers Rock Resort Tourist Information
Center, Ayers Rock
Tel: +61 (0) 8 8956 2240

Cradle Mountain
Tasmanian Travel and Information Center,
20F Davey Street, Hobart
Tel: +61 (0) 3 6230 8233

New Zealand
Tourism New Zealand, Fletcher Challenge
House, Level 16, PO Box 95, Wellington
Tel: +64 4 917 5400

THE PACIFIC

Galapagos
Corporacion Ecuatoriana de Turismo
Tel: +02 507 560

Tahiti
Tahiti Tourist Board (GIE)
Tel: +689 50 57 00

INDEX

222

CREDITS

Quarto would like to thank the following for the use of their pictures reproduced in this book:

Key: t = top, b = bottom, l = left, r = right, c = center

Alternative Travel Group, Oxford 108r

The Art Archive: Stephanie Colasanti 36, 83, 122, 123, 176tl, 179; Global Book Publishing 192; Nicolas Sapieha 120br; Neil Setchfield 34, 35t, 167b, 169

Axiom Photographic Agency 47t, 47b, 71tl, 71br, 109, 110, 110–111, 162r, 164b, 172–173, 186b, 187, 188–189

Mark Azavedo 53, 94b

Cameron-Cooper 106

Clark/Clinch 18r, 27tr, 94t, 104t, 128, 138l, 152–153

Corbis: Peter Adams/zefa 57; Steve Bein 158; Remi Benali 174–175; Randy Faris 151b; Lindsay Hebberd 177; Jon Hicks 82tl, 84; Jeremy Horner 120cl; Steve Kaufman 58; Wilfried Krecichwost/zefa 144tl; Danny Lehman 121; Chris Lisle 166t; Joe McDonald 56bl; Paul C. Pet/zefa 178; Joseph Sohm/Visions of America 56tl; José Fuste Raga 85; José Fuste Raga/zefa 99, 142br; Jim Richardson 127; Paul A. Souders 145; Hans Strand 142tl; Nevada Wier 168

Sylvia Cordaiy 7, 16tl, 22l, 60–61, 65b, 78l, 180–181, 190b, 193, 197

Ecoscene 15, 18l, 23r, 27br, 51l, 74–75, 76–77, 97, 182–183

ffotograff 116l, 116–117, 117t, 117b, 118–119, 119t

Lesley Garland 126, 129b

Getty: Theo Allofs/Photonica 38–39; Paul Chesley/Stone 166b; Jerry Driendl/The Image Bank 46; Peter Hendrie/Photographer's Choice 206–207; Wilfried Krecichwost/The Image Bank 199t; Hideo Kurihara/Stone 200l; John Lamb/ Stone 201; Mahaux Photography/Riser 146–147; Ted Mead 196; Neil Robinson/Stone 124–125; Martin Ruegner/The Image Bank 200tr; Travel Pix/Taxi 198

Nick Hanna 27bl

Image Bank 148l, 159t, 163, 173t, 208–209

Sally Jenkins 10, 51r

Joel Photo Library 30, 32bl, 32–33, 92, 98, 112–113, 149, 152t, 154t, 181b

John Man 6, 156l, 156–157

John Miles 164t

David Noble 20–21, 21tr, 24–25, 86–87, 92–93, 94–95, 139cr, 140t

Papilio 44, 45br, 48l, 49, 66–67, 67br, 68–69, 77tl, 80, 81tr, 81bl, 130–131

Pictures Colour Library 11, 48r, 50r, 63bl, 95r

Photo Visit Flåm www.visitflam.com: R.M. Sørensen 135

Geoffrey Roy/Kaa 68tr, 68bl, 75br, 77br

C. Schuller 115l, 115r

Skyscan 204l

Tony Stone 19, 54l, 64–65, 154–155, 159b, 164–165

Travel Ink 14, 16br, 16–17, 26, 40l, 45bl, 52, 54–55, 96, 160–161, 170, 173b, 195t

The Travel Library 22–23, 27tl, 28b, 28–29, 40–41, 41tl, 42–43, 70b, 78r, 101t, 102–103, 103r, 105, 112l, 113br, 114, 132–133, 139tl, 139tr, 140–141, 148r, 150b, 171, 181t, 203, 211, 214–215, 217, 218–219

World Pictures 50l, 62, 63br, 157r, 194–195, 213

All other photographs and illustrations are the copyright of Quarto Publishing plc. While every effort has been made to credit contributors, Quarto would like to apologize should there have been any omissions or errors—and would be pleased to make the appropriate correction for future editions of the book.